Critical essays on Chaucer's
Canterbury Tales

Edited by MALCOLM ANDREW

UNIVERSITY OF TORONTO PRESS
Toronto   Buffalo

First published in North America in 1991 by
University of Toronto Press
Toronto and Buffalo

ISBN 0–8020–5005–0 (cloth)
ISBN 0–8020–6936–3 (paper)

Canadian Cataloguing in Publication Data
Main entry under title:
Critical essays on Chaucer's Canterbury Tales
Includes index.
ISBN 0–8020–5005–0 (bound) ISBN 0–8020–6936–3 (pbk.)
1. Chaucer, Geoffrey, d. 1400. Canterbury Tales
I. Andrew Malcolm
PR1874.C75   1991   821'.1   C91–094479–2

Printed in Great Britain

Contents

Abbreviations

Abbreviated titles of works by Chaucer – several of which appear variously in the notes to the essays, chapters, and extracts reprinted in this volume – are not listed here. Lists of such abbreviations are provided in the standard editions of Chaucer.

Note on the text

Original punctuation and spelling have been retained throughout. Editorial amendments and additions, except for the correction of typographical errors and the re-numbering, where necessary, of Notes, are in square brackets.

Although every effort has been made, it has not proved possible to trace the holders of copyright on all original material reproduced here. The publishers would be pleased to hear from any copyright holders we failed to identify or trace.

Introduction

MALCOLM ANDREW

The first collection of reprinted essays and extracts on Chaucer was that of Edward Wagenknecht, published in 1959.[1] In the following two years, Richard Schoeck and Jerome Taylor edited two broadly similar volumes – the first devoted to the *Canterbury Tales*, the second to *Troilus and Criseyde* and other works.[2] The publication of three such volumes in consecutive years is striking. It suggests a concern both to take stock of established views and to make readily available a selection of significant critical writing. Though several other collections of essays and extracts have appeared since, none has rivalled the success of these pioneering volumes. Thirty years on, the time would seem ripe for new collections of criticism on Chaucer.

My intention in the present volume is to offer a stimulating and informative selection of essays and extracts on the *Canterbury Tales*. While the process of selection is, inevitably, at least somewhat arbitrary, it has been guided by some general principles. Above all, I have sought to represent the great variety of approaches, attitudes, concerns, and methodologies which have been reflected in critical writing on Chaucer. It has been my policy to include material on a substantial range of tales. When in doubt, I have tended to select material which deals with more than one tale or with some general issue or issues. I have felt it necessary to include several well-known essays which have proved particularly influential – especially those of G. L. Kittredge (1912) on the "marriage group" and E. Talbot Donaldson (1954) on the narrator – but have attempted to mingle these with some less familiar pieces, also deserving of recognition. Though I have devoted a relatively high proportion of the available space to materials published during the last thirty years, I have not neglected earlier writings on Chaucer, and have endeavoured to represent all the most significant phases of interpretation. Essays and extracts have been printed in chronological order, to facilitate appreciation of a developing and evolving tradition.

The collection begins with an extract from William Blake's *Descriptive Catalogue* (1809), in which he discusses his painting of the Canterbury pilgrims (perhaps better known as an etching). Though Blake's notion of the pilgrims as universal types may seem limited and impressionistic, his awareness of the implied pairings and groupings among them significantly anticipates subsequent views. The second piece was written a century later, in the early days of academic interpretation of Chaucer. John Livingston Lowes (1910) offers what has proved to be a highly influential reading of the Prioress's portrait – in which he detects "the delightfully imperfect submergence of the woman in the nun". This essay, later revised in Lowes' book, *Convention and Revolt in Poetry* (Boston: Houghton Mifflin, 1919), is notable for its combination of scholarliness and critical insight. Similar qualities distinguish the seminal essay of G. L. Kittredge entitled "Chaucer's Discussion of Marriage" (1912). Though best known for its presentation of the "marriage group" theory, this article is also important for its discussion of the implied relationships between teller and tale, between one tale and another, and between various tellers (especially in the links). If such approaches are based mainly on sensitive and imaginative response to the text, those of Walter Clyde Curry (1926) and John Matthews Manly (1926) depend on relating the text to external facts. The facts in question are, however, conspicuously divergent – as the two extracts, both on the portrait of the Reeve, will demonstrate. While Curry interprets the portrait by reference to the scholarly dicta of the pseudo-science of physiognomy, Manly takes it to reflect some actual contemporary events.

Critics writing on Chaucer during the remarkably productive decade of the 1950s have, on the whole, more in common with Lowes and Kittredge than with Curry and Manly. They investigate various crucial aspects of style, meaning, and form, and depend increasingly on close reading of the text. This last tendency is partially anticipated by John Speirs. The extract from one of his articles in *Scrutiny* (1943) focusses on some telling details from several of the less familiar tales – but perhaps at the cost of any sense of a whole. Charles A. Owen, Jr (1953), on the other hand, explores the symbolic and unifying function of five passages – each from a different tale – which he finds "symbolic of the whole work". He also considers the effect of multiple narration, and observes that Chaucer represents himself as "the simple reporter of experience". The latter point may be related to E. Talbot Donaldson's immensely influential essay, "Chaucer the Pilgrim" (1954). Donaldson stresses the essential fictiveness of the *Canterbury Tales*, arguing that Chaucer establishes in the *General Prologue* the persona of a sharply observant but profoundly obtuse narrator. Ralph Baldwin is concerned, rather, with the issue of structure. The brief extract from his quirky but illuminating study, *The Unity of the Canterbury Tales* (1955) provides a summary of his thesis: that the idea of pilgrimage functions as the key structural and thematic principle of the work. Charles Muscatine deals more broadly with issues of form, style, and meaning. The extract from his outstanding book *Chaucer and the French Tradition* (1957) investigates the nature and significance of the "mixed style" in relation to fictions of telling and fictive tellers, with special reference to the *Miller's Tale*.

Critical writing on the *Canterbury Tales* during the 1960s and 1970s develops in various ways, and reflects some notably antithetical urges – above all, that to interpret Chaucer according to rigid schema and that to explore how his work resists such categorization. The former position is, of course, associated with D. W. Robertson, Jr, who contends in his influential book *A Preface to Chaucer* (1962), that the essential purpose of Chaucer's writing is the promulgation of Christian charity. In the extract selected, Robertson relates the *Canterbury Tales* to the concepts of pilgrimage and of marriage in Christian thought and iconography (incidentally rejecting the "marriage group" theory). Paul G. Ruggiers (1965) examines a different set of categories. He considers the possible generic classification of the various tales, avoiding firm conclusions but emphasizing the great range of "literary types" used and the mixture of serious and "non-serious" material. The latter characteristic is also relevant to Gerhard Joseph's article (1970), which deals with the formula "game and ernest" and the concept of space, especially in the first fragment of the *Canterbury Tales*. Joseph discerns a contrast between space as location for serious experience in the *Knight's Tale* and as location for "play" in the subsequent *fabliaux*. Chaucer's treatment of antifeminist ideas and traditions is discussed by Hope Phyllis Weissman (1975). She draws special attention to the use of biblical echo, allusion, and parody in the creation of such figures as the Prioress and the Wife of Bath. Donald R. Howard (1976) takes issue with the notion of the *Canterbury Tales* as a literal or symbolic pilgrimage, relating it rather to the concept of the labyrinth. He compares the *House of Fame*, arguing that Chaucer regards poetry as based on "tidings" – and thus ultimately on experience – and conceives of truth as relative.

The essays and extracts from the 1980s reflect a continuing and developing range of themes, issues, and approaches. H. Marshall Leicester, Jr (1980), addresses the fundamental but elusive question of voices in the *Canterbury Tales*: how is the voice of any given teller to be related to that of the poet? Stressing the fictiveness of the frame and the reportage, he argues that the tales are "individually voiced" and are based on what he terms "impersonated artistry", in that Chaucer impersonates the various tellers. Elizabeth Salter (1983) compares the *Knight's Tale* with its main source, Boccaccio's *Teseida*. In an essay of sustained precision and intensity, she explores the ways in which Chaucer manages to "widen and deepen" the implications of his source. The developing subject of women's history is brought to bear on Chaucer's work by Michael M. Sheehan, CSB (1985). He sets up, as examples of major social groups, five women, identified with or derived from figures in the *Canterbury Tales*, and uses historical evidence to establish the typical rights and duties of each, at various crucial stages of life. This article is valuable especially for the wealth of information it presents concerning the norms to which Chaucer's fiction alludes. David Aers (1986) also addresses the issue of women's experience. He offers a radical and challenging account of medieval attitudes to women and marriage, as reflected in several tales. Finally, paired articles by Peggy A. Knapp and Traugott Lawler (1987) consider the potential for applying the techniques of deconstruction to the *Canterbury Tales*. Though, ostensibly, Knapp is arguing "pro" and Lawler "con," each proves open-minded and undogmatic – concerned rather to explore than to deny possibilities. These would seem particularly appropriate qualities for the interpreter to bring to a text as subtle, varied, and indeterminate as the *Canterbury Tales.*

Notes

1 Edward Wagenknecht, ed., *Chaucer: Modern Essays in Criticism* (New York: Oxford University Press, 1959).
2 Richard J. Schoeck and Jerome Taylor, eds, *Chaucer Criticism*, 2 vols. (Notre Dame and London: University of Notre Dame Press, 1960–61).

1 The Canterbury pilgrims

WILLIAM BLAKE

Originally published as part of number 3, "Sir Jeffery Chaucer and the nine and twenty Pilgrims on their journey to Canterbury", in William Blake's *Descriptive Catalogue* (London, 1809). The original pagination is recorded within square brackets. Two brief passages have been omitted, from p. 10 and pp. 16–17.

The characters of Chaucer's Pilgrims are the characters which compose all ages and nations: as one age falls, another rises, different to mortal sight, but to immortals only the same; for we see the same characters repeated again and again, in animals, vegetables, minerals, and in men; nothing new occurs in iden[10]tical existence; Accident ever varies, Substance can never suffer change nor decay.

Of Chaucer's characters, as described in his Canterbury Tales, some of the names or titles are altered by time, but the characters themselves for ever remain unaltered, and consequently they are the physiognomies or lineaments of universal human life, beyond which Nature never steps. Names alter, things never alter. I have known multitudes of those who would have been monks in the age of monkery, who in this deistical age are deists. As Newton numbered the stars, and as Linneus numbered the plants, so Chaucer numbered the classes of men. . . .

The Knight and Squire with the Squire's [11] Yeoman lead the procession, as Chaucer has also placed them first in his prologue. The Knight is a true Hero, a good, great, and wise man; his whole length portrait on horseback, as written by Chaucer, cannot be surpassed. He has spent his life in the field; has ever been a conqueror, and is that species of character which in every age stands as the guardian of man against the oppressor. His son is like him with the germ of perhaps greater perfection still, as he blends literature and the arts with his warlike studies. Their dress and their horses are of the first rate, without ostentation, and with all the true grandeur that unaffected simplicity when in high rank always displays. The Squire's Yeoman is also a great character, a man perfectly knowing in his profession:

"And in his hand he bare a mighty bow."

Chaucer describes here a mighty man; one who in war is the worthy attendant on noble heroes.

[12] The Prioress follows these with her female chaplain.

"Another Nonne also with her had she,
That was her Chaplaine and Priests three."

This Lady is described also as of the first rank; rich and honoured. She has certain peculiarities and little delicate affectations, not unbecoming in her, being accompanied with what is truly grand and really polite; her person and face, Chaucer has described with minuteness; it is very elegant, and was the beauty of our ancestors, till after Elizabeth's time, when voluptuousness and folly began to be accounted beautiful.

Her companion and her three priests were no doubt all perfectly delineated in those parts of Chaucer's work which are now lost; we ought to suppose them suitable attendants on rank and fashion.

[13] The Monk follows these with the Friar. The Painter has also grouped with these, the Pardoner and the Sompnour and the Manciple, and has here also introduced one of the rich citizens of London. Characters likely to ride in company, all being above the common rank in life or attendants on those who were so.

For the Monk is described by Chaucer, as a man of the first rank in society, noble, rich, and expensively attended: he is a leader of the age, with certain humourous accompaniments in his character, that do not degrade, but render him an object of dignified mirth, but also with other accompaniments not so respectable.

The Friar is a character also of a mixed kind.

"A friar there was, a wanton and a merry."

[B]ut in his office he is said to be a "full solemn man:" eloquent, amorous, witty, and satyri[14]cal; young, handsome, and rich; he is a complete rogue; with constitutional gaiety enough to make him a master·of all the pleasures of the world.

His neck was white as the flour de lis,
Thereto strong he was as a champioun.

It is necessary here to speak of Chaucer's own character, that I may set certain mistaken critics right in their conception of the humour and fun that occurs on the journey. Chaucer is himself the great poetical observer of men, who in every age is born to record and eternize its acts. This he does as a master, as a father, and superior, who looks down on their little follies from the Emperor to the Miller; sometimes with severity, oftener with joke and sport.

Accordingly Chaucer has made his Monk a great tragedian, one who studied poetical art. [15] So much so, that the generous Knight is, in the compassionate dictates of his soul, compelled to cry out

"Ho quoth the Knyght, good Sir, no more of this,
That ye have said, is right ynough I wis;

And mokell more, for little heaviness,
Is right enough for much folk as I guesse.
I say for me, it is a great disease,
Whereas men have been in wealth and ease;
To heare of their sudden fall alas,
And the contrary is joy and solas."

The Monk's definition of tragedy in the proem to his tale is worth repeating:

"Tragedie is to tell a certain story,
As old books us maken memory;
Of hem that stood in great prosperity.
And be fallen out of high degree,
Into miserie and ended wretchedly."

[16] Though a man of luxury, pride and pleasure, he is a master of art and learning, though affecting to despise it. Those who can think that the proud Huntsman, and noble Housekeeper, Chaucer's Monk, is intended for a buffoon or burlesque character, know little of Chaucer.

For the Host who follows this group, and holds the center of the cavalcade, is a first rate character, and his jokes are no trifles; they are always, though uttered with audacity, and equally free with the Lord and the Peasant, they are always substantially and weightily expressive of knowledge and experience; Henry Baillie, the keeper of the greatest Inn, of the greatest City; for such was the Tabarde Inn in Southwark, near London: our Host was also a leader of the age. . . .

[17] . . . But I have omitted to speak of a very prominent character, the Pardoner, the Age's Knave, who always commands and domineers over the high and low vulgar. This man is sent in every age for a rod and scourge, and for a blight, for a trial of men, to divide the classes of men, he is in the most holy sanctuary, and he is suffered by Providence for wise ends, and has also his great use, and his grand leading destiny.

His companion the Sompnour, is also a Devil of the first magnitude, grand, terrific, rich and honoured in the rank of which he holds [18] the destiny. The uses to society are perhaps equal of the Devil and of the Angel, their sublimity who can dispute.

"In daunger had he at his own gise,
The young girls of his diocese,
And he knew well their counsel, &c."

The principal figure in the next groupe, is the Good Parson; an Apostle, a real Messenger of Heaven, sent in every age for its light and its warmth. This man is beloved and venerated by all, and neglected by all: He serves all, and is served by none; he is, according to Christ's definition, the greatest of his age. Yet he is a Poor Parson of a town. Read Chaucer's description of the Good Parson, and bow the head and the knee to him, who, in every age sends us such a burning and a shining light. Search O ye rich and powerful, for these men and obey their counsel, then [19] shall the golden age return: But alas! you will not easily distinguish him from the Friar or the Pardoner, they also are "full solemn men," and their counsel, you will continue to follow.

I have placed by his side, the Sergeant at Lawe, who appears delighted to ride in his company, and between him and his brother, the Plowman; as I wish men of Law would always ride with them, and take their counsel, especially in all difficult points. Chaucer's Lawyer is a character of great venerableness, a Judge, and a real master of the jurisprudence of his age.

The Doctor of Physic is in this groupe, and the Franklin, the voluptuous country gentleman, contrasted with the Physician, and on his other hand, with two Citizens of London. Chaucer's characters live age after age. Every age is a Canterbury Pilgrimage; we all pass on, each sustaining one or other [20] of these characters; nor can a child be born, who is not one of these characters of Chaucer. The Doctor of Physic is described as the first of his profession; perfect, learned, completely Master and Doctor in his art. Thus the reader will observe, that Chaucer makes every one of his characters perfect in his kind, every one is an Antique Statue; the image of a class, and not of an imperfect individual.

This groupe also would furnish substantial matter, on which volumes might be written. The Franklin is one who keeps open table, who is the genius of eating and drinking, the Bacchus; as the Doctor of Physic is the Esculapius, the Host is the Silenus, the Squire is the Apollo, the Miller is the Hercules, &c. Chaucer's characters are a description of the eternal Principles that exist in all ages. The Franklin is voluptuousness itself most nobly pourtrayed:

[21]   "It snewed in his house of meat and drink."

The Plowman is simplicity itself, with wisdom and strength for its stamina. Chaucer has divided the ancient character of Hercules between his Miller and his Plowman. Benevolence is the plowman's great characteristic, he is thin with excessive labour, and not with old age, as some have supposed.

"He would thresh and thereto dike and delve
For Christe's sake, for every poore wight,
Withouten hire, if it lay in his might."

Visions of these eternal principles or characters of human life appear to poets, in all ages; the Grecian gods were the ancient Cherubim of Phoenicia; but the Greeks, and since them the Moderns, have neglected to subdue the gods of Priam. These Gods are visions of the eternal attributes, or divine names, which, when [22] erected into gods, become destructive to humanity. They ought to be the servants, and not the masters of man, or of society. They ought to be made to sacrifice to Man, and not man compelled to sacrifice to them; for when separated from man or humanity, who is Jesus the Saviour, the vine of eternity, they are thieves and rebels, they are destroyers.

The Plowman of Chaucer is Hercules in his supreme eternal state, divested of his spectrous shadow; which is the Miller, a terrible fellow, such as exists in all times and places, for the trial of men, to astonish every neighbourhood, with brutal strength and courage, to get rich and powerful to curb the pride of Man.

The Reeve and the Manciple are two characters of the most consummate worldly wisdom. The Shipman, or Sailor, is a similar genius of Ulyssean art; but with the highest courage superadded.

The Citizens and their Cook are each leaders [23] of a class. Chaucer has been somehow made to number four citizens, which would make his whole company, himself included, thirty-one. But he says there was but nine and twenty in his company.

"Full nine and twenty in a company."

The Webbe, or Weaver, and the Tapiser, or Tapestry Weaver, appear to me to be the same person; but this is only an opinion, for full nine and twenty may signify one more or less. But I dare say that Chaucer wrote "A Webbe Dyer," that is a Cloth Dyer.

"A Webbe Dyer and a Tapiser."

The Merchant cannot be one of the Three Citizens, as his dress is different, and his character is more marked, whereas Chaucer says of his rich citizens:

[24]   "All were yclothed in o liverie."

The characters of Women Chaucer has divided into two classes, the Lady Prioress and the Wife of Bath. Are not these leaders of the ages of men? The lady prioress, in some ages, predominates; and in some the wife of Bath, in whose character Chaucer has been equally minute and exact; because she is also a scourge and a blight. I shall say no more of her, nor expose what Chaucer has left hidden; let the young reader study what he has said of her: it is useful as a scare-crow. There are of such characters born too many for the peace of the world.

I come at length to the Clerk of Oxenford. This character varies from that of Chaucer, as the contemplative philosopher varies from the poetical genius. There are always these two classes of learned sages, the poetical and the philosophical. The painter has put them side by side, as if the youthful clerk had put him[25]self under the tuition of the mature poet. Let the Philosopher always be the servant and scholar of inspiration and all will be happy....

2 | Simple and coy. A note on fourteenth century poetic diction

JOHN LIVINGSTON LOWES

Originally published in *Anglia* 33 (1910):440–51. Reprinted by permission of Max Niemeyer Verlag. The original pagination is recorded within square brackets. The footnotes – in which Lowes supported his case with extensive references – have been omitted.

Nowhere else, perhaps, does Chaucer use with more consummate skill the subtle connotations of words and phrases than in his portraiture of the Prioress. His delicate irony — of the rare strain that has its roots in the perfect merging of artistic detachment with humorously sympathetic comprehension — is nowhere more pervasive; and the hovering of the worthy lady's spirit between "love celestiall" and "chere of court" is depicted with unerring art. And the key of the whole is set at once by the famous second line.

For (it is perhaps worth noting) not only this line but the entire description is steeped in reminiscences of the poetry of courtly love, and to the readers of Chaucer's day must have carried nuances which we, whose familiar reading is not theirs, are apt to miss. Even we, of course, cannot fail to catch certain salient points. The exquisite incongruity of the gentle nun's self-chosen name; the flash of association [441] from the rehearsal of her dainty manners to the distinctly more mundane than pious intent of precisely these same manners as enjoined (among other things) with due zest by La Vieille; and the happy ambiguity of the motto of the brooch — touches like these are manifest enough. Less obvious, perhaps, is the art of the five lines (152–56) in which the Prioress's features are described — every detail of which might have come from any fourteenth century lover's description of his mistress. Such descriptions, indeed, the lines must inevitably have recalled. And no less noteworthy than the skill with which they suggest still youthful flesh [442] and blood behind the well-pinched wimple is the restraint which forgoes the remainder of the inevitable inventory, and leaves the Prioress charmingly human, without a suggestion of the sensuous. In a word, not only in his account of the amiable foibles of the Prioress herself, but in his own choice of words and phrases, Chaucer suggests the delightfully imperfect submergence of the woman in the nun. And his "simple and coy", as it happens, is by no means the least effective touch.

For this phrase too belongs to the stock-in-trade of fourteenth century love poetry, and its associations are not without their interest. Too little attention, certainly, has been paid to Chaucer's individual use of conventional phraseology, and obviously conventions must be recognized as such before the individuality of their employment can be felt. Not only, then, for the particular interest of the phrase itself, but also as an indication of what might be done in other more important cases, an examination of the contemporary usage of "simple and coy" is perhaps worth while. At all events, it may serve to exemplify the qualities of a poetic diction beside whose deadly yet fascinating monotony that of the eighteenth century is kaleidoscopic in its variety. Yet amazing as the jargon is, it has its spell, and one comes in the end to snatch a fearful joy in the settled assurance of the sort of thing predestined to confront one when the next page is turned. For, given certain familiar contexts, one may as securely count on the probable appearance (for instance) of [443] a "simple et coie" as one relies on this or that plant turning up in its due environment. And Chaucer's use of the phrase is racy with the flavor of its soil.

Simple alone, it may be noted first, is one of the commonest words in the vocabulary of the "lovers that can make of sentement". . . . [444] Times without number the word is used to characterize the lady's look, her face, her voice, her speech, her bearing. It occurs frequently in conventional lists of feminine virtues . . .

[445] . . . Like simple, coi also belongs to the conventional vocabulary of courtly love. . . . [446] Simple and coi then, taken separately, are obviously conventional in their employment.

But the phrase simple et coie is no less a commonplace. One of its favorite habitats is the pastourelle. The engagingly frank and often frail young persons who are the heroines of the genre are uncommonly likely to be simple et coie. . . . [447] . . . The phrase, moreover, is very apt to turn up in the long-drawn catalogues of the lady's physical charms. . . .

[448] . . . In contexts with less of the savourous, the phrase appears as one of the stock conventions of the "sweet jargoning" of mediaeval lovers. It is common in Machaut, and Froissart, [449] and Jehannot de Lescurel; it occurs in Gower and Deschamps; it is a favorite locution of Christine de Pisan. And it is scattered broadcast through the pages of the other love poets of the day. . . . [450–51] . . . The gently ironical humor of Chaucer's delineation of [the Prioress's] engaging inconsistencies surely loses nothing from an attempt to catch once more the forgotten flavor — subtly suggestive of her beloved "chere of court"! — of a felicitously chosen phrase.

3 Chaucer's discussion of marriage[1]

G. L. KITTREDGE

Originally published in *MP* 9 (1912):435–67. Reprinted by permission of the University of Chicago Press. The original pagination is recorded within square brackets. The square brackets in the text from p. 449 are the author's. The endnotes originally appeared as footnotes and are here renumbered.

We are prone to read and study the *Canterbury Tales* as if each tale were an isolated unit and to pay scant attention to what we call the connecting links,—those bits of lively narrative and dialogue that bind the whole together. Yet Chaucer's plan is clear enough. Structurally regarded, the *Canterbury Tales* is a kind of Human Comedy. From this point of view, the Pilgrims are the *dramatis personae*, and their stories are only speeches that are somewhat longer than common, entertaining in and for themselves (to be sure), but primarily significant, in each case, because they illustrate the speaker's character and opinions, or show the relations of the travelers to one another in the progressive action of the Pilgrimage. In other words, we ought not merely to consider the general appropriateness of each tale to the character of the teller: we should also inquire whether the tale is not determined, to some extent, by the circumstances,—by the situation at the moment, by something that another Pilgrim has said or done, by the turn of a discussion already under way.

Now and then, to be sure, this point is too obvious to be overlooked, as in the squabble between the Summoner and the Friar and that between the Reeve and the Miller, in the Shipman's intervening to check the Parson, and in the way in which the gentles head off the Pardoner when he is about to tell a ribald anecdote. [436] But, despite these unescapable instances, the general principle is too often blinked or ignored. Yet its temperate application should clear up a number of things which are traditionally regarded as difficulties, or as examples of heedlessness on Chaucer's part.[2]

Without attempting to deny or abridge the right to study and criticize each tale in and for itself,—as legend, romance, *exemplum*, fabliau, or what-not,— and without extenuating the results that this method has achieved, let us consider certain tales in their relation to Chaucer's structural plan,—with reference, that is to say, to the Pilgrims who tell them and to the Pilgrimage to which their telling is incidental. We may begin with the story of Griselda.

This is a plain and straightforward piece of edification, and nobody has ever questioned its appropriateness to the Clerk, who, as he says himself, had traveled in Italy and had heard it from the lips of the laureate Petrarch. The Clerk's "speech," according to the General Prologue, was "sowning in moral vertu," so that this story is precisely the kind of thing which we should expect from his lips. True, we moderns sometimes feel shocked or offended at what we style the immorality of Griselda's unvarying submission. But this feeling is no ground of objection to the appropriateness of the tale to the Clerk. The Middle Ages delighted (as children still delight) in stories that exemplify a single human quality, like valor, or tyranny, or fortitude. In such cases, the settled rule (for which neither Chaucer nor the Clerk was responsible) was to show to what lengths this quality may conceivably go. Hence, in tales of this kind, there can be no question of conflict of duties, no problem as to the point at which excess of goodness becomes evil.[3] It is, then, absurd to censure a fourteenth-century Clerk for telling (or Chaucer for making him tell) a story which exemplifies in this hyperbolical way the virtue of fortitude under affliction. Whether [437] Griselda could have put an end to her woes, or ought to have put an end to them, by refusing to obey her husband's commands is *parum ad rem*. We are to look at her trials as inevitable, and to pity her accordingly, and wonder at her endurance. If we refuse to accept the tale in this spirit, we are ourselves the losers. We miss the pathos because we are aridly intent on discussing an ethical question that has no status in this particular court, however pertinent it may be in the general forum of morals.

Furthermore, in thus focusing attention on the morality or immorality of Griselda's submissiveness, we overlook what the Clerk takes pains to make as clear as possible,—the real lesson that the story is meant to convey,—and thus we do grave injustice to that austere but amiable moralist. The Clerk, a student of "Aristotle and his philosophye," knew as well as any of us that every virtue may be conceived as a mean between two extremes. Even the Canon's Yeoman, an ignorant man, was aware of this principle:

> "That that is overdoon, it wol nat preve
> Aright, as clerkes seyn,—it is a vyce."[4]

Chaucer had too firm a grasp on his *dramatis personae* to allow the Clerk to leave the true purport of his parable undefined. "This story is not told," says the Clerk in substance, "to exhort wives to imitate Griselda's humility, for *that* would be beyond the capacity of human nature. It is told in order that every man or woman, in whatever condition of life, may learn fortitude in adversity. For, since a woman once exhibited such endurance under trials inflicted on her by a mortal man, a fortiori ought *we* to accept patiently whatever tribulation God may send us. For God is not like Griselda's husband. He does not wantonly experiment with us, out of inhuman scientific curiosity. God *tests* us, as it is reasonable that our Maker should test his handiwork, but he does not *tempt* us. He allows us to be beaten with sharp scourges of adversity, not, like the Marquis Walter, to see if we can stand it, for he knoweth our frame, he remembereth that we are dust: all *his* affliction is for our better grace. Let us live, therefore, in manly endurance of the visitations of Providence."

[438] And then, at verse 1163, comes that matchless passage in which the Clerk (having explained the *universal* application of his parable,—having provided with scrupulous care against any misinterpretation of its serious purport) turns with gravely satiric courtesy to the Wife of Bath and makes the *particular* application of the story to her "life" and "all her sect."

Here one may appreciate the vital importance of considering the *Canterbury Tales* as a connected Human Comedy,—of taking into account the Pilgrims in their relations to one another in the great drama to which the several narratives are structurally incidental. For it is precisely at this point that Professor Skeat notes a difficulty. "From this point to the end," he remarks, "is the work of a later period, and in Chaucer's best manner, though unsuited *to the coy Clerk.*"[5] This is as much as to say that, in the remaining stanzas of the Clerk's Tale and in the Envoy, Chaucer has violated dramatic propriety. And, indeed, many readers have detected in these concluding portions Chaucer's own personal revulsion of feeling against the tale that he had suffered the Clerk to tell.[6]

Now the supposed difficulty vanishes as soon as we study vss. 1163–1212, not as an isolated phenomenon, but in their relation to the great drama of the Canterbury Pilgrimage. It disappears when we consider the lines in what we may call their dramatic context, that is (to be specific), when we inquire what there was in the situation to prompt the Clerk, after emphasizing the serious and universal moral of Griselda's story, to give his tale a special and peculiar application by annexing an ironical tribute to the Wife of Bath, her life, her "sect," and her principles. To answer this question we must go back to the Wife of Bath's Prologue.

[439] The Wife of Bath's Prologue begins a Group in the *Canterbury Tales*, or, as one may say, a new act in the drama. It is not connected with anything that precedes.[7] Let us trace the action from this point down to the moment when the Clerk turns upon the Wife with his satirical compliments.

The Wife had expounded her views at great length and with all imaginable zest. Virginity, which the Church glorifies, is not required of us. Our bodies are given us to use. Let saints be continent if they will. She has no wish to emulate them. Nor does she accept the doctrine that a widow or a widower must not marry again. Where is bigamy forbidden in the Bible, or octogamy either? She has warmed both hands before the fire of life, and she exults in the recollection of her fleshly delights:

> "But lord Crist! whan that it remembreth me
> Upon my youthe and on my iolitee,
> It tikleth me aboute myn herte rote;
> Unto this day it doth myn herte bote
> That I have had my world as in my time!"[8]

True, she is willing to admit, for convention's sake, that chastity is the ideal state. But it is not *her* ideal. On the contrary, her admission is only for appearances. In her heart she despises virginity. Her contempt for it is thinly veiled, or rather, not veiled at all. Her discourse is marked by frank and almost obstreperous animalism. Her whole attitude is that of scornful, though good-humored, repudiation of what the Church teaches in that regard.

Nor is the Wife content with this single heresy. She maintains also that wives should rule their husbands, and she enforces this doctrine by an account of her own life, and further illustrates it by her tale of the knight of King Arthur who learned that

> Wommen desiren to have sovereyntee
> As wel over hir housband as hir love,
> And for to been in maistrie him above,

[440] and who accepted the lesson as sound doctrine. Then, at the end of her discourse, she sums up in no uncertain words:

> And Iesu Crist us sende
> Housbandes meke, yonge, and fresshe abedde,
> And grace to overbyde hem that we wedde;
> And eek I preye Iesu shorte her lyves
> That wol nat be governed by her wyves.[9]

Now the Wife of Bath is not *bombinans in vacuo*. She addresses her heresies not to *us* or to the world at large, but to her fellow-pilgrims. Chaucer has made this point perfectly clear. The words of the Wife were of a kind to provoke comment,—and we have the comment. The Pardoner interrupts her with praise of her noble preaching:

> "Now, dame," quod he, "by God and by seint Iohn,
> Ye been a noble prechour in this cas!"[10]

The adjective is not accidental. The Pardoner was a judge of good preaching: the General Prologue describes him as "a noble ecclesiaste"[11] and he shows his ability in his own sermon on Covetousness. Furthermore, it is the Friar's comment on the Wife's preamble that provokes the offensive words of the Summoner, and that becomes thereby the occasion for the two tales that immediately follow in the series. It is manifest, then, that Chaucer meant us to imagine the *dramatis personae* as taking a lively interest in whatever the Wife says. This being so, we ought to inquire what effect her Prologue and Tale would have upon the Clerk.

Of course the Clerk was scandalized. He was unworldly and an ascetic,— he "looked holwe and therto sobrely." Moral virtue was his special study. He had embraced the celibate life. He was grave, devout, and unflinchingly orthodox. And now he was confronted by the lust of the flesh and the pride of life in the person of a woman who flouted chastity and exulted that she had "had her world as in her time." Nor was this all. The woman was an heresiarch, or at best a schismatic. She set up, and aimed to establish, a new and dangerous sect, whose principle was that the wife should rule the husband. The Clerk kept silence for the moment. Indeed, he had no chance to utter his sentiments, unless he interrupted,—[441] something not to be expected of his quiet ("coy") and sober temperament. But it is not to be imagined that his thoughts were idle. He could be trusted to speak to the purpose whenever his opportunity should come.

Now the substance of the Wife's false doctrines was not the only thing that must have roused the Clerk to protesting answer. The very manner of her discourse was a direct challenge to him.[12] She had garnished her sermon with scraps of Holy Writ and rags and tatters of erudition, caught up, we may infer, from her last husband. Thus she had put herself into open competition with the guild of scholars and theologians, to which the Clerk belonged. Further, with her eye manifestly upon this sedate philosopher, she had taken pains to gird at him and his fellows. At first she pretends to be modest and apologetic,—"so that the clerkes be nat with me wrothe" (vs. 125),—but later she abandons all pretense and makes an open attack:

> "For trusteth wel, it is an impossible
> That any clerk wol speken good of wyves,
> But-if it be of holy seintes lyves,
> Ne of noon other womman never the mo.
> . . . .
> The clerk, whan he is old, and may noght do
> Of Venus werkes worth his olde sho,
> Than sit he doun, and writ in his dotage
> That wommen can nat kepe hir mariage."[13]

And there was more still that the Wife made our Clerk endure. Her fifth husband was, like him, a "clerk of Oxenford"—surely this is [442] no accidental coincidence on Chaucer's part. He had abandoned his studies ("had left scole"), and had given up all thought of taking priest's orders. The Wife narrates, with uncommon zest, how she intrigued with him, and cajoled him, and married him (though he was twenty and she was forty), and how finally she made him utterly subservient to her will,—how she got "by maistrie al the soveraynetee." This was gall and wormwood to our Clerk. The Wife not only trampled on his principles in her theory and practice, but she pointed her attack by describing how she had subdued to her heretical sect a clerk of Oxenford, an alumnus of our Clerk's own university.[14] The Wife's discourse is not malicious. She is too jovial to be ill-natured, and she protests that she speaks in jest ("For myn entente nis but for to pleye," vs. 192). But it none the less embodies a rude personal assault upon the Clerk, whose quiet mien and habitual reticence made him seem a safe person to attack. She had done her best to make the Clerk ridiculous. He saw it; the company saw it. He kept silent, biding his time.

All this is not speculation. It is nothing but straightforward interpretation of the text in the light of the circumstances and the situation. We can reject it only by insisting on the manifest absurdity (shown to be such in every headlink and endlink) that Chaucer did not visualize the Pilgrims whom he had been at such pains to describe in the Prologue, and that he never regarded them as associating, as looking at each other and thinking of each other, as becoming better and better acquainted as they jogged along the Canterbury road.

Chaucer might have given the Clerk a chance to reply to the wife immediately. But he was too good an artist. The drama of the Pilgrimage is too natural and unforced in its development under the master's hand to admit of anything so frigidly schematic. The very liveliness with which he conceived his individual *dramatis personae* forbade. The Pilgrims were interested in the Wife's harangue, but it was for the talkative members of the company to thrust themselves forward. The Pardoner had already interrupted her with humorous comments before she was fully under way[15] and [443] had exhorted her to continue her account of the "praktike" of marriage. The Friar, we may be confident, was on good terms with her before she began: she was one of those "worthy wommen of the toun" whom he especially cultivated.[16] He, too, could not refrain from comment:

> The Frere lough, whan he had herd al this:
> "Now, dame," quod he, "so have I ioye or blis,
> This is a long preamble of a tale!"
>
> (D. 829–31)

The Summoner reproved him, in words that show not only his professional enmity but also the amusement that the Pilgrims in general were deriving from the Wife's disclosures.[17] They quarreled, and each threatened to tell a story at the other's expense. Then the Host intervened roughly, calling for silence and bidding the Wife go ahead with her story. She assented, but not without a word of good-humored, though ironical, deference to the Friar:

> "Al redy, sir," quod she, "right as yow lest,
> If I have licence of this worthy Frere."[18]

And, at the very beginning of her tale, she took humorous vengeance for his interruption in a characteristic bit of satire at the expense of "limitours and other holy freres."[19] This passage, we note, has nothing whatever to do with her tale. It is a side-remark in which she is talking at the Friar, precisely as she has talked at the Clerk in her prologue.

The quarrel between the Summoner and the Friar was in abeyance until the Wife finished her tale. They let her end her story and proclaim her moral in peace,—the same heretical doctrine that we have already noted, that the wife should be the head of the house.[20] Then the Friar spoke, and his words are very much to our present purpose. He adverts in significant terms both to the subject and to the manner of the Wife's discourse,—a discourse, we should observe, that was in effect a doctrinal sermon illustrated (as the fashion of preachers was) by a pertinent *exemplum*:[21]

> [444]   "Ye have here touched, al-so moot I thee,
>   In scole-matere greet difficultee."[22]

She has handled a hard subject that properly belongs to scholars. She has quoted authorities, too, like a clerk. Such things, he says, are best left to ecclesiastics:

> "But, dame, here as we ryden by the weye,
> Us nedeth nat to speken but of game,
> And lete auctoritees, on Goddes name,
> To preching and to scole eek of clergye."[23]

This, to be sure, is but a device to "conveyen his matere,"—to lead up to his proposal to "telle a game" about a summoner. But it serves to recall our minds to the Wife's usurpation of clerkly functions. If we think of the Clerk at all at this point (and assuredly Chaucer had not forgotten him), we must feel that here is another prompting (undesigned though it be on the Friar's part) to take up the subject which the Wife has (in the Clerk's eyes) so shockingly maltreated.

Then follows the comic interlude of the Friar and the Summoner,[24] in the course of which we may perhaps lose sight of the serious subject which the Wife had set abroach,—the status of husband and wife in the marriage relation. But Chaucer did not lose sight of it. It was a part of his design that the Host should call on the Clerk for the first story of the next day.

This is the opportunity for which the Clerk has been waiting. He has not said a word in reply to the Wife's heresies or to her personal attack on him and his order. Seemingly she has triumphed. The subject has apparently been dismissed with the Friar's words about leaving such matters to sermons and to school debates. The Host, indeed, has no idea that the Clerk purposes to revive the discussion; he does not even think of the Wife in calling upon the representative of that order which has fared so ill at her hands.

> "Sir clerk of Oxenford," our hoste sayde,
> "Ye ryde as coy and stille as doth a mayde
> Were newe spoused, sitting at the bord;
> This day ne herde I of your tonge a word.
> I trowe ye studie aboute som sophyme."[25]

[445] Even here there is a suggestion (casual, to be sure, and, so far as the Host is concerned, quite unintentional) of *marriage*, the subject which is occupying the Clerk's mind. For the Host is mistaken. The Clerk's abstraction is only apparent. He is not pondering syllogisms; he is biding his time.

"Tell us a tale," the unconscious Host goes on, "but don't preach us a Lenten sermon—tell us som mery thing of aventures." "Gladly," replies the demure scholar. "I will tell you a story that a worthy *clerk* once told me at Padua—Francis Petrarch, God rest his soul!"

At this word *clerk*, pronounced with grave and inscrutable emphasis, the Wife of Bath must have pricked up her ears. But she has no inkling of what is in store, nor is the Clerk in any hurry to enlighten her. He opens with tantalizing deliberation, and it is not until he has spoken more than sixty lines that he mentions marriage. "The Marquis Walter," says the Clerk, "lived only for the present and lived for pleasure only—

> "As for to hauke and hunte on every syde,—
> Wel ny al othere cures leet he slyde;

> And eek he nolde, and that was worst of alle,
> Wedde no wyf, for noght that may bifalle."

These words may or may not have appeared significant to the company at large. To the Wife of Bath, at all events, they must have sounded interesting. And when, in a few moments, the Clerk made Walter's subjects speak of "soveraynetee," the least alert of the Pilgrims can hardly have missed the point:

> "Boweth your nekke under that blisful yok
> Of soveraynetee, noght of servyse,
> Which that men clepeth spousaille or wedlok."[26]

"Sovereignty" had been the Wife's own word:

> "And whan that I hadde geten unto me
> By maistrie al the soveraynetee"
>
> (D. 817–18)

> "Wommen desyren to have sovereyntee
> As wel over hir housband as hir love,
> And for to been in maistrie him above"
>
> (D. 1038–40)

[446] Clearly the Clerk is catching up the subject proposed by the Wife. The discussion is under way again.

Yet, despite the cheerful view that Walter's subjects take of the marriage yoke, it is by no means yet clear to the Wife of Bath and the other Pilgrims what the Clerk is driving at. For he soon makes Walter declare that "liberty is seldom found in marriage," and that, if he weds a wife, he must exchange freedom for servitude.[27] Indeed, it is not until vss. 351–57 are reached that Walter reveals himself as a man who is determined to rule his wife absolutely. From that point to the end there is no room for doubt in any Pilgrim's mind: *the Clerk is answering the Wife of Bath*; he is telling of a woman whose principles in marriage were the antithesis of hers; he is reasserting the orthodox view in opposition to the heresy which she had expounded with such zest and with so many flings and jeers at the clerkly profession and character.

What is the tale of Griselda? Several things, no doubt—an old *märchen*, an *exemplum*, a *novella*, what you will. Our present concern, however, is primarily with the question what it seemed to be to the Canterbury Pilgrims, told as it was by an individual Clerk of Oxford at a particular moment and under the special circumstances. The answer is plain. To them it was a retort (indirect, impersonal, masterly) to the Wife of Bath's heretical doctrine that the woman should be the head of the man. It told them of a wife who had no such views,—who promised ungrudging obedience and kept her vow. The Wife of Bath had railed at her husbands and badgered them and cajoled them: Griselda never lost her patience or her serenity. On its face, then, the tale appeared to the Pilgrims to be a dignified and scholarly narrative, derived from a great Italian clerk who was dead, and now utilized by their fellow-pilgrim, the Clerk of Oxford, [447] to demolish the heretical structure so boisterously reared by the Wife of Bath in her prologue and her tale.

But Chaucer's Clerk was a logician—"unto logik hadde he longe ygo." He knew perfectly well that the real moral of his story was not that which his hearers would gather. He was aware that Griselda was no model for literal imitation by ordinary womankind. If so taken, his tale proved too much; it reduced his argument *ad absurdum*. If he let it go at that, he was playing into his opponent's hands. Besides, he was a conscientious man. He could not misrepresent the lesson which Petrarch had meant to teach and had so clearly expressed,—the lesson of submissive fortitude under tribulation sent by God. Hence he does not fail to explain this moral fully and in unmistakable terms, and to refer distinctly to Petrarch as authority for it:

> And herkeneth what this auctor seith therfore.
>
> This storie is seyd, nat for that wyves sholde
> Folwen Griselde as in humilitee,
> For it were importable, though they wolde;
> But for that every wight, in his degree,
> Sholde be constant in adversitee
> As was Grisilde; therfor Petrark wryteth
> This storie, which with heigh style he endyteth.
>
> For, sith a womman was so pacient
> Un-to a mortal man, wel more us oghte
> Receyven al in gree that God us sent;
> For greet skile is, he preve that he wroghte.
> But he ne tempteth no man that he boghte,
> As seith seint Iame, if ye his pistel rede;
> He preveth folk al day, it is no drede,
>
> And suffreth us, as for our exercyse,
> With sharpe scourges of adversitee
> Ful ofte to be bete in sondry wyse;
> Nat for to knowe our wil, for certes he,
> Er we were born, knew al our freletee;
> And for our beste is al his governaunce:
> Lat us than live in vertuous suffrance.[28]

[448] Yet the Clerk has no idea of failing to make his point against the Wife of Bath. And so, when the tale is finished and the proper Petrarchan moral has been duly elaborated, he turns to the Wife (whom he has thus far sedulously refrained from addressing) and distinctly applies the material to the purpose of an ironical answer, of crushing force, to her whole heresy. There is nothing inappropriate to his character in this procedure. Quite the contrary. Clerks were always satirizing women—the Wife had said so herself—and this particular Clerk had, of course, no scruples against using the powerful weapon of irony in the service of religion and "moral vertu." In

this instance, the satire is peculiarly poignant for two reasons: first, because it comes with all the suddenness of a complete change of tone (from high seriousness to biting irony, and from the impersonal to the personal); and secondly, because, in the tale which he has told, the Clerk has incidentally refuted a false statement of the Wife's, to the effect that

> "It is an impossible
> That any clerk wol speke good of wyves,
> But if it be of holy seintes lyves,
> Ne of noon other womman never the mo."[29]

Clerks *can* "speak well" of women (as our Clerk has shown), when women deserve it; and he now proceeds to show that they can likewise speak well (with biting irony) of women who do *not* deserve it—such women as the Wife of Bath and all her sect of domestic revolutionists.

It now appears that the form and spirit of the conclusion and the Envoy[30] are not only appropriate to clerks in general, but peculiarly and exquisitely appropriate to this particular clerk under these particular circumstances and with this particular task in hand,—the duty of defending the orthodox view of the relations between husband and wife against the heretical opinions of the Wife of Bath: "One word in conclusion,[31] gentlemen. There are few Griseldas now-[449]a-days. Most women will break before they will bend. Our companion, the Wife of Bath, is an example, as she has told us herself. Therefore, though I cannot sing, I will recite a song in honor, not of Griselda (as you might perhaps expect), but of the Wife of Bath, of the sect of which she aspires to be a doctor, and of the life which she exemplifies in practice—

> "For the wyves love of Bathe,
> Whos lif and al hir secte God mayntene
> In high maistrye, and elles were it scathe."

Her *way of life*—she had set it forth with incomparable zest. Her *sect*—she was an heresiarch or at least a schismatic. The terms are not accidental: they are chosen with all the discrimination that befits a scholar and a rhetorician. They refer us back (as definitely as the words "Wife of Bath" themselves) to that prologue in which the Wife had stood forth as an opponent of the orthodox view of subordination in marriage, as the upholder of an heretical doctrine, and as the exultant practicer of what she preached.[32]

And then comes the Clerk's Envoy,[33] the song that he recites in honor of the Wife and her life and her sect, with its polished lines, its ingenious rhyming, and its utter felicity of scholarly diction. Nothing could be more in character. To whom in all the world should such a masterpiece of rhetoric be appropriate if not to the Clerk of Oxenford? It is a mock encomium, a sustained ironical commendation of what the Wife has taught:

"O noble wives, let no clerk ever have occasion to write such a story of you as Petrarch once told me about Griselda. Follow your great leader, the Wife of Bath. Rule your husbands, as she did; rail at them, as she did; make them jealous, as she did; exert yourselves to get lovers, as she did. And all this you must do whether you are fair or foul [with manifest allusion to the problem of beauty or ugliness presented in the Wife's story]. Do this, I say, and you will fulfil the precepts that she has set forth and achieve the great end which she has proclaimed as the object of marriage: that is, *you will make your husbands miserable, as she did!*"

[450]   "Be ay of chere as light as leef on linde,
          And lat him care and wepe and wringe and waille!"

And the Merchant (hitherto silent, but not from inattention) catches up the closing words in a gust of bitter passion:

"Weping and wayling, care and other sorwe
I know ynough on even and amorwe,"
Quod the Merchant, "and so don othere mo
That wedded ben."

The Clerk's Envoy, then, is not only appropriate to his character and to the situation: it has also a marked dynamic value. For it is this ironical tribute to the Wife of Bath and her dogmas that, with complete dramatic inevitability, calls out the Merchant's *cri de cœur*. The Merchant has no thought of telling a tale at this moment. He is a stately and imposing person in his degree, by no means prone (so the Prologue informs us) to expose any holes there may be in his coat.[34] But he is suffering a kind of emotional crisis. The poignant irony of the Clerk, following hard upon the moving story of a patient and devoted wife, is too much for him. He has just passed through his honeymoon (but two months wed!) and he has sought a respite from his thraldom under color of a pilgrimage to St. Thomas.

"I have a wyf, the worste that may be!"

She would be an overmatch for the devil himself. He need not specify her evil traits: she is bad in every respect.[35]

"There is a long and large difference
Bitwix Grisildis grete pacience
And of my wyf the passing crueltee."

The Host, as ever, is on the alert. He scents a good story:

"Sin ye so muchel knowen of that art,
Ful hertely I pray yow telle us part."

The Merchant agrees, as in duty bound, for all the Pilgrims take care never to oppose the Host, lest he exact the heavy forfeit established as the penalty for rebellion.[36] But he declines to relate his [451] own experiences, thus leaving us to infer, if we choose,—for nowhere is Chaucer's artistic reticence more effective,—that his bride has proved false to him, like the wife of the worthy Knight of Lombardy.

And so the discussion of marriage is once more in full swing. The Wife of Bath, without intending it, has opened a debate in which the Pilgrims have become so absorbed that they will not leave it till the subject is "bolted to the bran."

The Merchant's Tale presents very noteworthy features, and has been much canvassed, though never (it seems) with due attention to its plain significance in the Human Comedy of the Canterbury Pilgrimage. In substance, it is nothing but a tale of bawdry, one of the most familiar of its class. There is nothing novel about it except its setting, but that is sufficiently remarkable. Compare the tale with any other version of the Pear-Tree Story,—their name is legion,—and its true significance comes out in striking fashion. The simple fabliau devised by its first author merely to make those laugh whose lungs are tickle o' the sere, is so expanded and overlaid with savage satire that it becomes a complete disquisition on marriage from the only point of view which is possible for the disenchanted Merchant. Thus considered, the cynicism of the Merchant's Tale is seen to be in no way surprising, and (to answer another kind of comment which this piece has evoked) in no sense expressive of Chaucer's own sentiments, or even of Chaucer's momentary mood. The cynicism is the Merchant's. It is no more Chaucer's than Iago's cynicism about love is Shakspere's.

In a word, the tale is the perfect expression of the Merchant's angry disgust at his own evil fate and at his folly in bringing that fate upon himself. Thus, its very lack of restraint—the savagery of the whole, which has revolted so many readers—is dramatically inevitable. The Merchant has schooled himself to hide his debts and his troubles. He is professionally an adept at putting a good face on matters, as every clever business man must be. But when once the barrier is broken, reticence is at an end. His disappointment is too fresh, his disillusion has been too abrupt, for him to measure his words. He speaks in a frenzy of contempt and hatred. The hatred is for women; the contempt is for himself and all other fools who will not take warning by example. For we should not [452] forget that the satire is aimed at January rather than at May. That egotistical old dotard is less excusable than his young wife, and meets with less mercy at the Merchant's hands.

That the Merchant begins with an encomium on marriage which is one of the most amazing instances of sustained irony[37] in all literature, is not to be wondered at. In the first place, he is ironical because the Clerk has been ironical. Here the connection is remarkably close. The Merchant has fairly snatched the words out of the Clerk's mouth ("And lat him care and wepe and wringe and waile"—"Weping and wayling, care and other sorwe"), and his mock encomium on the wedded state is a sequel to the Clerk's mock encomium on the Wife of Bath's life and all her sect. The spirit is different, but that is quite proper. For the Clerk's satire is the irony of a logician and a moral philosopher, the irony of the intellect and the ethical sense: the Merchant's is the irony of a mere man, it is the irony of passion and personal experience. The Clerk is a theorist,—he looks at the subject from a point of philosophical detachment. The Merchant is an egotist,—he feels himself to be the dupe whose folly he depicts. We may infer, if we like, that he was a man in middle age and that he had married a young wife.

There is plenty of evidence that the Merchant has been an attentive listener. One detects, for instance, a certain similarity between January and the Marquis Walter (different as they are) in that they have both shown themselves disinclined to marriage. Then again, the assertion that a wife is never weary of attending a sick husband—

> "She nis nat wery him to love and serve,
> Thogh that he lye bedrede til he sterve"[38]—

must have reminded the Pilgrims of poor Thomas, in the Summoner's Tale, whose wife's complaints to her spiritual visitor had precipitated so tremendous a sermon.[39] But such things are trifles compared with the attention which the Merchant devotes to the Wife of Bath.

So far, in this act of Chaucer's Human Comedy, we have found that the Wife of Bath is, in a very real sense, the dominant figure. [453] She has dictated the theme and inspired or instigated the actors; and she has always been at or near the center of the stage. It was a quarrel over her prologue that elicited the tale of the Friar and that of the Summoner. It was she who caused the Clerk to tell of Griselda—and the Clerk satirizes her in his Envoy. "The art" of which the Host begs the Merchant to tell is *her* art, the art of marriage on which she has discoursed so learnedly. That the Merchant, therefore, should allude to her, quote her words, and finally mention her in plain terms is precisely what was to be expected.

The order and method of these approaches on the Merchant's part are exquisitely natural and dramatic. First there are touches, more or less palpable, when he describes the harmony of wedded life in terms so different from the Wife's account of what her husbands had to endure. Then—after a little—comes a plain enough allusion (put into January's mouth) to the Wife's character, to her frequent marriages, and to her inclination to marry again,[40] old as she is:

> "And eek thise olde widwes, God it wot,
> They conne so muchel craft on Wades boot,
> So muchel broken harm, whan that hem leste,
> That with hem sholde I never live in reste!
> For sondry scoles maken sotil clerkis:
> Wommen of many scoles half a clerk is."[41]

Surely the Wife of Bath was a woman of many schools, and her emulation of clerkly discussion had already been commented on by the Pardoner[42] and the Friar.[43] Next, the Merchant lets Justinus quote some of the Wife's very words—though without naming her: "God may apply the trials of marriage, my dear January, to your salvation. Your wife may make you go straight to heaven without passing through purgatory."

> "Paraunter she may be your purgatorie!
> She may be Goddes mene, and Goddes whippe;
> Than shal your soule up to hevene skippe
> Swifter than doth an arwe out of the bowe."[44]

This is merely an adaptation of the Wife of Bath's own language in speaking of her fourth husband:

[454]   "By God, in erthe I was his purgatorie,
          For which I hope his soule be in glorie."[45]

Compare also another phrase of hers, which Justinus echoes: "Myself have been the whippe."[46] And finally, when all the Pilgrims are quite prepared for such a thing, there is a frank citation of the Wife of Bath by name, with a reference to her exposition of marriage:

> "My tale is doon:—for my wit is thinne.
> Beth not agast herof, my brother dere.
> *But lat us waden out of this matere:*
> *The Wyf of Bathe, if ye han understonde,*
> *Of marriage, which we have on honde,*
> *Declared hath ful wel in litel space.*
> Fareth now wel, God have yow in his grace."[47]

Are the italicized lines a part of the speech of Justinus, or are they interpolated by the Merchant, in his own person, in order to shorten Justinus' harangue? Here is Professor Skeat's comment: "These four parenthetical lines interrupt the story rather awkwardly. They obviously belong to the narrator, the Merchant, as it is out of the question that Justinus had heard of the Wife of Bath. Perhaps it is an oversight." Now it makes no difference whether we assign these lines to Justinus or to the Merchant, for Justinus, as we have seen, has immediately before quoted the Wife's very words, and he may as well mention her as repeat her language. Either way, the lines are exquisitely in place. *Chaucer* is not speaking, and there is no violation of dramatic propriety on *his* part. It is not Chaucer who is telling the story. It is the Merchant. And the Merchant is telling it as a part of the discussion which the Wife has started. It is dramatically proper, then, that the Merchant should quote the Wife of Bath and that he should refer to her. And it is equally proper, from the dramatic point of view, for Chaucer to let the Merchant make Justinus mention the Wife. In that case it is the Merchant—*not Chaucer*—who chooses to have one of his characters fall out of his part for a moment and make a "local allusion." Chaucer is responsible for making the *Merchant* speak in character; the Merchant, in his turn, is responsible for *Justinus*. That the Merchant should put into the mouth of Justinus a remark that Justinus [455] could never have made is, then, not a slip on Chaucer's part. On the contrary, it is a first-rate dramatic touch, for it is precisely what the Merchant might well have done under the circumstances.

Nor should we forget the exquisitely comic discussion between Pluto and Proserpine which the Merchant has introduced near the end of his story. This dialogue is a flagrant violation of dramatic propriety—not on Chaucer's part, however, but on the Merchant's. And therein consists a portion of its merit. For the Merchant is so eager to make his point that he rises superior to all artistic rules. He is bent, not on giving utterance to a masterpiece of narrative construction, but on enforcing his lesson in every possible way. And Chaucer is equally bent on making him do it. Hence the Queen of the Lower World is brought in, discoursing in terms that befit the Wife of Bath (the presiding genius of this part of the *Canterbury Tales*), and echoing some of her very doctrines. The Wife had said:

> "Thus shal ye speke and bere hem wrong on honde;
> For half so boldely can ther no man
> Swere and lyen as a womman can.
> I say nat this by wyves that ben wyse,
> But-if it be whan they hem misavyse.
> A wys wyf, if that she can hir good,
> Shal beren him on hond the cow is wood,
> And take witnesse of his owene mayde."[48]

Now hear Proserpine:

> "Now, by my modres sires soule I swere,
> That I shal yeven hir suffisaunt answere,
> And alle wommen after, for hir sake;
> That, though they be in any gilt ytake,
> With face bold they shulle hemself excuse,
> And bere hem doun that wolden hem accuse.
> For lakke of answere noon of hem shal dyen.
> Al hadde man seyn a thing with bothe his yen,
> Yit shul we wommen visage it hardily,
> And wepe, and swere, and chyde subtilly,
> So that ye men shul been as lewed as gees."[49]

And note that Pluto (who is as fond of citing authorities as the Wife's last husband) yields the palm of the discussion to Proserpine:

> [456]   "Dame," quod this Pluto, "be no lenger wrooth;
> I yeve it up."[50]

This, too, was the experience of the Wife's husbands:

> "I ne owe hem nat a word that is not quit.
> I broghte it so aboute by my wit
> That they moste yeve it up, as for the beste."[51]

The tone and manner of the whole debate between Pluto and his queen are wildly absurd if regarded from the point of view of gods and goddesses, but in that very incongruity resides their dramatic propriety. What we have is not Pluto and Proserpine arguing with each other, but the Wife of Bath and one of her husbands attired for the nonce by the cynical Merchant in the external semblance of King Pluto and his dame.[52]

The end of the Merchant's Tale does not bring the Marriage Chapter of the *Canterbury Tales* to a conclusion. As the Merchant had commented on the Clerk's Tale by speaking of his own wife, thus continuing the subject which the Wife had begun, so the Host comments on the Merchant's story by making a similar application:

> "Ey, Goddes mercy," seyde our Hoste tho,
> "Now such a wyf I pray God kepe me fro!"

"See how women deceive us poor men, as the Merchant has shown us. However, *my* wife is true as any steel; but she is a shrew, and has plenty of other faults." And just as the Merchant had referred expressly to the Wife of Bath, so also does the Host refer to her expressly: "But I must not talk of these things. If I should, it would be told to her by some of this company. I need not say by whom, 'sin wommen connen outen swich chaffare.'"[53] Of course the Host points this remark by looking at the Wife of Bath. There are but three women in the company. Neither the highborn and dainty Prioress nor the pious nun who accompanies her is likely to gossip with Harry Baily's spouse. It is the Wife, a woman of the Hostess's own rank and temper, who will tattle when the party returns to the Tabard. And so we find the Wife of Bath still in the [457] foreground, as she has been, in one way or another, for several thousand lines.

But now the Host thinks his companions have surely had enough of marriage. It is time they heard something of love, and with this in view he turns abruptly to the Squire, whom all the Pilgrims have come to know as "a lovyer and a lusty bachiler."

> "Squier, com neer, if it your wille be,
> And set somewhat of *love*; for certes ye
> Connen theron as muche as any man."[54]

The significance of the emphasis on *love*, which is inevitable if the address to the Squire is read (as it should be) continuously with the Host's comments on marriage, is by no means accidental.

There is no psychology about the Squire's Tale,—no moral or social or matrimonial theorizing. It is pure romance, in the mediaeval sense. The Host understood the charm of variety. He did not mean to let the discussion drain itself to the dregs.

But Chaucer's plan in this Act is not yet finished. There is still something lacking to a full discussion of the relations between husband and wife. We have had the wife who dominates her husband; the husband who dominates his wife; the young wife who befools her dotard January; the chaste wife who is a scold and stirs up strife. Each of these illustrates a different kind of marriage,—but there is left untouched, so far, the ideal relation, that in which love continues and neither party to the contract strives for the mastery. Let this be set forth, and the series of views of wedded life begun by the Wife of Bath will be rounded off; the Marriage Act of the Human Comedy will be concluded. The Pilgrims may not be thinking of this; but there is at least *one* of them (as the sequel shows) who has the idea in his head. And who is he? The only pilgrims who have not already told their tales are the yeoman, two priests, the five tradesmen (haberdasher, carpenter, weaver, dyer, and tapicer), the parson, the plowman, the manciple, and the franklin. Of all these there is but one to whom a tale illustrating this ideal would not be inappropriate—the Franklin. To him, then, must Chaucer assign it, or leave the debate unfinished.

[458] At this point, the dramatic action and interplay of characters are beyond all praise. The Franklin is not brought forward in formal fashion to address the company. His summons is incidental to the dialogue.[55] No sooner has the Squire ended his chivalric romance, than the Franklin begins to compliment him:

> "In feyth, squier, thou hast thee well yquit
> And gentilly. I preise wel thy wit,"
> Quod the frankeleyn, "considering thy youthe.
> So felingly thou spekest, sir, I allow the!
> As to my doom, there is noon that is here
> Of eloquence that shal be thy pere,
> If that thou live: God yeve thee good chaunce
> And in vertu sende thee continuance,
> For of thy speche I have great deyntee!"[56]

"You have acquitted yourself well and *like a gentleman!*" *Gentillesse*, then, is what has most impressed the Franklin in the tale that he has just heard. And the reason for his enthusiasm soon appears. He is as we know, a rich freeholder, often sheriff in his county. Socially, he is not quite within the pale of the gentry, but he is the kind of man that may hope to found a family, the kind of man from whose ranks the English nobility has been constantly recruited. And that such is his ambition comes out naïvely and with a certain pathos in what he goes on to say: "I wish my son were like you:

> "I have a sone, and, by the Trinitee,
> I hadde lever than twenty pound worth lond,
> Though it right now were fallen in myn hond,
> He were a man of swich discrecioun
> As that ye been! Fy on possessioun
> But-if a man be vertuous with-al!
> I have my sone snibbed, and yet shal,
> For he to vertu listeth nat entende;
> But for to pleye at dees, and to despende,
> And lese al that he hath, is his usage;
> And he hath lever talken with a page
> Than to commune with any gentil wight
> Ther he mighte lerne gentillesse aright."[57]

[459] It is the contrast between the Squire and his own son, in whom his hopes are centered, that has led the Franklin's thoughts to *gentillesse*, a subject which is ever in his mind.

But the Host interrupts him rudely: "Straw for your gentillesse! It is your turn to entertain the company:

"Telle on thy tale withouten wordes mo!"

The Franklin is, of course, very polite in his reply to this rough and unexpected command. Like the others, he is on his guard against opposing the
Host and incurring the forfeit:

> "I wol yow nat contrarien in no wise,
> As fer as that my wittes wol suffise."[58]

Here, then, as in the case of the Merchant, the Host has taken advantage of
a spontaneous remark on some Pilgrim's part to demand a story. Yet the
details of the action are quite different. On the previous occasion, the Merchant is requested to go on with an account of his marriage, since he has
already begun to talk about it; and, though he declines to speak further of his
own troubles, he does continue to discuss and illustrate wedlock from his
own point of view. In the present instance, on the contrary, the Host
repudiates [460] the topic of *gentillesse*, about which the Franklin is discoursing to the Squire. He bids him drop the subject and tell a story. The Franklin
pretends to be compliant, but after all, he has his own way. Indeed, he takes
delicate vengeance on the Host by telling a tale which thrice exemplifies
gentillesse—on the part of a knight, a squire, and a clerk. Thus he finishes his
interrupted compliment to the Squire, and incidentally honors two other
Pilgrims who have seemed to him to possess the quality that he values so
highly. He proves, too, both that *gentillesse* is an entertaining topic and that it
is not (as the Host has roughly intimated) a theme which he, the Franklin, is
ill-equipped to handle.

For the Franklin's Tale is a gentleman's story, and he tells it like a gentleman. It is derived, he tells us, from "thise olde *gentil* Britons."[59] Dorigen
lauds Arveragus' *gentillesse* toward her in refusing to insist on soveraynetee
in marriage.[60] Aurelius is deeply impressed by the knight's *gentillesse* in
allowing the lady to keep her word, and emulates it by releasing her:

> Fro his lust yet were him lever abyde
> Than doon so heigh a churlish wrecchednesse
> Agaynes franchyse and alle gentillesse.[61]

> I see his grete gentillesse.[62]

> Thus can a squyer don a gentil dede
> As wel as can a knyght, withouten drede.[63]

> Arveragus, of gentillesse,
> Had lever dye in sorwe and in distresse
> Than that his wyf were of her trouthe fals.[64]

And finally, the clerk releases Aurelius, from the same motive of generous
emulation:

> This philosophre answerde, "Leve brother,
> Everich of yow dide gentilly til other.

Thou art a squyer, and he is a knight;
But God forbede, for his blisful might,
But-if a clerk coude doon a gentil dede
As wel as any of yow, it is no drede!"[65]

[461] Thus it appears that the dramatic impulse to the telling of the Franklin's Tale is to be found in the relations among the Pilgrims and in the effect that they have upon each other,—in other words, in the circumstances, the situation, and the interplay of character.

It has sometimes been thought that the story, either in subject or in style, is too fine for the Franklin to tell. But this objection Chaucer foresaw and forestalled. The question is not whether this tale, thus told, would be appropriate to a typical or "average" fourteenth-century franklin. The question is whether it is appropriate to this particular Franklin, under these particular circumstances, and at this particular juncture. And to this question there can be but one answer. Chaucer's Franklin is an individual, not a mere type-specimen. He is rich, ambitious socially, and profoundly interested in the matter of *gentillesse* for personal and family reasons. He is trying to bring up his son as a gentleman, and his position as "St. Julian in his country" has brought him into intimate association with first-rate models. He has, under the special circumstances, every motive to tell a gentleman's story and to tell it like a gentleman. He is speaking under the immediate influence of his admiration for the Squire and of his sense of the inferiority of his own son. If we choose to conceive the Franklin as a mediaeval Squire Western and then to allege that he could not possibly have told such a story, we are making the difficulty for ourselves. We are considering—not Chaucer's Franklin (whose character is to be inferred not merely from the description in the General Prologue but from all the other evidence that the poet provides)— not Chaucer's Franklin, but somebody quite different, somebody for whom Chaucer has no kind of responsibility.[66]

In considering the immediate occasion of the Franklin's Tale, we have lost sight for a moment of the Wife of Bath. But she was not absent from the mind of the Franklin. The proper subject of his tale, as we have seen, is *gentillesse*. Now that (as well as marriage) was a subject on which the Wife of Bath had descanted at [462] some length. Her views are contained in the famous harangue delivered by the lady to her husband on the wedding night: "But for ye speken of swich gentillesse," etc.[67] Many readers have perceived that this portentous curtain-lecture clogs the story, and some have perhaps wished it away, good as it is in itself. For it certainly seems to be out of place on lips of the *fée*. But its insertion is (as usual in such cases) exquisitely appropriate to the teller of the tale, the Wife of Bath, who cannot help dilating on subjects which interest her, and who has had the advantage of learned society in the person of her fifth husband. Perhaps no *fée* would have talked thus to her knightly bridegroom on such an occasion; but it is quite in character for the Wife of Bath to use the *fée* (or anybody else) as a mouthpiece for her own ideas, as the Merchant had used Proserpine to point his satire.

Thus the references to Dante, Valerius, Seneca, Boethius, and Juvenal—so deliciously absurd on the lips of a *fée* of King Arthur's time—are perfectly in place when we remember who it is that is reporting the monologue. The Wife was a citer of [463] authorities—she makes the *fée* cite authorities. How comical this is the Wife did not know, but Chaucer knew, and if we think he did not, it is our own fault for not observing how dramatic in spirit is the *Canterbury Tales.*

A considerable passage in the curtain-lecture is given to the proposition that "such gentillesse as is descended out of old richesse" is of no value: "Swich arrogance is not worth an hen."[68] These sentiments the Franklin echoes:

> "Fy on possessioun
> But-if a man be vertuous withal!"[69]

But, whether or not the Wife's digression on *gentillesse* is lingering in the Franklin's mind (as I am sure it is), one thing is perfectly clear: the Franklin's utterances on marriage are spoken under the influence of the discussion which the Wife has precipitated. In other words, though everybody else imagines that the subject has been finally dismissed by the Host when he calls on the Squire for a tale of *love*, it has no more been dismissed in fact than when the Friar attempted to dismiss it at the beginning of his tale.[70] For the Franklin has views, and he means to set them forth. He possesses, as he thinks, the true solution of the whole difficult problem. And that solution he embodies in his tale of *gentillesse.*

The introductory part of the Franklin's Tale sets forth a theory of the marriage relation quite different from anything that has so far emerged in the debate. And this theory the Franklin arrives at by taking into consideration both *love* (which, as we remember, was the subject that the Host had bidden the Squire treat of) and *gentillesse* (which is to be the subject of his own story).

Arveragus had of course been obedient to his lady during the period of courtship, for obedience was well understood to be the duty of a lover. Finally, she consented to marry him—

> To take him for hir housbande and hir lord,
> Of swich lordshipe as men han over her wyves.[71]

Marriage, then, according to the orthodox doctrine (as held by Walter and Griselda) was to change Arveragus from the lady's servant to her master. But Arveragus was an enlightened and chivalric [464] gentleman, and he promised the lady that he would never assert his marital authority, but would content himself with the mere name of sovereignty, continuing to be her servant and lover as before. This he did because he thought it would ensure the happiness of their wedded life.

> And for to lede the more in blisse hir lyves,
> Of his free wil he swoor hir as a knight,
> That never in al his lyf he, day ne night,

> Ne sholde up-on him take no maistrye
> Agayn hir wil, ne kythe hir ialousye,
> But hir obeye, and folwe hir wil in al,
> As any lovere to his lady shal;
> Save that the name of soveraynetee,
> That wolde he have for shame of his degree.[72]

But, just as Arveragus was no disciple of the Marquis Walter, so Dorigen was not a member of the sect of the Wife of Bath. She promised her husband obedience and fidelity in return for his *gentillesse* in renouncing his sovereign rights.

> She thanked him, and with ful greet humblesse
> She seyde, "Sire, sith, of your gentillesse,
> Ye profre me to have so large a reyne,
> Ne wolde never God bitwixe us tweyne,
> As in my gilt, were outher werre or stryf.
> Sir, I wol be your humble trewe wyf,
> Have heer my trouthe, til that myn herte breste."[73]

This, then, is the Franklin's solution of the whole puzzle of matrimony, and it is a solution that depends upon love and *gentillesse* on both sides. But he is not content to leave the matter in this purely objective condition. He is determined that there shall be no misapprehension in the mind of any Pilgrim as to his purpose. He wishes to make it perfectly clear that he is definitely and formally offering this theory as the only satisfactory basis of happy married life. And he accordingly comments on the relations between his married lovers with fulness, and with manifest reference to certain things that the previous debaters have said.

The arrangement, he tells the Pilgrims, resulted in "quiet and rest" for both Arveragus and Dorigen. And, he adds, it is the only [465] arrangement which will ever enable two persons to live together in love and amity. Friends must "obey each other if they wish to hold company long."

> "Love wol nat ben constreyned by maistrye;
> Whan maistrie comth, the god of love anon
> Beteth hise winges, and farewel! he is gon!
> Love is a thing as any spirit free;
> Wommen of kinde desiren libertee,
> And nat to ben constreyned as a thral;
> And so don men, if I soth seyen shal.
> Loke who that is most pacient in love,
> He is at his avantage al above.
> Pacience is an heigh vertu certeyn;
> For it venquisseth, as thise clerkes seyn,
> Thinges that rigour sholde never atteyne.
> For every word men may nat chyde or pleyne.
> Lerneth to suffre, or elles, so moot I goon,
> Ye shul it lerne, wher-so ye wole or noon."[74]

Hence it was that this wise knight promised his wife "suffraunce" and that she promised him never to abuse his goodness.

> Heer may men seen an humble wys accord;
> Thus hath she take hir servant and hir lord,
> Servant in love, and lord in mariage;
> Than was he bothe in lordship and servage;
> Servage? nay, but in lordshipe above,
> Sith he hath bothe his lady and his love;
> His lady, certes, and his wyf also,
> The which that lawe of love accordeth to.[75]

The result, the Franklin adds, was all that could be desired. The knight lived "in blisse and in solas." And then the Franklin adds an encomium on the happiness of true marriage:

> "Who coude telle, but he had wedded be,
> The ioye, the ese, and the prosperitee
> That is bitwixe an housbonde and his wyf?"[76]

This encomium echoes the language of the Merchant:

> "A wyf! a Seinte Marie! *benedicite!*
> How mighte a man han any adversitee
> That hath a wyf? Certes, I can nat seye!
> The blisse which that is bitwixe hem tweye
> Ther may no tonge telle or herte thinke."[77]

[466] The Franklin's praise of marriage is sincere; the Merchant's had been savagely ironical. The Franklin, we observe, is answering the Merchant, and he answers him in the most effective way—by repeating his very words.

And just as in the Merchant's Tale we noted that the Merchant has enormously expanded the simple *fabliau* that he had to tell, inserting all manner of observations on marriage which are found in no other version of the Pear-Tree Story, so also we find that the Franklin's exposition of the ideal marriage relation (including the pact between Arveragus and Dorigen) is all his own, occurring in none of the versions that precede Chaucer.[78] These facts are of the very last significance. No argument is necessary to enforce their meaning.

It is hardly worth while to indicate the close connection between this and that detail of the Franklin's exposition and certain points that have come out in the discussion as conducted by his predecessors in the debate. His repudiation of the Wife of Bath's doctrine that men should be "governed by their wives"[79] is express, as well as his rejection of the opposite theory. Neither party should lose his liberty; neither the husband nor the wife should be a thrall. Patience (which clerks celebrate as a high virtue) should be mutual, not, as in the Clerk's Tale, all on one side. The husband is to be both servant and lord—servant in love and lord in marriage. Such servitude is true lordship. Here there is a manifest allusion to the words of Walter's subjects in the Clerk's Tale:

> That blisful yok
> Of sovereynetee, noght of servyse,[80]

as well as to Walter's rejoinder:

> "I me reioysed of my libertee,
> That selde tyme is founde in mariage;
> Ther I was free, I moot been in servage."[81]

It was the regular theory of the Middle Ages that the highest type of chivalric love was incompatible with marriage, since marriage [467] brings in mastery, and mastery and love cannot abide together. This view the Franklin boldly challenges. Love *can* be consistent with marriage, he declares. Indeed, without love (and perfect, *gentle* love) marriage is sure to be a failure. The difficulty about mastery vanishes when mutual love and forbearance are made the guiding principles of the relation between husband and wife.

The soundness of the Franklin's theory, he declares, is proved by his tale. For the marriage of Arveragus and Dorigen was a brilliant success:

> Arveragus and Dorigene his wyf
> In sovereyn blisse leden forth hir lyf.
> Never eft ne was ther angre hem bitwene;
> He cherisseth hir as though she were a quene;
> And she was to him trewe for evermore.
> Of this two folk ye gete of me na-more.[82]

Thus the whole debate has been brought to a satisfactory conclusion, and the Marriage Act of the Human Comedy ends with the conclusion of the Franklin's Tale.

Those readers who are eager to know what Chaucer thought about marriage may feel reasonably content with the inference that may be drawn from his procedure. The Marriage Group of Tales begins with the Wife of Bath's Prologue and ends with the Franklin's Tale. There is no connection between the Wife's Prologue and the group of stories that precedes; there is no connection between the Franklin's Tale and the group that follows. Within the Marriage Group, on the contrary, there is close connection throughout. That act is a finished act. It begins and ends an elaborate debate. We need not hesitate, therefore, to accept the solution which the Franklin offers as that which Geoffrey Chaucer the man accepted for his own part. Certainly it is a solution that does him infinite credit. A better has never been devised or imagined.[83]

Notes

1 The Marriage Group of the *Canterbury Tales* has been much studied, and with good results. Hitherto, however, scholars have been concerned with the order of the tales, or with their several dates, not with Chaucer's development of the theme (see especially a paper by Mr. George Shipley in *Modern Language Notes*, X. 273–76).

2 Since the *Canterbury Tales* is an unfinished work, the drama of the Pilgrimage is of course more or less fragmentary, and, furthermore, some of the stories (being old material, utilized for the nonce) have not been quite accurately fitted to their setting. Such defects, however, need not trouble us. They are patent enough whenever they occur, and we can easily allow for them. Indeed, the disturbance they cause is more apparent than real. Thus the fact that the Second Nun speaks of herself as a "son of Eve" does not affect our argument. The contradiction would eventually have been removed by a stroke of Chaucer's pen, and its presence in no wise prevents the Legend of St. Cecilia from being exquisitely appropriate to the actual teller.

3 This fact was admirably brought out, long ago, by Professor Hales (in his *Folia Litteraria*, 90–93).

4 G. 645–46.

5 Whether vss. 1163–1212 are later than the bulk of the Clerk's Tale, when the Tale was written, and whether it was originally intended for the Clerk, or for the *Canterbury Tales* at all, are questions that do not here concern us, for they in no way affect the present investigation. It makes no difference in our argument whether Chaucer translated the story of Griselda in order to put it into the Clerk's mouth, or whether he created the Clerk in order to give him the story of Griselda, or whether, having translated the story and created the Clerk as independent acts, he noticed that the story suited the Clerk, and so brought the two together. It is enough for us that the Tale was sooner or later allotted to the Clerk and that it fits his character without a wrinkle.

6 Against this particular view I have nothing to object, for (manifestly) the theory that Chaucer relieved his own feelings in this fashion does not conflict at all with my opinion that the passage is dramatically consistent with the Clerk's character and with the circumstances.

7 What connection Chaucer meant to make between the Wife's Prologue and the portion of the *Canterbury Tales* that comes before it we need not conjecture. Probably he had not determined. For us the question is of no immediate interest. It is enough for us that the Prologue begins a group and opens a new subject of discussion.

8 D. 469–73.

9 D. 1258–62.

10 D. 164–65.

11 A. 708.

12 We may note that the tale which Chaucer first gave to the Wife, as it seems, but afterwards transferred to the Shipman, had also a personal application. It was aimed more or less directly at the Monk, and its application was enforced by the Host's exhortation to the company: "Draweth no monkes more unto your in" (B. 1632). And it contained also a roving shot at the Merchant. Compare the General Prologue:

> Ther wiste no wight that he was in dette,
> So estatly was he of his governaunce,
> With his bargaynes and with his chevisaunce.
>
> (A. 280–82)

with the words of the Merchant in the Shipman's Tale:

> For of us chapmen, also God me save,
> And by that lord that cleped is Seint Yve,
> Scarsly amonges twelve ten shul thryve
> Continuelly, lasting unto our age.

> We may wel make chere and good visage,
> And dryve forth the world as it may be,
> And kepen our estaat in privetee
> Til we be deed, or elles that we pleye
> A pilgrimage, or goon out of the weye.
>
> (B. 1416–24)

13 D. 688–91, 707–10.

14 The Wife's clerk gave himself to "worldly occupacioun" (vs. 684). Our Clerk was not "so worldly for to have offyce" (Prologue, vs. 292).

15 "Abyde!" quod she, "my tale is not bigonne" (D. 169).

16 Prologue, vs. 217. The Wife "was a worthy woman al hir lyve" (Prologue, vs. 459).

17 "Thou lettest our disport in this manere" (D. 839).

18 D. 854–55.

19 D. 864–81.

20 D. 1258–62.

21 We remember that this is also the form of the Pardoner's Tale (which even included a text, "Radix malorum est cupiditas"), and that the Nun's Priest's Tale is in effect but a greatly expanded *exemplum*, without a text, to be sure, but with an appropriate moral ("taketh the moralitee," B. 4630), an address to the hearers ("good men"), and a formal benediction (B. 4634–36).

22 D. 1271–72.

23 D. 1274–77.

24 Note also the comic interlude (Miller, Reeve, Cook) that follows the Knight's Tale, and the dramatic manner in which it is brought in and continued.

25 E. 1–5.

26 E. 113–15. Petrarch has "ut coniugio scilicet animum applices, collumque non liberum modo sed imperiosum legitimo subjicias iugo." Chaucer may or may not have understood this Latin, but he certainly did not think that he was translating it. He was rewriting to suit himself. It may be an accident that the ideas he expressed and the words he chose are so extremely apropos. If accident is to be assumed, however, the present argument is in no way affected. Grant that the translation was made before Chaucer had even conceived the idea of a Canterbury Pilgrimage, and it remains true that, in utilizing this translation as the Clerk's Tale and in putting it into its present position, he found these words *sovereynetee* and *servyse* particularly apt, and that the Pilgrims (who were living men and women to Chaucer) found them equally pertinent. It is Chaucer's final design, I repeat, that we are considering, not the steps by which he arrived at it.

27 Petrarch has "delectabat omnimoda libertas, quae in coniugio rara est"; but "Ther I was free, I moot been in servage" (E. 147) is the Clerk's own addition.

28 E. 1141–62.

29 D. 688–91. When the clerk is too old for Venus, says the Wife, he sits down and writes "that wommen can nat kepe hir mariage." But our Clerk is not old, and he has told of a woman who kept her marriage under difficult conditions.

30 E. 1163–1212.

31 "Er I go" is a mere formula (derived from the technique of the wandering narrator) for "before I finish." Its use does not indicate that either Chaucer or the Clerk has forgotten the situation.

32 As to the Wife's "life" see her expressions in D. 111–12, 469–73, 615–26.

33 The scribe's rubric "Lenvoy *de Chaucer*" should not mislead us, any more than the world *auctor* does when attached by the scribe to E. 995–1001 (a stanza which is expressly ascribed by the Clerk to "sadde folk in that citee").

34 "Ther wiste no wight that he was in dette" (Prol., vs. 280).
35 "She is a shrewe at al" (E. 1222). *Shrew* has, of course, a general sense. It is not here limited to the specific meaning of "scold."
36 "Who-so be rebel to my iuggement
   Shal paye for al that by the weye is spent" (Prologue, vss. 833–34).
37 Twice in the course of this encomium the speaker drops his irony for an instant – with superb dramatic effect – once in vs. 1318 and again in vss. 1377–78. In the latter case there is a quick turn in the next verse.
38 E. 1291–92.
39 D. 1823 ff.
40 "Welcome the sixte, whan that ever he shal!" says the Wife (D. 45).
41 E. 1423–28.
42 D. 165.
43 D.1270–77.
44 E. 1670–73.
45 D. 489–90.
46 D. 175.
47 E. 1682–88.
48 D. 226–33.
49 E. 2265–75.
50 E. 2311–12.
51 D. 425–27.
52 We should not forget that this discussion between Pluto and Proserpine is the Merchant's own addition to the Pear-Tree Story.
53 E. 2419–40.
54 F. 1–3.
55 Just as the summons to the Merchant was incidental to his comments on the Clerk's Tale.
56 F. 673–81.
57 F. 682–94.
58 The Host's conduct and the bearing of the Pilgrims toward him are alike noteworthy. He has been appointed "judge and reporter" of the tales and general manager of the pilgrimage. The penalty for "rebellion" against his authority is to pay the traveling expenses of the whole troop, a sufficiently heavy fine (A. 803–18, 832–34). More than once he magnifies his office, sometimes in terms so arbitrary as to warrant the suspicion that he is trying to irritate his interlocutor so that the forfeit may be exacted. But at such times the person addressed is always significantly deferential. Thus he "speaks as lordly as a king" when he interrupts the Reeve's preamble: "The devil made a reve for to preche" (A. 3899–3908). His words to the Man of Law are courteous, but decided:

"Acquiteth yow, and holdeth your biheste,
Than have ye doon your devoir atte leste"

(B. 33–38)

And the lawyer's reply is a full acknowledgment of the Host's legal rights in the case (B. 39–44). The Host accuses the Parson, jocosely but not very politely, of being a Lollard (B. 1172–77). His rude criticism of Chaucer's own "Sir Thopas" is famous (B. 2109–25). The badinage with which he addresses the dignified Monk is so broad that Chaucer feels constrained to comment upon the victim's patient endurance of it: "This worthy monk took al in pacience." (B. 3155). His address to the Nun's Priest is described as "rude speche and bold" (B. 3998), but the Priest's answer is merely a hearty and eager assent (B. 4006). He reproves the Friar and the Summoner in drastic terms: "Ye fare as folk that dronken been of ale"

(D. 852). The only case of rebellion is the Miller's refusal to give way to the Monk (A. 3118–34); but here, in effect, the rebel claims a drunken man's privilege, and it is accorded him. The momentary quarrel between the Pardoner and the Host (C. 956–68) does not involve insubordination (cf. *Atlantic Monthly*, December, 1893, LXXII, 832–33). The fine courtesy of the Host's invitation to the Prioress (B. 1635–41) – in contrast with his habitual lordly roughness – shows what an impression that most charming of mediaeval ladies has made upon the company.

59 F. 709–15.
60 F. 754–55.
61 F. 1522–24.
62 F. 1527.
63 F. 1543–44.
64 F. 1595–97.
65 F. 1607–12.
66 How elaborate a compliment the Franklin pays the Squire is not always perceived by us moderns, prone as we are to read each tale in and for itself as if it were an isolated unit. The point may be appreciated in all its force, however, if one will take the trouble to compare the Franklin's description (F. 925–34, 943–52) of Aurelius (who is the real hero of the story) with Chaucer's description of our Squire in the General Prologue (A. 79–100). The resemblance extends even to verbal details. There is also a point of contact between the Franklin's Tale and the Merchant's, in that the demeanor of Aurelius in love is much like that of Damian (both of whom are squires), though the character of Aurelius is so different from Damian's (E. 1866 ff.; F. 941 ff.). Both were at first afraid to tell their love to the lady and each expressed his passion in lyric verse. Compare

> In a lettre wroot he al his sorwe
> In maner of a compleynt or a lay
> Unto his faire fresshe lady May.
>
> (E. 1880–82)

with

> He was despeyred, no-thing dorste he seye,
> Save in his songes somwhat wolde he wreye
> His wo, as in a general compleyning:
> He seyde he lovede, and was biloved no-thing:
> Of swich matere he made manye layes,
> Songes, compleintes, roundels, virelayes.
>
> (F. 943–48)

This similarity brings out the more strongly the contrast between May's and Dorigen's reception of the confession when it is finally made. The antithesis may well have been intended by the Franklin. At all events, the conduct of Dorigen fits admirably the words of the Merchant in pointing his satirical praise of the compassionate May:

> Som tyrant is, as ther be many oon,
> That hath an herte as hard as any stoon,
> Which wolde han lete him sterven in the place
> Wel rather than han graunted him hir grace,
> And hem reioysen in hir cruel pryde,
> And rekke nat to been an homicyde.
>
> (E. 1989–94)

For Aurelius had protested that his life depended on Dorigen's mercy:

Madame, reweth upon my peynes smerte,
For with a word ye may me sleen or save,
Heer at your feet God wolde that I were grave!
I ne have as now no leyser more to seye;
Have mercy, swete, or ye wol do me deye.

(F. 974–78)

These things, it is true, are all conventions. But (1) they are conventions that Chaucer used not mechanically, but with consciousness of their significance, and (2) I mention them merely for what they are worth, not as necessary parts of my argument.

67 D. 1109–76.
68 D. 1109 ff.
69 F. 686–87.
70 D. 1274–77.
71 The sly suggestion of this line was certainly not missed by the Pilgrims.
72 F. 744–52.
73 F. 753–59.
74 F. 764–78.
75 F. 791–98.
76 F. 803–5.
77 E. 1337–41.
78 The original point of the story is, of course, preserved in the question "Which was the moste free?" (F. 1622) – the same question that occurs in other versions. The peculiarity consists in the introduction of the pact of mutual love and forbearance and in dwelling upon the lesson which it teaches.
79 D. 1261–62.
80 E. 113–14.
81 E. 145–47.
82 F. 1551–56.
83 Professor Lowes's important paper on "Chaucer and the *Miroir de Mariage*", (*Modern Philology*, VIII, 165–86, 305–34) may here be cited as incidentally but powerfully confirmatory of the views which are set forth in the present essay.

4 The Reeve

WALTER CLYDE CURRY

Originally published as the first part of chapter 4 in Walter Clyde Curry, *Chaucer and the Mediaeval Sciences* (New York: Oxford University Press, 1926, pp. 71–75). The original pagination is recorded within square brackets. The endnotes originally appeared on p. 251. In the rest of chapter 4, Curry goes on to discuss the Miller. The chapter is based on an article: "Chaucer's Reeve and Miller," *PMLA* 35 (1920):189–209.

A mediaeval audience's comprehension of the personalities attributed to those delightful rascals, the Reeve and the Miller, must have been greatly facilitated by virtue of the fact that Chaucer has bodied them forth with the evident aid of physiognomical principles. It could not be maintained that the poet has created these personages mechanically according to certain rules and regulations known to his audience, but in presenting an exact correspondence between personal appearances and characters he has, while apparently detracting nothing from the lifelike qualities of the personalities introduced, succeeded in rendering them more vivid, natural, and significant to anyone with the mediaeval point of view.

Though the description of the Reeve's person is meager enough, it doubtless sufficed to indicate to the well informed men and women of the fourteenth century most of what Chaucer wanted to develop in the Reeve's character:

> The Reve was a sclendre colerik man,
> His berd was shave as ny as ever he can,
> His heer was by his eres round y-shorn,
> His top was dokked lyk a preest biforn.
> Ful longe were his legges, and ful lene,
> Y-lyk a staf, there was no calf y-sene.

(*C. T.*, A, 587 ff.)

[72] Now, may we ask again just what did these few items of personal appearance, perhaps only amusing to modern readers, signify to the mediaeval audience? The Reeve's custom of shaving his beard and of wearing his hair closely cropped need not detain us; it merely indicated in Middle

English times a man of low caste or, more especially, an obedient and humble servant. This ostentatious display of humility affected by the Reeve was doubtless a part of his general programme of hoodwinking his young lord and of privately increasing his own store of goods; he could so "plesen subtilly" that, in addition to what he stole during the year, he had the confidence and thanks of his lord together with special gifts of coats and hoods besides. Everybody in Chaucer's time, it may be presumed, knew something about the four complexions of men, so that the artist thought it necessary to suggest only two characteristics of the choleric man in his description of the Reeve. The Middle English *Secreta Secretorum*, some version of which the poet certainly knew, has this to say: "The colerike (man) by kynde he sholde be lene of body; his body is light and drye, and he shal be sumwhat rogh; and lyght to wrethe and lyght to peyse; of sharpe witt, wyse and of good memorie, a greete entremyttere; he louyth hasty wengeaunce; desyrous of company of women moore than hym nedyth."[1] A large part of the delineation of the Reeve's character, in the General Prologue, is taken up with illustrative material bearing out the fact that he is of "a sharpe witt, wyse, and of good memorie." He understands the art of husbandry; the raising of cattle, chickens, poultry, and swine is a [73] congenial and profitable occupation; and, it is said, he has been accustomed to tampering so skilfully with the annual reports made to his lord that, in spite of his rascality, no man might bring him in arrears. Many of the under-servants have known him for a thief all along, of course, but according to his choleric nature he is generally so "hasty" of his "wengeaunce" that they have maintained a discreet silence:

> They were adrad of him as of the deeth
>
> (A, 605) [reference corrected]

The Reeve is a choleric man and, therefore, cunning and crafty. So Chaucer presents him in the General Prologue to the *Canterbury Tales*.

When we come to the Reeve's Prologue, however, Oswald the Carpenter seems, upon first acquaintance, to be quite another man; at any rate, emphasis is there placed upon other, different elements of his character. Without further preparation, apparently, than the suggestion that "in his youth" he learned a good trade, we suddenly find that he is an old man, easily angered and as easily appeased, indulging in certain preachments upon old age and the follies of youth — to the disgust of the Host (*C. T.*, A, 3899 ff.) [reference corrected]. He is here revealed in his true colors; he is a lecher of the worst sort, a churl, a pitiful example of the burnt-out body in which there still lives a concupiscent mind. Youth with its follies is past; his hairs are white with age and perhaps from illicit association and women;[2] he is like rotten fruit. Yet he still boasts of having a "coltes tooth," and though the power to gratify his physical desires is gone, he still mentally hops to folly while the world pipes. [74] And worst of all he shamelessly publishes the viciousness of his imagination:

> For in oure wil there stiketh ever a nayl,
> To have an hoor heed and a grene tayl
> As hath a leek; for thogh our might be goon,
> Our wil desireth folie ever in oon,
> For when we may nat doon, than wol we speke;
> Yet in our asshen olde is fyr y-reke
>   (*C. T.*, A, 387 ff.) [reference corrected]

This unexpected change in the character of the Reeve might well seem to be a serious blemish upon the poet's artistic workmanship; Oswald, an aged reprobate reveling in memories of follies committed in youth and prime, appears to come into direct conflict with the cunning and wide-awake Reeve of the General Prologue. But Chaucer is, for the most part, the conscious artist. Rightly understood, he rarely leaves out any element that might be considered essential to the unity and consistency of his characterizations. In the General Prologue — precisely where it should be — there is the emphatic statement that the Reeve has exceedingly small legs. This apparently innocent observation contains by implication most of what the poet later develops in the Reeve's hidden personality.

For it must be remembered that whenever Chaucer takes the trouble to impress upon his reader's notice the special physical peculiarities of his Pilgrims, we may rest assured that he intends for them to be straightway interpreted in terms of character. What, then, should small legs like those of the Reeve signify? The physiogno[75]mists do not leave us in doubt. Aristotle himself affirms[3] that "whoever has thin, sinewy legs is luxurious or voluptuous by nature and is to be referred to birds." Polemon, the greatest and probably the father of most of the mediaeval physiognomists, is still more explicit in his discussion, "De signis crurum":[4] "And if, moreover, the legs are slender so that the tendons are visible, such persons should be judged as being given to much cupidity and lust." An anonymous author of the eleventh century — and a follower of Polemon — is of a like opinion:[5] "People who are of a white color and have slender legs as if the tendons were stretched are lustful and intemperate in their sensual desires"; and the Middle English *Secreta Secretorum* says that "tho men whyche haue smale legges and synowye bene luchrus." When we remember, moreover, that one of the chief characteristics of the "colerik" man is that he is "Desyrous of the company of women moore than hym nedyth," it is apparent that Chaucer has made in the General Prologue ample preparation for the revelations which come in the Reeve's Prologue. His personal appearance betrays the Reeve to any ordinary observer — with the mediaeval point of view —, and his later confession need cause no surprise.

Notes

1 *Secreta Secretorum*, ed. R. Steele, EETS. E. S., LXXIV, p. 220. With this should be compared by Lydgate and Burgh, *Secrees of Old Philosoffres*, ed. Steele, EETS. E. S., LXVI, p. 104.

2 Richard Saunders, *Physiognomie, and Chiromancie, Metoposcopie, Dreams, and the Art of Memory*, London, 1671, p. 189.
3 Aristotle's *Physiognomonika*, ed. R. Foerster, *Scriptores Physiognomonici*, I, 55.
4 *Polemonis de physiognomonia liber Arabice et Latine*, ed. G. Hoffman, in Foerster, *op. cit.*, I, 204. This work is edited also in I. G. F. Franzius's *Scriptores physiognomoniae veteres*, 1780, pp. 209 ff.
5 *Anonymi de physiognomonia liber Latinus*, ed. Foerster, II, 133.

5 | The Reeve

JOHN MATTHEWS MANLY

Originally published as the middle section of chapter 3 in John
Matthews Manly, *Some New Light on Chaucer* (New York: Holt,
1926, pp. 84–94). The original pagination is recorded within square
brackets. Two passages have been omitted: a quotation (of the
portrait of the Reeve in the *General Prologue* [lines 587–622] from
pp. 84–85, and a brief passage from pp. 86–87. In chapter 3, Curry
discusses the Host, the Reeve, and the Miller.

You will readily recall the picturesque and highly individualized description
of the Reeve in the Prologue.... [85] ... Three features of this description
first suggested that Chaucer had in mind a definite person. One was the
statement that the Reeve came from Norfolk, beside a town called Baldeswelle; the second was the description of his house as situated on a heath and
well shaded by green trees; the third was the specific statement that he had
had charge of the manor since his lord was twenty years of age. The last two
sounded like bits of per[86]sonal observation by Chaucer, the first suggested
the question why Baldeswelle—an insignificant village, far from London,
almost in the "ferthest end of Norfolk"—should be mentioned, unless
Chaucer had some particular reason for interest in it.

The main facts in regard to Baldeswelle—the modern Bawdeswell—were
not hard to find. Blomefield's great *History of Norfolk* tells us that it is a
hamlet partly in the manor of Foxley, which in the fourteenth century
belonged to the estates of the earls of Pembroke. These facts did not,
however, suffice to explain why Chaucer's attention was attracted to the
Reeve and especially why his presentation of him is always and everywhere
charged with malice.... [87] ...

Fortunately a study of the facts regarding the earls of Pembroke and their
estates threw some light on the subject. John Hastings, second earl of Pembroke, whose father had died in 1348, came of age on September 12, 1368.
Before the following April he went abroad in the retinue of the Prince of
Wales and, with the exception of brief visits to England, remained in foreign
service until his death in 1375. Here, at once, is a curiously close agreement
with the lines:

And by his covenaunt yaf the rekening
Sin that his lord was twenty year of age.

[GP I (A) 600–1]

[88] On one of the earl's brief visits home he arranged that if he should die without an heir, all his property that was transferable should go to his cousin Sir William de Beauchamp, younger brother of the Earl of Warwick, on condition that he take the whole arms of Pembroke and get the King to allow him to assume the title of Earl of Pembroke. As a son and heir was born to Pembroke in September 1372, this plan did not take effect. But as the heir was a minor on the death of his father in 1375 he and the estates which were held in chief fell into the hands of the king and provision had to be made for them. The heir was allowed to remain in the custody of his mother and grandmother; the estates in England and Wales were variously disposed of. After a faithful inventory had been made, by two clerks appointed by the king, of the stock and other things in the lordships, manors, and lands, including those assigned in dower to the earl's widow, Anne, the custody of two-thirds of the lands in England exclusive of those in Kent was on January 22, 1376 committed to the Countess Anne and her mother Margaret Marshall, the [89] famous and powerful countess of Norfolk, daughter of Edmund de Brotherton and aunt of king Edward III. A week later, January 29, certain manors in Kent were committed to the custody of the king's esquire, John de Beverle, and on March 9, 1378, King Richard granted the custody of the estates in Wales to Sir William de Beauchamp. In this last transaction the mainpernors or sureties for Sir William de Beauchamp were two: John de Beverle and Geoffrey Chaucer of London. Whether these mainpernors were personal or official we do not know, and we need not stop to inquire whether the appointment implies that Geoffrey Chaucer was a large landowner, though we can hardly believe that either the king or the mother and grandmother of the heir would regard the responsibility of the sureties as of no importance. The other surety, John de Beverle, who had long been in service as one of the king's esquires, was a man of considerable wealth, as is evident from the numerous large grants made to him by the king and the land transactions recorded of him and his wife. Moreover, it was to John de Beverle [90] that the custody of the Pembroke estates in Kent had been granted in January 1376.

The public for which Chaucer wrote would infallibly recognize immediately his allusion to one of the manors belonging to the Pembroke estates and would be interested in anything concerning the affairs of so great a family. Chaucer himself had additional personal reasons for interest, because of his relations with Sir William de Beauchamp in connection both with the Pembroke lands and with his own trial for the raptus of Cecilia Chaumpaigne in 1380, when Beauchamp appeared as witness in his behalf.

On the mismanagement of some of the estates the records are interesting. Even before the death of the second earl two of his receivers had been called to account, as we learn from the *Calendar of Close Rolls* for 1374. After the death of the earl in 1375 we have no reason to believe that the management improved while the estates were in the hands of the king. Sir William de Beauchamp was much engaged in the king's business in Scotland and France and from 1384 to 1392 was captain of Calais. He could hardly have [91] given much personal attention to the lordships and lands committed to him. In the autumn of 1386 investigation of his management was officially begun and in 1387 (February 22 and October 6) an arrangement was made between Sir William de Beauchamp on the one side and the young earl's grandmother on the other (his mother having died in 1384). It was agreed that Sir William should be relieved of the custody of the lands and should receive the annual grant from the king of 100*m.* charged upon the estates and further should be free from any claim for waste committed after Easter next (i.e., 1388) on condition that he should appoint two of his council to meet two or three of the council of the countess and the young earl to view the waste in the Pembroke lands. The deputies were to collect what moneys they could to the profit of the said earl from those who had committed wastes.

From the facts just given it is evident that some of the Pembroke estates had been mismanaged from the time the second earl went abroad, soon after his twenty-first birthday, and that some continued to be mismanaged [92] at least until very near the time at which Chaucer was writing. On the mismanagement of the Norfolk lands I have as yet been unable to get any documentary evidence. They had long been in the sole custody of the young heir's grandmother, Margaret Marshall countess of Norfolk, for Anne countess of Pembroke had in 1376 granted to her mother both all her own property and the custody of all the lordships, manors and lands granted to her by the king as guardian of the heir of Pembroke. But Chaucer represents the Reeve of Baldeswelle as a rascal whose tricks might be suspected but could hardly be proved. How he obtained this information we can only guess. It is possible that he was chosen as one of the two deputies of Sir William to view the waste committed on the lands in his custody. The other mainpernor, John de Beverle, had died in 1381 and apparently had not been replaced. Chaucer had, so far as we know, no official or other duties to prevent him from taking part in such an investigation. It may even be suspected that before this time he had been concerned [93] about this matter. According to a recently discovered record, on June 23, 1383, he was granted permission to execute the controllership of wool, hides, and woolfells by Henry Gisors as deputy until Allhallows next (about four months) because "he is like to be so much occupied upon particular business that for a certain time he may not without grievous disturbance attend to that office;" and on November 25, 1384 he was given leave of absence for one month for the same reason. Whether he viewed the waste or not, it is likely that, as one personally concerned, he was present at the meeting held at Framlingham to discuss the transfer of the lands in Wales from the custody of Sir William de Beauchamp to that of the countess of Norfolk. If so he may, then and there, have heard reports of the tricky Reeve of Baldeswelle.

Three lines, at least, of the account of the Reeve sound as if Chaucer had
visited Baldeswelle:

> They were adrad of hym as of the deeth.
> His wonyng was ful faire upon an heeth;
> With grene trees yshadwed was his place.

[605–7]

[94] The records indicate that Sir William de Beauchamp did not willingly
give up the custody of the Pembroke lands that had been committed to him,
and it is perhaps not unjustifiable to assume that he and his friends—among
whom we can surely count the poet—took no little pleasure in this portrayal
of the sly Norfolk Reeve, whose petty thieving had so long been successfully
carried on under the very eyes of Sir William's antagonist, the masterful
countess of Norfolk. Chaucer's malicious sketch must have been highly
entertaining to the great folk at court, all of whom were certainly familiar
with the facts concerning the Pembroke lands.

6

Chaucer (II):
the Canterbury Tales (I)

JOHN SPEIRS

Originally published as the beginning of an article in *Scrutiny*
11 (1943):189–211. The original pagination is recorded within
square brackets. In the rest of the article, Speirs discusses the
General Prologue and the *Wife of Bath's Prologue*.

In the *Divine Comedy* states of perdition and deprivation at one extreme, and
the evil of human nature, of Dante's Italy in particular, and of the world in
general, all the grades of being in between, and, at the other extreme, the
higher and highest possibilities and states of beatitude, are placed and
apprehended. In the *Canterbury Prologue* and *Tales* the human order, as it
actually existed, with all its deficiencies, in England at Chaucer's moment
is more singly—more fragmentarily perhaps—the object of contemplation.
What has struck readers of the *Canterbury Prologue* and *Tales*—readers so
different as Dryden and Blake—is the variety of the human world they
mirror. But, as Blake alone perhaps seems to perceive ('They are the physiognomies or lineaments of universal human life') this surface variety has its
corresponding depth. Chaucer is in a seemingly modern way so realistic in
his foreground and at the same time so humane that, reading superficially we
are apt to miss the depth of difference behind. But the richness of significance
of that foreground is lent it from the unfamiliar depth. By the time the best
of the *Canterbury Tales* were composed Chaucer had behind him long years
of poetic practice. The accomplishment—so 'seemingly unstudied' as Coleridge remarked—of the versification is sufficient proof of that. But that
technical mastery was already remarkable in *Troilus and Criseyde* and indeed
was achieved at a very early stage. The depth, the ripeness of the *Prologue*
and the best of the *Tales*, is more than a thing of the maximum technical
accomplishment but is a depth of acquired meaning and achieved understanding. Habits of mind, ways of feeling—a whole way of life different from
our own—by comparison with which our own seems to many crude and
unsatisfactory—goes to the composing of that Chaucerian depth.

The simplifications of religious feeling distinguish a number of the *Tales*.
Most of these are probably among the earliest in date of composition—but it
is never safe to feel sure about this—and later inserted into the framework of
the *Canterbury Tales* to relate it to the religious occasion that the Pilgrimage

officially was. They are so "un-modern" (that may partly account for their charm for us) that they in this respect also contrast with the maturest of the *Tales* [190] and with the *Prologue*. Such phrases—of a singularly tender and haunting beauty—as these from the *A.B.C.*, a probably early translation outside the Canterbury framework:

> And bringest him out of the crooked strete . . .
>
> [70]
>
> And ledest us in-to the hye tour . . .
>
> [154]

are nearer such phrases as these from the *Man of Lawe's Tale*:

> The whyte lamb, that hurt was with the spere . . .
>
> [II (B¹) 459]
>
> The child stood, loking in the kinges face . . .
>
> [1015]

than either seems to be to anything in the *Prologue, The Nonne Prestes Tale, The Wyf of Bath's Prologue, The Pardoneres Tale, The Marchantes Tale.* Yet the complexity and subtlety of these latter, which are exactly those which *seem* most 'modern' to us, is found on analysis to be composed of elements which are just as 'un-modern'. As we dig down through the successive levels of these we come again upon their quite 'un-modern' foundations of allegory and personification by which their complex meaning is sustained.

The *Prioresses Tale*, unlike the *Seconde Nonnes*, the *Man of Lawe's*, the *Clerkes* and the *Monkes*, seems to have been specially composed for its *persona*, but though dramatically and otherwise robuster than these close translations and adaptations it is like them in that it belongs for us to an unescapably different world—less of dogmatic intellectual belief, however, than of Catholic folk-belief that was half superstitious credulity and naïve wonder; the gaping crowd confront the miracle of the Virgin. The humanity of Chaucer's—the Prioresse's—appreciation of the 'litel clergeon' and his 'prymer' further substantialises the Tale, his daily progress to and from school, the 'povre widwe' waiting vainly with a mother's anxious distress for the child's return. But the repetition in the child's mouth of the 'O Alma redemptoris'—of the meaning of the Latin the child, like the folk, is innocent—sustains to the miraculous climax a quite *other* note of religious exaltation caught from the choir-singing of the church services:

> Twyes a day it passed thurgh his throte,
> To scoleward and homward whan he wente.
>
> [VII 548–49; B² 1738–39]

The child has acquired the passivity—'it passed thurgh his throte'—of an instrument or vehicle of the divinity. There is further an exaggerated folk-rumour horror about a child-murder having taken place up an alley that is curiously combined with the naïve religious ecstasy. And combined with the miraculousness there is a curiously physical element:

> Ther he with throte y-corven lay upright,
> He 'Alma redemptoris' gan to singe
> So loude, that al the place gan to ringe . . .
>
> [611–13; 1801–3]

[191]   This holy monk, this abbot, him mene I,
> Him tonge out-caughte, and took a-wey the greyn,
> And he yaf up the goost ful softely . . .
>
> [670–72; 1860–62]

Something like this earthly-unearthly or other-earthly note—'there is better life in other place' [VIII (G) 323]—occurs again in the *Seconde Nonnes Tale* of Seinte Cecile; where it is more exactly perhaps sensual super-sensual in quality.

An angel:

> I have an angel which that loveth me
>
> [VIII (G) 152]

has brought Cecile and Valerian roses and lilies from Paradise. Tiburce, Valerian's brother, speaks:

> . . . 'I wondre, this tyme of the yeer,
> Whennes that sote savour cometh so
> Of rose and lilies that I smelle heer . . .
> The sote smel that in myn herte I finde
> Hath chaunged me al in another kinde'.
>
> [VIII (G) 246–52]

There is the beautiful and profound metaphysical recognition:

> Tiburce answerde, 'seistow this to me
> In soothnesse, or in dreem I herkne this?'
> 'In dremes', quod Valerian, 'han we be
> Unto this tyme, brother myn, y-wis.
> But now at erst in trouthe our dwelling is'.
>
> [VIII (G) 260–64]

But having less of the backbone of folkiness than the *Prioresses Tale*, this Tale is more a bookish product; the sweet savour of roses and lilies of Paradise seems a little sickly; its *persona* is appropriately an uncharacterized nun.

The *Man of Lawe's Tale* of Constance is rather more satisfying, in spite of its inordinate diffusion, because, being a tale of moment to all Christendom as opposed to all Heathendom, it is less private. Constance is compelled not only to leave parents and those with whom she has been brought up for strangers and an unknown husband, but also to leave Christian land for a barbarous nation and to come under the spells of a 'sowdanesse, rote of iniquitee'. The tale is evidently a tale of Christian constancy—Constance is in the first instance a personification; it manifests, besides the preservation of innocence by God's power in the midst of darkness, solitude, evil and death. The allusions to past miracles (*exempla*) of divine intervention (lines 470–490):

> Who saved Daniel in the horrible cave . . .
> Who kept hir fro the drenching in the see . . .

condense and accumulate the strength of religious feeling behind the [192] theme. In association with this supernatural, superterrestrial element there is the overflowing fountain of tenderness enveloping, as frequently in Chaucer, the child image—here the double image of mother and child:

> Hir litel child lay weping in hir arm,
> And kneling, pitously to him she seyde,
> 'Pees, litel sone, I wol do thee non harm'.
> With that hir kerchef of hir heed she breyde,
> And over his litel yen she it leyde;
> And in hir arm she lulleth it ful faste,
> And in-to heven hir eyn up she caste.

$$[\text{II} \ (\text{B}^1) \ 834-40]$$

This feeling evidently originates in, and derives its quality from the mediaeval worship of Mary and the child Christ.

> In him triste I, and in his moder dere,
> That is to me my seyl and eek my stere . . .

$$[832-33]$$

There is a corresponding feeling about Griselda and her child in the *Clerkes Tale*—particularly when the child is threatened by the monstrous brutality of man in the huge male person of the sergeant. In this passage explicitly religious associations, those of the Crucifixion, appear:

> But, sith I thee have marked with the croys,
> Of thilke fader blessed mote thou be,
> That for us deyde up-on a croys of tree.

$$[\text{IV} \ (\text{E}) \ 556-58]$$

The grotesqueness, to the modern mind, of the *Clerkes Tale*, a translation of Petrarch's Latin version of the tale of Griselda, largely disappears once we recognize that Griselda is not a completely human character at all, and should not be judged as such, but is again a kind of personification or, in this case, a type of wifely obedience and patience. As we see her first she is a type of daughterly perfection which merges into her assumption, and typification throughout the tale, of wifely perfection to the extremity of the violence that is done to her perfection as a mother; for if, by her incredible yielding up of her son, she continues the perfect image of the obedient wife it is at the expense of having become a very imperfect image of a mother. The tale of her sufferings, borne by her with a more than human passivity and resignation, seems to have some kind of further, more generalized significance, as that of Constance has also, as an allegory of the disciplinary trials of the soul.

Griselda, then, is both human and non-human. She is lent human substance as a peasant girl.

> And in greet reverence and charitee
> Hir olde povre fader fostred she;
> [193]   A fewe sheep spinning on feeld she kepte,
> She wolde noght been ydel til she slepte.

> And whan she hoomward cam, she wolde bringe
> Wortes or othere herbes tymes ofte,
> The whiche she shredde and seeth for hir livinge,
> And made hir bed ful harde and no-thing softe.
>
> [221-28]

But she and the village folk, with their beasts, are translated to a spiritual plane by the Christian idea of the blessedness of poverty and of labour performed 'in reverence and charitee' (compare the Plowman of the *Prologue*). The apparent contradiction between 'th' erthe yaf hem habundance' and 'povre folk' [203-4] is perhaps explainable in this context in terms of God's providing the fruits of the earth for His children as for the birds and beasts. The religious overtones of the poetry arise from remote but perceptible Biblical allusions.

> And as she wolde over hir threshfold goon,
> The markis cam and gan hir for to calle;
> And she set doun hir water-pot anoon,
> Bisyde the threshfold, in an oxes stalle,
> And doun up-on hir knees she gan to falle,
> And with sad contenance kneleth stille
> Til she had herd what was the lordes wille.
>
> [288-94]

The 'oxes stalle', taking up the resonance from previous lines (206):

> But hye god som tyme senden can
> His grace in-to a litel oxes stalle

half-consciously recalls the manger in which the infant Christ was laid. The 'markis' calling the peasant girl half seems God calling the soul; and her act of obeisance to her feudal lord:

> And doun up-on hir knees she gan to falle

—seems rather an act of worship. In such a context the water-pot (*cf.* 220, To fechen water at a welle is went) again dimly awakens Biblical virgin-at-the-well associations. The pomp of the marriage that follows owes some of its significance to the suggestion of the soul's espousals. Such an interpretation of the *Clerkes Tale* as having grown out of religious allegory should not be pressed too far. But the peculiar tenderness of the feeling cannot wholly be explained by the partially grotesque facts of the *human* story pitiful as these are.

Chaucer's version of the Hugolino story in the *Monkes Tale* is again not without traces of the religious feeling, if not the idea, which governed its occurrence as an episode in the *Divine Comedy*. The pity which in the *Divine Comedy*, as an element of that ordered [194] context, ultimately resolves the horror of the episode seems to suffuse, as a partially detached self-contained feeling, Chaucer's version, dissolving away the original horror. The children, in Chaucer's version, are childish, thus touching the gentler feelings.

> The eldeste scarsly fyf yeer was of age.
> Allas, fortune! it was greet crueltee
> Swiche briddes for to putte in swiche a cage!
>
> [vii 2412–14; B² 3602–04]

The metaphor associates them with what is small, helpless, innocent and pitiable.

> And on a day bifil that, in that hour,
> Whan that his mete wont was to be broght,
> The gayler shette the dores of the tour.
> He herde it wel,—but he ne spak right noght,
> And in his herte anon ther fil a thoght,
> That they for hunger wolde doon him dyen.
>
> [2423–28; 3613–18]

Following the sudden shock of this agonized recognition comes the gentler pathos of the common humanity of the child hungry for its 'potage' and the father's helplessness to relieve its hunger. (This is wholly Chaucer's addition).

> His yonge sone, that three yeer was of age,
> Un-to him seyde, 'fader, why do ye wepe?
> Whan wol the gayler bringen our potage,
> Is ther no morsel breed that ye do kepe?
> I am so hungry that I may nat slepe'.
>
> [2431–35; 3621–25]

The child, through the extremity of its suffering, begins to pass beyond the normal child consciousness:

> Now wolde god that I mighte slepen ever;
> Than sholde nat hunger in my wombe crepe
>
> [2436–37; 3626–27]

hunger being, moreover, imaged as a kind of beast that creeps into the 'wombe'. The child's simple acceptance of death, described with Chaucerian, un-Elizabethan absence of fuss:

> Til in his fadres barme adoun it lay,
> And seyde, 'far-wel, fader, I moot dye'.
> And kiste his fader, and deyde the same day
>
> [2440–42; 3630–32]

contrasts with the animal-like action of the distraught father:

> For wo his armes two he gan to byte.
>
> [2444; 3634]

But finally the horrible and repulsive is transformed into the sublimely pathetic when the two surviving children touchingly mis[195]understand that action and their love expresses itself in a sacrificial offer that would be grotesque if it did not recall the sacraments of religion:

> His children wende that it for hunger was
> That he his armes gnow, and nat for wo,
> And seyde, 'fader, do nat so, allas!
> But rather eet the flesh upon us two;
> Our flesh thou yaf us, tak our flesh us fro'.
>
> [2447–51; 3637–41]

As in the other tales it is the mother and son, in this it is the father and his sons in the tower who form what are felt as partially symbolic images.

Yet these poems for all their unique and touching beauty are too slight to possess that profounder seriousness which Arnold missed in Chaucer when he compared him with Dante, Homer, and Shakespeare—and even perhaps with Milton and Wordsworth. That profounder seriousness is to be discovered, where perhaps Arnold least thought of looking for it, at the basis of the great *Prologue* itself, the *Wife of Bath's Prologue*, the *Nonne Preestes Tale*, the *Marchantes Tale*, and some others of the maturest, and wisest, of the *Canterbury Tales*. These Arnold no doubt relegated to the inferior category of the "comic". But *Don Juan* (to take an example nearly contemporary with Arnold himself) is, at bottom, more *serious* than any other poem of the early 19th century with the exception perhaps of the *Prelude* and some other poems of Wordsworth, the *Induction* to the revised *Hyperion* and, possibly, the *Mask of Anarchy*.

7

The crucial passages in five of the *Canterbury Tales*: a study in irony and symbol

CHARLES A. OWEN, Jr

Originally published in *JEGP* 52 (1953):294–311. Reprinted by permission of the author and of the University of Illinois Press. The original pagination is recorded within square brackets. The endnotes originally appeared as footnotes.

Chaucer's art in the *Canterbury Tales* projects a complex world. To the dramatic pose of simplicity already adopted by Chaucer in many of his narrative poems is added the complication of a group of observed narrators. The intrinsic value of each of the tales is not its final one. Behind the artificial world created in the tale are the conscious purposes of the narrator and the self-revelation, involuntary and often unconscious, involved in all artistic effort. The simplest of the plots in the *Canterbury Tales* is that of the frame. It makes the same demand of each character involved, that he ride in the company of the others to Canterbury and back and participate in the creative activity of the tale-telling. Each character projects his tale, the limited vision it embodies, and his limiting personality into the world of the pilgrimage. The plot is simple but dynamic. For each vision has the potentiality of bringing into new focus those that preceded and of influencing those that will follow. The possibilities are soon unlimited. They lead to a richness that defies final analysis but finds its most concentrated expression in passages that at once embody and expose the limited vision of created character and creating narrator. These passages foreshadow in the unwitting speech or opinion of a character the outcome of the plot and help to create symbolic values that give the narrative an added and unifying dimension. They are in a sense symbolic of the whole work: in the contrast between what *is* and what men see—of themselves and of others—lies Chaucer's deepest vein of comedy.

Passages that foreshadow the outcome in the unwitting speech of a character are fairly numerous in the *Canterbury Tales*,[1] but I have found only five that perform also a symbolic and unifying function.[2] [295] These five passages occur in five of the most important tales. It will be the purpose of this paper to analyze the five passages and to explore the multiple meanings, both within the tales and in the world of the pilgrimage, which they epitomize.

I

One of the clearest of the symbolic passages is the speech in the *Franklin's Tale*, where Dorigen softens her refusal to Aurelius and at the same time expresses her love for her husband:

> But after that in pley thus seyde she:
> "Aurelie," quod she, "by heighe God above,
> Yet wolde I graunte you to been youre love,
> Syn I yow se so pitously complayne,
> Looke what day that endelong Britayne
> Ye remoeve alle the rokkes, stoon by stoon,
> That they ne lette ship ne boot to goon.
> I seye, whan ye han maad the coost so clene
> Of rokkes that there nys no stoon ysene,
> Thanne wol I love yow best of any man,
> Have heer my trouthe, in al that evere I kan."
>
>   v (F) 988–98

This speech of Dorigen provides the final element necessary to the plot. The happy marriage, the temporary absence of Arveragus, the enduring love of Aurelius, have all been presented. The wife's rash promise is the catalytic element that sets the others to reacting.

But because of the view we have had of Dorigen's grief, in which the rocks played so menacing a part, the rash promise is at the same time an expression of Dorigen's love for her husband. Her mention of the rocks tells us even more certainly than her refusal that she is entirely devoted to her husband. This speech introduces for the first time in the tale the contrast, extremely important later, between the appearance of things and the reality. On the surface the speech is an agreement under certain conditions to commit adultery. Beneath the surface it is an expression of conjugal loyalty.

In fact Dorigen has endeavored without realizing it to transform the symbolic meaning of the rocks. Up to this point they have represented to her the menace of natural forces to her husband's life. Hereafter their permanence is a guarantee of her enduring love for her husband. The rocks occur to her not only because her husband's life is in danger from them but because their immutability is like her love. She has seen beyond the menacing appearance of the rocks and [296] has invoked the symbolic value of their endurance at the same time that she has finally accepted their reality.

The changed significance of the rocks is emphasized in several ways by Chaucer. Before her rash promise Dorigen questions on grounds of reason the purpose of the rocks in God's world and prays

> "But wolde God that alle thise rokkes blake
> Were sonken into helle for his sake!
> Thise rokkes sleen myn herte for the feere."
>
>   v (F) 891–93

After her promise to Aurelius it is his turn to pray for the removal of the rocks. Instead of Eterne God, he addresses Apollo, and asks him to persuade his sister Lucina to cause a two-year flood tide high enough to cover the rocks with five fathoms, or, if this is not feasible,

> "Prey hire to synken every rok adoun
> Into hir owene dirke regioun
> Under the ground, ther Pluto dwelleth inne,
> Or nevere mo shal I my lady wynne."
>
> v (F) 1076

The parallelism of the prayers emphasizes the transformation of the symbol. The removal of the rocks is now the menace to the marriage. In both the prayers the desire to see the rocks removed is a sign of weakness, of unwillingness to accept the real world. Dorigen transcends her weakness when she accepts the permanence of the rocks. Aurelius transcends his weakness when he recognizes the quality of Dorigen's and Arveragus's love as superior to his own passion.

The rocks play an important part in the contrast between appearance and reality. There is never any question of doing away with the rocks: Aurelius's brother doesn't expect to achieve that when he proposes the trip to Orleans, v (F) 1157 ff., nor can the magician do more than make them *seem* to vanish.

> But thurgh his magik, for a wyke or tweye,
> It semed that alle the rokkes were aweye.
>
> v (F) 1296

Aurelius responds at first to the appearance of things.

> he knew that ther was noon obstacle,
>   That voyded were thise rokkes everychon.
>
> v (F) 1301

But gradually he finds that the obstacles are still there. He himself makes no demand of Dorigen but merely reminds her of her promise. And when he hears of Arveragus's "gentillesse" and sees Dorigen's distress, he gallantly releases her. The real obstacles, like the rocks, [297] only seem to have vanished. They are the honor, the decency, the gentility of all the people involved, and the true love of Dorigen and Arveragus for one another.

Dorigen's rash promise also functions in the tale in a way not intended by the Franklin. In addition to its other meanings it is an expression of "gentillesse" in its superficial sense. Dorigen tempers her absolute refusal in a way that makes it sound courteous, though in her heart she knows of the removal of the rocks,

> "It is agayns the proces of nature."
>
> v (F) 1345

Even while accepting the natural order, she is shirking a part of her duty in the moral. That the rocks play so great a part in the thought and fate of this soft-hearted woman is a further irony. When faced at the end with the disappearance of the rocks and the necessity of keeping her promise, she will propose to herself suicide but allow her purpose to disintegrate as she calls to mind the sad fate of women who firmly carried out such a purpose.[3] Arveragus alone displays a firmness to which the rocks have relevance. His temporary absence makes possible the rash promise and his decision at the crisis forces Aurelius to see the "obstacles" that have only seemed to vanish. The superficial gentility of Dorigen's promise foreshadows and contrasts with the gentility of the ending, and the tale becomes a criticism of some aspects of gentility, more subtle than the Host's in the prologue to the tale, v (F) 695, and more justified.

The Franklin presents in his tale an ideal of marriage and of "gentillesse," and manages at the same time to compliment the Knight, the Squire, and the Clerk. But his story is, without his realizing it, a critique of "gentillesse," for it is Dorigen's courteous softening of her refusal that makes the exhibition of gentility at the end necessary. The rocks which suggest the enduring value of gentility also suggest the distinctions which the Franklin in his easy acceptance of the good things of life fails to make.

II

The crucial passage in the *Merchant's Tale*[4] comes in the middle of the epithalamion and sends echoes and reverberations through the two consultations and the marriage to a crowning climax in the [298] garden scene at the end. The Merchant is showing us January's reasons for wanting to marry:

> Mariage is a ful greet sacrement.
> He which that hath no wyf, I holde him shent;
> He lyveth helplees and al desolat, –
> I speke of folk in seculer estaat.
> And herke why, I sey nat this for noght,
> That womman is for mannes helpe ywroght.
> The hye God, whan he hadde Adam maked,
> And saugh him al allone, bely-naked,
> God of his grete goodnesse seyde than,
> "Lat us now make an helpe unto this man
> Lyk to hymself"; and thanne he made him Eve.
> Heere may ye se, and heerby may ye preve,
> That wyf is mannes helpe, and his confort,
> His paradys terrestre, and his disport.
> So buxom and so vertuous is she
> They moste nedes lyve in unitee.
> O flessh they been, and o flessh, as I gesse
> Hath but oon herte, in wele and in distresse.
>
> IV (E) 1319–36

The concept of marriage as an earthly paradise[5] has come to January late but with the blinding light of revelation: it has taken complete possession of his mind. The cautious habits and the short-sighted shrewdness of old age will be called on to support rather than examine this new vision. As in his judicious exclusion of the clergy and his appeal to example, he will use the forms of wisdom but not its substance. Marriage will carry all before it because it promises to combine the self-indulgence he has practised all his life with two things that old age makes vital to him for the first time—help for his physical weakness and the salvation of his soul. His lust for pleasure and his desire for salvation combine in the first consultation scene to blind him to the danger inherent in taking a young wife. The only danger he can foresee by the time he has chosen the girl and called his friends together the second time is so much felicity in marriage as to ruin his chance of a blissful after-life.

Besides epitomizing the precise and willful blindness of his attitude toward marriage, the passage foreshadows many of the details of his fate. The helpfulness that he anticipates in a wife will serve May as excuse for being in Damian's arms in the pear tree, and it will take the form before his very eyes of a nakedness similar to Adam's, [299] her smock upon her breast (2395). But as he sees in Adam's story a proof of marital bliss, so he will see in the pear tree only what his wife wants him to, an example of her care for his welfare. The "unitee" and "o flessh" receive an ironical fulfillment in the blind old man's constant clutch on his buxom and perforce virtuous May, and an additional twist in the line from his invitation to the garden,

> "No spot of thee ne knew I al my lyf,"
>
> IV (E) 2146

where the irony of the contrast between his ugly passion and the romantic imagery and sacred associations of the Song of Songs (which is Solomon's!) matches the irony of his being as unconscious of the physical spot he is even then touching as he will later be of the moral spot—adultery—when he is looking at it with miraculously unblinded eyes.

The controlling images in the poem, however, are the linked ones of the garden, the blindness, and the tree. They are linked for the first time in this passage. "Heere may ye se," says the Merchant for January. But you can see in the story of Adam and Eve that a wife is man's earthly paradise, only if you are blind to the tree of the knowledge of good and evil and the forbidden fruit. As January is blind in the Garden of Eden, so is he blind in the paradise (1822) of his wife's arms:

> "A man may do no synne with his wyf,
> Ne hurte hymselven with his owene knyf."
>
> IV (E) 1840

Adam and Eve and the first sin link up in these fatuous lines with Damian,

> Which carf biforn the knyght ful many a day
>
> IV (E) 1773

and the sin soon to be committed in January's private paradise. The garden that January builds is the consummation of his folly and the symbol of his marriage. Its beauty is May, and the stone wall with which it is "enclosed al aboute" is the jealous precautions of the blind January as well as the inescapable unpleasantness of his lovemaking. There is no stone of tyranny (1990) in May's nature, and in fact we find her pliancy which January expected to be like warm wax (1430) taking a ready impression (1978) from Damian's wooing. The silver key to the garden which is January's alone is his privilege as husband, but from the warm wax of May's nature a suitable replica is provided for Damian—his privilege as lover. The blindness is the physical counterpart of the ignorance of marriage and of women that January has shown all along. It prevents him to the end from seeing the tree [300] in the garden and the knowledge of evil which it represents. And the regaining of his sight wipes out even the alertness to danger which accompanied the blindness.

The tree plays a further and more striking part in the tale. January fails to see it in the Garden of Eden, but brings it in as an image of his own virility in the first consultation with his friends:

> "Though I be hoor, I fare as dooth a tree
> That blosmeth er that fruyt ywoxen bee
> And blosmy tree nys neither drye ne deed.
> I feele me nowhere hoor but on myn heed;
> Myn herte and alle my lymes been as grene
> As laurer thurgh the yeer is for to sene."
>
> IV (E) 1461–66

The image bears fruit in the final part of the story. In January's private paradise, his arms around the trunk of the pear tree, he serves his wife as stepping stone to the forbidden fruit of adultery. At the same time he becomes the symbol of his folly, cuckolded in the branches which spring from his head as horns.[6]

The imagery of growth has structural significance. The story is essentially the growth of an idea to complete fulfillment. Starting in the mind of January, a germ with all that develops already implicit, it attains in each part of the story a new mode of actualization—first verbal expression in general terms; then the fixing of the dream to a specific woman; then the literal fulfillment. At each stage January's blindness to his own folly achieves some new fatuity linked to the imagery in which he first clothed his "vision."[7] But the story does not stop with a single literal fulfillment. Through Proserpina's vow it suggests repetition through the ages. And it creates in the literal world the symbolic fulfillment of the idea. The garden and the blindness, in January's mind from the beginning, are now fully materialized. No miracle can make him see the tree as horns growing from his head, nor make him see the adultery committed before his very eyes.

The Merchant has taken care to tell us that this tale is not autobiographical:

> [301]   "of myn owene soore,
> For soory herte, I telle may namoore."
>
> IV (E) 1244

Moved by the ironical moral of the *Clerk's Tale*, he will join the discussion opened by the Wyf of Bath and present directly a male view of marriage. The Wife and her theories are clearly in his mind for he commits the anachronism of having Justinus refer to her in the tale. His real intentions in telling the story are clear from two passages. In the prologue he says,

> "We wedded men lyven in sorwe and care. . . .
> As for the moore part, I say nat alle."

IV (E) 1231

And in the tale itself, speaking of Argus,

> Yet was he blent, and, God woot, so been mo,
> That wenen wisly that it be nat so.
> Passe over is an ese, I sey namoore.

IV (E) 2115

For the Merchant January is the type of that *rara avis*—the happily married man: Not all married men are miserable; some are blind.

The Merchant participates in the blindness of his creature January in not realizing the extent to which he is talking of his own sore in the tale. His imperceptiveness extends even to thinking that he can disguise the vulgarity of his tale in circumlocution. The circumlocutions in fact call attention to the vulgarity,[8] just as January's blissful ignorance contrasts with but does not conceal the Merchant's disillusionment. The creator of January is evidently a converted idealist, and the bitterness of his cynicism is the measure of his former folly. He can be so penetrating in exposing January's reasons for marriage because he is really looking at his own from beyond the gulf of two shattering months of marital experience. The cynical egoist looks at the delusions of an idealistic egoist and cannot see that his bitterness betrays him.

III

The *Wife of Bath's Tale* is ostensibly a two-part exposition of the Wife's thesis that marriages are happy only when the woman is the master. The crucial passage occurs when the "olde wyf" at the juncture of the two parts reiterates in stronger terms her demand that the knight marry her:

> "Nay thanne," quod she, "I shrewe us bothe two!
> For thogh that I be foul, and oold, and poore,
> [302]   I nolde for al the metal, ne for oore,
> That under erthe is grave, or lith above,
> But if thy wyf I were, and eek thy love."

III (D) 1066

The old woman's demand is not only the conclusion of the quest plot, the price the knight pays for his life, but it is also the point of departure for the husband's dilemma. The woman must first secure her man before she can offer him her alternatives. The Wife of Bath's story passes with this speech from its public to its private demonstration of the thesis. The world-wide scene of the quest dwindles to the marriage-bed of the dilemma. We pass from generally accepted theory to the practice of one woman in achieving first sovereignty then happiness in her marriage.

But the husband's dilemma and the Wife of Bath's thesis are merely the surface of the story. The old woman has already demanded that the knight marry her. In her reiteration she reveals her real desire. She wants not just a husband but a husband's love. The phrase "and eek thy love" brought here into conjunction with the woman's ugliness, age, and poverty suggests that the real dilemma in the second part of the story is the wife's rather than the husband's; it foreshadows the necessity for miracle at the end and reveals for the story a second and more valid theme, operating on the instinctive level beneath the Wife's and her heroine's theories—the quest for love.

On this level the tale as a whole progresses from rape to marriage to love with each of the three crises of the story presenting a common pattern. In each there is a problem, a theoretical solution, and a modification of theory in practice. At the beginning of the story the knight's crime of rape is to be punished by death until the ladies intervene and send him off in quest of crucial information about women. The second problem, what women most desire, is solved theoretically by the answer the knight gives the court. But it is clear from the "olde wyf's" demand that in practice one woman wants not sovereignty over husband and lover, but merely a husband and his love. The final problem is the obtaining of the husband's love, theoretically solved when he leaves the choice in his dilemma and thus the sovereignty to his wife. Actually the wife attains the knight's love by magically slipping between the horns of the dilemma and giving him exactly what he wants. The happy married life that results differs markedly from the blue-print of the Wife's thesis:

> And she obeyed hym in every thyng
> That myghte doon hym plesance or likyng.
>
> III (D) 1256

[303] The Wife of Bath had good reason to tell the story she did. It provided what she considered a good demonstration of her theory. It gave her an opportunity of discussing a number of the questions close to her heart such as the true meaning of "gentillesse," and of parodying Arthurian romance with its unrealistic notions of life and love. It had the further appeal of an imaginative wish-fulfillment, for it presented an old woman who gained a young husband and magically changed herself into everything he could desire in a wife. As a story of the quest for love it was the artistic counterpart of her life.

In its continuing contrast between theory and practice the tale repeats the unconscious revelation of the Wife's prologue. For her theory of marriage and her own practise have been worlds apart. In her first three marriages she did maintain her sovereignty, but the marriages were not happy. No doubt the Wife enjoyed the cowed submission she so cleverly exacted from her old dotards. But she is forced to admit,

> And yet in bacon hadde I nevere delit.
>
> III (D) 418

The fourth husband with his paramour aroused her jealousy and, to her satisfaction, became jealous in his turn. The Wife of Bath took refuge in travel, and the marriage was little more than nominal. Only with the fifth, her clerk of Oxenford, did she find happiness. Jankyn she cannot name without a blessing. But in the fifth marriage the relationship of the first three was simply reversed. This time she was twice his age and forced to sign over her property before the ceremony. Like the old woman in her tale she had to win his love. At the same time, she would have us believe, she won the upper hand in the marriage. That the triumph, like that of the heroine in her tale, is nominal her own words confess:

> After that day we hadden never debaat.
> God helpe me so, I was to him as kynde
> As any wyf from Denmark unto Ynde,
> And also trewe, and so was he to me.
>
> III (D) 825

We have further proof of the clerk's influence over her in the stress she puts on authorities in her discussions, on the clear memory she has for the stories in the book she made him burn, and in the strange distortion she makes of the Midas story in her tale. Jankyn left his mark on more than her "ribbes," more than her hearing.

The Wife of Bath enjoyed theory on one level and life on another. Her enjoyment of both was intense and convincing, so much so that [304] most critics and readers have appreciated her gusto without noticing the contrast between her theory and practice in both prologue and tale.

IV

In the *Pardoner's Tale*[9] the crucial passage occurs at the point where the revelers find the pile of gold under the tree:

> No lenger thanne after Deeth they soughte.
>
> VI (C) 772

On the primary level of the revelers' limited vision the wealth has driven all thought of their search for Death from their minds. They now think of the pleasures the gold will buy them and plan how to get it home safely. At the same time the statement foreshadows their end. They no longer seek Death because they have found him.

The single line marks a fundamental division in the tale. On the one hand is the drunken search for Death, marked by an unwonted and a deluded altruism. They are sworn brothers. They will slay Death. Drink has given them a mission, stature, pride, contempt for others. The gold has both a sobering and a deflating effect. It brings them back to the real world from their illusions of brotherhood and of slaying Death. Yet their drunken intentions were closer to the final outcome than their sober planning and counter-planning to secure the treasure. The gold has brought them back to their narrow world. It both focuses and limits their vision. These two sections of the tale, as we shall see later, have a symbolic value for the Pardoner.

But first we must explore the complex set of meanings in the tale as a whole. What happens to the gold in the story happens to the story itself. Its value is determined by the human motives focused upon it. In itself it may be an effective warning against cupidity, showing how greed turns gold into death. But as a part of the sermon habitually delivered by the Pardoner to the "lewed peple" it is at the same time the instrument of the Pardoner's greed. And as a part of the confession made to the other pilgrims it is the expression of the Pardoner's vanity. The pilgrimage gives him the opportunity to display to an intelligent audience the full measure of his cleverness and cynicism. He hopes so to dazzle and shock them that they will fail to see the motive that drives him to the compensation of hypocrisy and greed.

The Pardoner's physical disability has isolated him from some of [305] the normal satisfactions in life. In revenge he has rejected the professed morality of other people and uses it against them to attain the power and comfort that wealth brings. His income is thus a symbol of his victory over physical inadequacy and of his superiority over the normal and stupid louts who are his victims. But the victory is not one that he can fully reveal in his daily life. Here, before the pilgrims, stimulated by the intelligence of his audience and with neither the necessity nor the possibility of assuming his customary role, he can for once reveal the extent of his success, impress his companions with the amount of his income, and shock them with the cynicism that makes it all possible. He seeks at the same time to conceal the emptiness and isolation of his life by reference to the comforts and gaieties he enjoys:

> "I wol have moneie, wolle, chese, and whete....
> Nay, I wol drynke licour of the vyne,
> And have a joly wenche in every toun."
>
> vi (C) 453

The task he has set himself in his confession is as wild and deluded as the drunken revelers' quest in the first part of the tale. Like the quest it has a wider range than his customary hypocrisy and is nearer the ultimate truth. But hypocrisy is his normal and sober world, and like the revelers' vision in the second part of the tale it is narrow and limited. The presumption of the pilgrim and the hypocrisy of the "noble ecclesiaste" both end in isolation. The Pardoner has also found death without recognizing it. His life is an exemplum of the futility of cynicism. And in the world of the pilgrimage, where we see the Pardoner but he cannot see himself, the crucial passage again functions.

V

The crucial passage in the *Nun's Priest's Tale*[10] is not so obviously a fore-shadowing of the plot as in the other instances. It comes at the juncture between the discussion of dreams and the action of the near-fatal third of May. Chauntecleer is speaking:

> "Now let us speke of myrthe, and stynte al this.
> Madame Pertelote, so have I blis,
> Of o thyng God hath sent me large grace;
> For whan I se the beautee of youre face,
> Ye been so scarlet reed aboute youre yen,
> It maketh al my drede for to dyen;
> [306] For al so siker as *In principio*,
> *Mulier est hominis confusio*—
> Madame, the sentence of this Latyn is,
> 'Womman is mannes joye and al his blis.'
> For whan I feele a-nyght your softe syde,
> Al be it that I may nat on yow ryde,
> For that oure perche is maad so narwe, allas!
> I am so ful of joye and of solas,
> That I diffye bothe sweven and dreem."
>
> VII 3157–3171 (B 4347–4361)

Here the ultimate victim employs the same technique in his deception of his wife as is later to be used by the fox on him—deceitful flattery. Behind the fair words of his translation, designed to smooth the ruffled feathers of Pertelote, whose laxatives have just been scorned, lurks the malicious dig of the Latin. The cock will later be "hoist with his own petard,"

> As man that koude his traysoun nat espie
> So was he ravysshed with his flaterie
>
> VII 3324 (B 4514)

Furthermore the cock is delighted with the sound of his own voice. In the long discourse on dreams, of which this is the conclusion, he has displayed the smug assurance of the born raconteur. And it is a moot point here whether his wife's beauty or his own cleverly barbed praise of it most attracts him. The cock is indeed ready to believe that other people admire his voice.

This speech of Chauntecleer brings out the pedantry implicit from the beginning in his actions. He alone can witness and appreciate the victory he has won over his wife. The victory is a pedant's triumph and contrasts strikingly with the one the fox later wins over him, which calls forth a universal clamor.

The cock's vast learning has furthermore contributed to the easy fatalism he has fallen into as a result of his learned rebuttal on dreams. The original dream was clearly a warning dream. The beast in it, which with all his learning the cock can describe but cannot recognize as his natural enemy the fox,

"wolde han maad areest
Upon my body, and wolde han had me deed"

VII 2901 (B 4091)

But in the examples which he uses to refute his wife's skepticism people either fail to heed the warning or they have no chance of evading the fate foretold in their dreams. The cock in effect wins the argu[307]ment and forgets the dream that occasioned it. His pedantry has led him into a smug fatalism that contemplates his own coming "adversitee" (3151–53) as merely the concluding proof of the truth of dreams. No effort is called for—only the pursuit of what the soon-to-be-shipwrecked victim in one of the dreams called "my thynges" and the assumption of the courageous pose which Pertelote recommended and which his prowess makes ridiculous.

The cock, warned by dream and instinct against the fox and prepared by his own deft use of flattery against the technique the fox is to use, unwittingly gives himself a further warning, which he is either not learned enough or too pedantic to apply. Just as truly as the words of St. John's Gospel, woman is man's confusion, he tells his wife in Latin. But the words from the Gospel are *In principio*, in the beginning; and in the beginning Eve was Adam's confusion. So far is he from heeding the warning that the passage which contains it is full of the uxorious passion usually attributed to Adam. The cock's appreciation of his wife's charms diverts him from further thought of his own danger. Here in effect is another Adam, succumbing to the attractions of his wife when he should be using his reason. The Adam-and-Eve parallel, thus suggested for the cock-and-hen story, contributes to the mock heroics.

The passage is rich in other contributions to the mock heroic effect. It unites the language of exalted human passion with details of hen anatomy and barnyard architecture. The exalted language and the deflating details give the passage a quality that is typical of the whole poem. The courtly behavior and refined pretensions of Chauntecleer are constantly betrayed by the ludicrous activities and ignoble motives contingent upon chicken nature. The suggestion is clear: Objectively viewed, human pride and vanity are similarly betrayed. Only the simple life with frank acceptance of the necessities and limitations of the human lot, as exemplified by the widow and her menage, can have real dignity.

The contrast between Chauntecleer and his owner has a dramatic value in the Canterbury Tales. The Host in calling on the Prioress a little earlier addressed her in terms of the most exaggerated respect. Her Priest, however, he addresses with peremptory intimacy, making game of his poverty. When we remember the Prioress's pains

to countrefete cheere
Of court, and to been estatlich of manere,
And to ben holden digne of reverence,

I (A) 141

[308] we can glimpse a guarded purpose. The sexes of the characters in the tale are reversed, as is also the ownership, but the essential relationship between poverty and wealth, between simplicity and pretension is there. The drama is carried a step further when the Priest falls into overt criticism of women (3252–59). This he does at the expense of the complexity of his tale. The advice of his wife is, as we have seen, a minor detail in the cock's decision. But it is a theme that the Priest attacks with evident relish. He brings himself up sharp with the thought of whom he might be offending, then returns to the attack indirectly by referring his listeners to the "auctors," and finally tries to ascribe the whole thing to the cock:

> "Thise ben the cokkes wordes, and nat myne;
> I kan noon harm of no womman divyne."
>
> VII 3266 (B 4456)

The inner conflict of the misogynist employed by a woman has come for a moment to the surface; then it is pushed back behind the artifice of the story, where it has been operating secretly all along. The Host's reaction to the story has thus a double irony. Not only has he failed to see the point, but he imagines the Priest, if he were only a layman, a prodigious treader of hens!

The pedantry, ridiculed in the portrait of Chauntecleer, is also attacked by the Nun's Priest in his criticism of the rhetoricians. The satire is most highly comic when Friday and Master Gaufred are brought in at the climax of the story, and Venus is reproached for not protecting her devotee on her day, when it was her influence that was partly responsible for Chauntecleer's plight. It is possible, however, to ridicule a thing and be guilty of it on occasion oneself. This trap the Nun's Priest falls into at least once when he gets himself involved in a discussion of free will and God's fore-knowledge—as a result of elaborating too far on a mock heroic color, VII 3230–50 (B 4420–40). Like Chauntecleer he is for a moment hoist with his own petard. And in struggling to get back to his tale, he suddenly finds himself involved in the criticism of women. Pedantry which leads to a criticism of women recalls the crucial passage and the cock's gibe, "*In principio,/Mulier est hominis confusio.*" The Priest in fact makes the same charge:

> Wommanes conseil broghte us first to wo,
> And made Adam fro Paradys to go,
> Ther as he was ful myrie and wel at ese.
>
> VII 3259 (B 4449)

[309] Whatever the cause for the Priest's misogyny (it may well be a combination of intellectual contempt and involuntary attraction), there is no mistaking the animus with which he follows his hero's lead in attributing man's ills to woman. This blanket condemnation of women is a very different thing from his implied criticism of the Prioress's pretensions. In his better moments he knows, as his portrait of Chauntecleer indicates, the real significance of Adam and Eve for mankind. *Hominis confusio* is man's own frailty.

That the Priest lashes out at women as his stupid cock had done measures the strength of his feelings. In a sense these *are* the cock's words, and the Priest's recognition of their unworthiness enables him to recover his composure and his story.

On the primary level then the *Nun's Priest's Tale* is a brilliant and complex exposure of vanity, self-esteem, and self-indulgence through the mock heroic treatment of a beast fable. On the secondary level, the Nun's Priest joins the discussions of the Pilgrims on poverty (Man of Law and Wife of Bath), women's advice (Merchant), rhetoric (Host and Squire), and marriage. He is also presenting in the contrast between the widow and Chauntecleer a veiled comment on his position vis-à-vis the Prioress. Finally, on the level of involuntary revelation, he falls into the pedantry that he is ridiculing and uncovers for a moment in his confusion the feelings of a misogynist dependent on a woman. In this moment there is revealed a second conflict, the conflict between the artist, building with the materials of his art a world where his feelings achieve symbolic and universal expression, and the man, expressing his feelings directly.

CONCLUSION

The symbols which Chaucer employed are unobtrusive; they fit in their contexts of sentimental romance or crude realism without "shake or bind." Nothing in the tale forces them to the symbolic level. Yet the consistency with which the rocks are developed in the *Franklin's Tale* gives the obvious charm of the story a focused integrity which can be felt even when not clearly analyzed. The linked images of garden, tree, and blindness of the *Merchant's Tale* add to the bitter unity of tone an underlying unity of action: the seed of January's folly grows from the fertile soil of his figurative blindness into the successive realizations of word, fixed purpose, and deed, until it attains full maturity in the garden, the blindness, and the tree-born fruit of adultery, with the head that conceived realistically behorned.

[310] The focus and additional dimension which symbol and image provide in the tales are also attained by the contrast or ambiguity of the narrative elements involved. The intentional pattern of the *Wife of Bath's Tale* and the zest with which she tells it lose none of their literal value when we see the ambiguity of the elements she uses to prove her thesis. The nature of love and marriage resists the warping efforts of her dogged feminism and provides the counterpoint of a contrasting and more valid pattern. The quest for love which dominated her life dominates her tale. The greed in which the Pardoner has taken refuge creates the skillful weapon of his tale. With one edge he cynically dupes peasants; with the other he seeks to shock the pilgrims into a recognition of his importance. For the deluded vanity of the second purpose as well as the hypocrisy of the first, the two parts of his tale present analogies; at the very center the symbol of gold as unrecognized death reveals the futile emptiness of both efforts. The concealed purpose of the Nun's Priest finds urbane expression in the contrast between the simple

dignity of the people and the ostentation of the chickens in his tale. But a momentary lapse into the pedantry he is mocking in Chauntecleer confuses him and he breaks through the artifice of beast fable to direct expression of his purpose. The artistic expression, where *hominis confusio* is man's own foolish presumption, forms an ironic background for the priest's lapse into an indiscriminate and direct antifeminism.

Chaucer, unlike the Nun's Priest, never expresses his intention directly. Present himself on the pilgrimage and in the occasional asides to the audience, he pictures himself as the simple reporter of experience, not responsible because unable to judge the questions of morals and propriety raised by the tales. Only in his own experience as narrator does the mask become penetrable, and then not to the pilgrims, his imaginary audience, who acquiesce in the Host's misunderstanding and crude estimate of *Sir Thopas* and get for their reward the prosy and long-winded idealism of the *Melibeus*. There is implied in the episode, as in the Man of Law's wrong-headed praise while cudgeling his brains for a tale, a comment on the popular taste and on Chaucer's relation to his real audience. Chaucer did not expect to be understood fully by all his readers. Certain of his effects depend on a knowledge which few of them could have. Others, like the crucial passages that have just been analyzed, are the subtle elaborations by the artist of a design already present. They suggest a personal standard and private satisfaction in his art.

[311] But the simplicity adopted as a mask in the tales is not entirely ironical. It is a token for the deeper simplicity that receives impressions freely and refuses to interpose the eager evaluations, artistic and moral, that prevent full recognition. This deeper simplicity reflects faithfully the paradoxes of personality, the contradictions of experience. It becomes through its forbearance a rare and delicate instrument for evaluation and judgment, and presents a total vision not to be fully appreciated from the mental and spiritual posture of the Host, nor from that of the *homme moyen du moyen âge*, whom Chaucer could not only entertain but also see beyond.

Notes

1 Of special note are the two comments on learning by John the carpenter in the *Miller's Tale*, I (A) 3449–64, and Symkin the miller in the *Reeve's Tale*, I (A) 4120–26; and the twin laments at the end of Part I of the *Knight's Tale*, which set a pattern of parallel and paradox carried through to the end of the tale and thematically important. The lecture on anger that the Friar gives Thomas in the *Summoner's Tale*, III (D) 1981–2092, lacks the concentration of the passages under discussion but performs the same functions.

2 Two of the passages, those in the *Franklin's Tale* and *The Pardoner's Tale*, are discussed by Germaine Dempster, *Dramatic Irony in Chaucer*, Stanford, 1932, 63–65 and 78. Mrs. Dempster, though concerned principally with the dramatic irony in the passages and the extent to which it is original with Chaucer, is clearly aware of other values. Her discussion of the linked ironies in the *Merchant's Tale*, with respect especially to wax, p. 51, and trees, p. 53 and n. 107, also points toward the findings of this paper.

3 See James Sledd, "Dorigen's Complaint," *MP*, xlv (1947), 36 ff.
4 In this analysis I am indebted to G. G. Sedgewick, "Structure of the *Merchant's Tale*," *UTQ*, xvii (1947–48), 337 ff.
5 First stated at the beginning of the tale, iv (E) 1258–65, in a passage that adumbrates the one under discussion.
6 The *OED* gives 1430–40 as the first instance of the cuckold's horns in English, but Robinson suggests a possible reference to them in the *Miller's Prologue*, i (A) 3161, and the notion was certainly current on the continent. See, for instance, Boccaccio's *Decameron*, 5th Story, 7th Day.
7 In the first consultation with January's friends there is the tree-virility passage already quoted. In the second consultation there is the fear "That I shal have myn hevene in erthe heere," iv (E) 1647. And in the marriage section there is the passage already quoted about sin and knives.
8 For instance in iv (E) 1950 f., 1961 f., and 2361–63.
9 I am indebted in this analysis to Curry, *Chaucer and the Medieval Sciences*, 54 ff., and G. G. Sedgewick, "The Progress of Chaucer's Pardoner, 1880–1940," *MLQ*, i (1940), 431 ff.
10 I am indebted in this analysis to J. B. Severs, "Chaucer's Originality in the *Nun's Priest's Tale*," *SP*, xliii (1946), 22 ff.

8 Chaucer the pilgrim

E. TALBOT DONALDSON

Originally published in *PMLA* 60 (1954):928–36. Reprinted by permission of the Modern Language Association of America. The original pagination is recorded within square brackets.

Verisimilitude in a work of fiction is not without its attendant dangers, the chief of which is that the responses it stimulates in the reader may be those appropriate not so much to an imaginative production as to an historical one or to a piece of reporting. History and reporting are, of course, honorable in themselves, but if we react to a poet as though he were an historian or a reporter, we do him somewhat less than justice. I am under the impression that many readers, too much influenced by Chaucer's brilliant verisimilitude, tend to regard his famous pilgrimage to Canterbury as significant not because it is a great fiction, but because it seems to be a remarkable record of a fourteenth-century pilgrimage. A remarkable record it may be, but if we treat it too narrowly as such there are going to be certain casualties among the elements that make up the fiction. Perhaps first among these elements is the fictional reporter, Chaucer the pilgrim, and the role he plays in the Prologue to the *Canterbury Tales* and in the links between them. I think it time that he was rescued from the comparatively dull record of history and put back into his poem. He is not really Chaucer the poet—nor, for that matter, is either the poet, or the poem's protagonist, that Geoffrey Chaucer frequently mentioned in contemporary historical records as a distinguished civil servant, but never as a poet. The fact that these are three separate entities does not, naturally, exclude the probability—or rather the certainty—that they bore a close resemblance to one another, and that, indeed, they frequently got together in the same body. But that does not excuse us from keeping them distinct from one another, difficult as their close resemblance makes our task.

The natural tendency to confuse one thing with its like is perhaps best represented by a school of Chaucerian criticism, now outmoded, that pictured a single Chaucer under the guise of a wide-eyed, jolly, rolypoly little man who, on fine Spring mornings, used to get up early, while the dew was still on the grass, and go look at daisies. A charming portrait, this, so charming, indeed, that it was sometimes able to maintain itself to the exclusion of any Chaucerian other side. It has every reason to be charming, since it was lifted almost *in toto* from the version Chaucer gives of himself in the Prologue to the *Legend of Good Women*, though I imagine it owes some of its popularity to a rough analogy with Wordsworth—a sort of *Legend of Good Poets*. It was this version of Chaucer that Kittredge, in a page of great importance to Chaucer criticism, demolished with his assertion that "a naïf Collector of Customs would be a paradoxical monster." He might well have added that a naïve creator of old January would be even more monstrous.

[929] Kittredge's pronouncement cleared the air, and most of us now accept the proposition that Chaucer was sophisticated as readily as we do the proposition that the whale is a mammal. But unhappily, now that we've got rid of the naïve fiction, it is easy to fall into the opposite sort of mistake. This is to envision, in the *Canterbury Tales*, a highly urbane, literal-historical Chaucer setting out from Southwark on a specific day of a specific year (we even argue somewhat acrimoniously about dates and routes), in company with a group of persons who existed in real life and whom Chaucer, his reporter's eye peeled for every idiosyncrasy, determined to get down on paper—down, that is, to the last wart—so that books might be written identifying them. Whenever this accurate reporter says something especially fatuous—which is not infrequently—it is either ascribed to an opinion peculiar to the Middle Ages (sometimes very peculiar), or else Chaucer's tongue is said to be in his cheek.

Now a Chaucer with tongue-in-cheek is a vast improvement over a simple-minded Chaucer when one is trying to define the whole man, but it must lead to a loss of critical perception, and in particular to a confused notion of Chaucerian irony, to see in the Prologue a reporter who is acutely aware of the significance of what he sees but who sometimes, for ironic emphasis, interprets the evidence presented by his observation in a fashion directly contrary to what we expect. The proposition ought to be expressed in reverse: the reporter is, usually, acutely unaware of the significance of what he sees, no matter how sharply he sees it. He is, to be sure, permitted his lucid intervals, but in general he is the victim of the poet's pervasive—not merely sporadic—irony. And as such he is also the chief agent by which the poet achieves his wonderfully complex, ironic, comic, serious vision of a world which is but a devious and confused, infinitely various pilgrimage to a certain shrine. It is, as I hope to make clear, a good deal more than merely fitting that our guide on such a pilgrimage should be a man of such naïveté as the Chaucer who tells the tale of *Sir Thopas*. Let us accompany him a little distance.

It is often remarked that Chaucer really liked the Prioress very much, even though he satirized her gently—very gently. But this is an understatement: Chaucer the pilgrim may not be said merely to have liked the Prioress very much—he thought she was utterly charming. In the first twenty-odd lines of her portrait (A 118 ff.) he employs, among other superlatives, the adverb *ful* seven times. Middle English uses *ful* where we use *very*, and if one translates the beginning of the portrait into a kind of basic English (which is what, in a way, it really is), one gets something like this: "There was also a Nun, a Prioress, who was very sincere and modest in the way she smiled; her biggest oath was only 'By saint Loy'; and she was called Madame Eglantine. She sang the divine service very [930] well, intoning it in her nose very prettily, and she spoke French very nicely and elegantly"—and so on, down to the last gasp of sentimental appreciation. Indeed, the Prioress may be said to have transformed the rhetoric into something not unlike that of a very bright kindergarten child's descriptive theme. In his reaction to the Prioress Chaucer the pilgrim resembles another—if less—simple-hearted enthusiast: the Host, whose summons to her to tell a tale must be one of the politest speeches in the language. Not "My lady prioresse, a tale now!" but, "as curteisly as it had been a mayde,"

> My lady Prioresse, by youre leve,
> So that I wiste I sholde yow nat greve,
> I wolde demen that ye tellen sholde
> A tale next, if so were that ye wolde.
> Now wol ye vouche sauf, my lady deere?

(B 1636–41)

Where the Prioress reduced Chaucer to superlatives, she reduces the Host to subjunctives.

There is no need here to go deeply into the Prioress. Eileen Power's illustrations from contemporary episcopal records show with what extraordinary economy the portrait has been packed with abuses typical of fourteenth-century nuns. The abuses, to be sure, are mostly petty, but it is clear enough that the Prioress, while a perfect lady, is anything but a perfect nun; and attempts to whitewash her, of which there have been many, can only proceed from an innocence of heart equal to Chaucer the pilgrim's and undoubtedly directly influenced by it. For he, of course, is quite swept away by her irrelevant *sensibilité*, and as a result misses much of the point of what he sees. No doubt he feels that he has come a long way, socially speaking, since his encounter with the Black Knight in the forest, and he knows, or thinks he knows, a little more of what it's all about: in this case it seems to be mostly about good manners, kindness to animals, and female charm. Thus it has been argued that Chaucer's appreciation for the Prioress as a sort of heroine of courtly romance *manquée* actually reflects the sophistication of the living Chaucer, an urbane man who cared little whether amiable nuns were good nuns. But it seems a curious form of sophistication that permits itself to babble superlatives; and indeed, if this is sophistication, it is the kind generally seen in the least experienced people—one that reflects a wide-eyed wonder at the glamor of the great world. It is just what one might expect of a bourgeois exposed to the splendors of high society, whose values, such as they are, he eagerly accepts. And that is precisely what Chaucer the pilgrim is, and what he does.

If the Prioress's appeal to him is through elegant femininity, the Monk's is through imposing virility. Of this formidable and important prelate the pilgrim does not say, with Placebo,

[931]   I woot wel that my lord kan moore than I:
           What that he seith, I holde it ferme and stable,
                                                        (E 1498–9)

but he acts Placebo's part to perfection. He is as impressed with the Monk as the Monk is, and accepts him on his own terms and at face value, never sensing that those terms imply complete condemnation of Monk *qua* Monk. The Host is also impressed by the Monk's virility, but having no sense of Placebonian propriety (he is himself a most virile man) he makes indecent jokes about it. This, naturally, offends the pilgrim's sense of decorum: there is a note of deferential commiseration in his comment, "This worthy Monk took al in pacience" (B 3155). Inevitably when the Monk establishes hunting as the highest activity of which religious man is capable, "I seyde his opinion was good" (A 183). As one of the pilgrim's spiritual heirs was later to say, Very like a whale; but not, of course, like a fish out of water.

Wholehearted approval for the values that important persons subscribe to is seen again in the portrait of the Friar. This amounts to a prolonged gratulation for the efficiency the deplorable Hubert shows in undermining the fabric of the Church by turning St. Francis' ideal inside out:

Ful swetely herde he confessioun,
And plesaunt was his absolucioun.

For unto swich a worthy man as he
Acorded nat, as by his facultee,
To have with sike lazars aqueyntaunce.
                                    (A 221–222, 243–245)

It is sometimes said that Chaucer did not like the Friar. Whether Chaucer the man would have liked such a Friar is, for our present purposes, irrelevant. But if the pilgrim does not unequivocally express his liking for him, it is only because in his humility he does not feel that, with important people, his own likes and dislikes are material: such importance is its own reward, and can gain no lustre from Geoffrey, who, when the Friar is attacked by the Summoner, is ready to show him the same sympathy he shows the Monk (see D 1265–67).

Once he has finished describing the really important people on the pilgrimage the pilgrim's tone changes, for he can now concern himself with the bourgeoisie, members of his own class for whom he does not have to show such profound respect. Indeed, he can even afford to be a little patronizing at times, and to have his little joke at the expense of the too-busy lawyer. But such indirect assertions of his own superiority do not prevent him from giving substance to the old cynicism that the only motive recognized by the middle class is the profit motive, for his interest and admiration for the bourgeois pilgrims is centered mainly in their material prosperity and their ability to increase it. He starts, properly enough, with the out-and-out money-grubber, the Merchant, [932] and after turning aside for that *lusus naturae*, the non-profit-motivated Clerk, proceeds to the Lawyer, who, despite the pilgrim's little joke, is the best and best-paid ever; the Franklin, twenty-one admiring lines on appetite, so expensively catered to; the Gildsmen, cheered up the social ladder, "For catel hadde they ynogh and rente" (A 373); and the Physician, again the best and richest. In this series the portrait of the Clerk is generally held to be an ideal one, containing no irony; but while it is ideal, it seems to reflect the pilgrim's sense of values in his joke about the Clerk's failure to make money: is not this still typical of the half-patronizing, half-admiring *un*understanding that practical men of business display towards academics? But in any case the portrait is a fine companion-piece for those in which material prosperity is the main interest both of the characters described and of the describer.

Of course, this is not the sole interest of so gregarious—if shy—a person as Chaucer the pilgrim. Many of the characters have the additional advantage of being good companions, a faculty that receives a high valuation in the Prologue. To be good company might, indeed, atone for certain serious defects of character. Thus the Shipman, whose callous cruelty is duly noted, seems fairly well redeemed in the assertion, "And certeinly he was a good felawe" (A 395). At this point an uneasy sensation that even tongue-in-cheek irony will not compensate for the lengths to which Chaucer is going in his approbation of this sinister seafarer sometimes causes editors to note that *a good felawe* means "a rascal." But I can find no evidence that it ever meant a rascal. Of course, all tritely approbative expressions enter easily into ironic connotation, but the phrase *means* a good companion, which is just what Chaucer means. And if, as he says of the Shipman, "Of nyce conscience took he no keep" (A 398), Chaucer the pilgrim was doing the same with respect to him.

Nothing that has been said has been meant to imply that the pilgrim was unable to recognize, and deplore, a rascal when he saw one. He could, provided the rascality was situated in a member of the lower classes and provided it was, in any case, somewhat wider than a barn door: Miller, Manciple, Reeve, Summoner, and Pardoner are all acknowledged to be rascals. But rascality generally has, after all, the laudable object of making money, which gives it a kind of validity, if not dignity. These portraits, while in them the pilgrim, prioress-like conscious of the finer aspects of life, does deplore such matters as the Miller's indelicacy of language, contain a note of ungrudging admiration for efficient thievery. It is perhaps fortunate for the pilgrim's reputation as a judge of men that he sees through the Pardoner, since it is the Pardoner's particular tragedy that, except in Church, every one can see through him at a glance; but in Church he remains to the pilgrim "a noble ecclesiaste" (A 708). The equally repellent Summoner, a practicing bawd, is partially redeemed [933] by his also being a good fellow, "a gentil harlot and a kynde" (A 647), and by the fact that for a moderate bribe he will neglect to summon: the pilgrim apparently subscribes to the popular definition of the best policeman as the one who acts the least policely.

Therefore Chaucer is tolerant, and has his little joke about the Summoner's small Latin—a very small joke, though one of the most amusing aspects of the pilgrim's character is the pleasure he takes in his own jokes, however small. But the Summoner goes too far when he cynically suggests that purse is the Archdeacon's hell, causing Chaucer to respond with a fine show of righteous respect for the instruments of spiritual punishment. The only trouble is that his enthusiastic defense of them carries *him* too far, so that after having warned us that excommunication will indeed damn our souls—

> But wel I woot he lyed right in dede:
> Of cursyng oghte ech gilty man him drede,
> For curs wol slee right as assoillyng savith—
>
> (A 659–661)

he goes on to remind us that it will also cause considerable inconvenience to our bodies: "And also war hym of a *Significavit*" (A 662). Since a *Significavit* is the writ accomplishing the imprisonment of the excommunicate, the line provides perhaps the neatest—and most misunderstood—Chaucerian anticlimax in the Prologue.

I have avoided mentioning, hitherto, the pilgrim's reactions to the really good people on the journey—the Knight, the Parson, the Plowman. One might reasonably ask how his uncertain sense of values may be reconciled with the enthusiasm he shows for their rigorous integrity. The question could, of course, be shrugged off with a remark on the irrelevance to art of exact consistency, even to art distinguished by its verisimilitude. But I am not sure that there is any basic inconsistency. It is the nature of the pilgrim to admire all kinds of superlatives, and the fact that he often admires superlatives devoid of—or opposed to—genuine virtue does not inhibit his equal admiration for virtue incarnate. He is not, after all, a bad man; he is, to place him in his literary tradition, merely an average man, or mankind: *homo*, not very *sapiens* to be sure, but with the very best intentions, making his pilgrimage through the world in search of what is good, and showing himself, too frequently, able to recognize the good only when it is spectacularly so. Spenser's Una glows with a kind of spontaneous incandescence, so that the Red Cross Knight, mankind in search of holiness, knows her as good; but he thinks that Duessa is good, too. Virtue concretely embodied in Una or the Parson presents no problems to the well-intentioned observer, but in a world consisting mostly of imperfections, accurate evaluations are difficult for a pilgrim who, like mankind, is naïve. The pilgrim's ready appreciation for the virtuous characters is perhaps the greatest tribute [934] that could be paid to their virtue, and their spiritual simplicity is, I think, enhanced by the intellectual simplicity of the reporter.

The pilgrim belongs, of course, to a very old—and very new—tradition of the fallible first person singular. His most exact modern counterpart is perhaps Lemuel Gulliver who, in his search for the good, failed dismally to perceive the difference between the pursuit of reason and the pursuits of reasonable horses: one may be sure that the pilgrim would have whinnied with the best of them. In his own century he is related to Long Will of *Piers Plowman,* a more explicit seeker after the good, but just as unswerving in his inability correctly to evaluate what he sees. Another kinsman is the protagonist of the *Pearl,* mankind whose heart is set on a transitory good that has been lost—who, for very natural reasons, confuses earthly with spiritual values. Not entirely unrelated is the protagonist of Gower's *Confessio Amantis,* an old man seeking for an impossible earthly love that seems to him the only good. And in more subtle fashion there is the teller of Chaucer's story of *Troilus and Cressida,* who, while not a true protagonist, performs some of the same functions. For this unloved "servant of the servants of love" falls in love with Cressida so persuasively that almost every male reader of the poem imitates him, so that we all share the heartbreak of Troilus and sometimes, in the intensity of our heartbreak, fail to learn what Troilus did. Finally, of course, there is Dante of the *Divine Comedy,* the most exalted member of the family and perhaps the immediate original of these other first-person pilgrims.

Artistically the device of the *persona* has many functions, so integrated with one another that to try to sort them out produces both over-simplification and distortion. The most obvious, with which this paper has been dealing—distortedly, is to present a vision of the social world imposed on one of the moral world. Despite their verisimilitude most, if not all, of the characters described in the Prologue are taken directly from stock and recur again and again in medieval literature. Langland in his own Prologue and elsewhere depicts many of them: the hunting monk, the avaricious friar, the thieving miller, the hypocritical pardoner, the unjust stewards, even, in little, the all-too-human nun. But while Langland uses the device of the *persona* with considerable skill in the conduct of his allegory, he uses it hardly at all in portraying the inhabitants of the social world: these are described directly, with the poet's own voice. It was left to Chaucer to turn the ancient stock satirical characters into real people assembled for a pilgrimage, and to have them described, with all their traditional faults upon them, by another pilgrim who records faithfully each fault without, for the most part, recognizing that it is a fault and frequently felicitating its possessor for possessing it. One result—though not the only result—is a moral realism much more significant than the literary realism which is a part of it and [935] for which it is sometimes mistaken; this moral realism discloses a world in which humanity is prevented by its own myopia, the myopia of the describer, from seeing what the dazzlingly attractive externals of life really represent. In most of the analogues mentioned above the fallible first person receives, at the end of the book, the education he has needed: the pilgrim arrives somewhere. Chaucer never completed the *Canterbury Tales,* but in the Prologue to the *Parson's Tale* he seems to have been doing, rather hastily, what his contemporaries had done: when, with the sun nine-and-twenty degrees from the horizon, the twenty-nine pilgrims come to a certain—unnamed—*thropes ende*

(I 12), then the pilgrimage seems no longer to have Canterbury as its destination, but rather, I suspect, the Celestial City of which the Parson speaks. If one insists that Chaucer was not a moralist but a comic writer (a distinction without a difference), then the device of the *persona* may be taken primarily as serving comedy. It has been said earlier that the several Chaucers must have inhabited one body, and in that sense the fictional first person is no fiction at all. In an oral tradition of literature the first person probably always shared the personality of his creator: thus Dante of the *Divine Comedy* was physically Dante the Florentine; the John Gower of the *Confessio* was also Chaucer's friend John Gower; and Long Will was, I am sure, some one named William Langland, who was both long and wilful. And it is equally certain that Chaucer the pilgrim, "a popet in an arm t'enbrace" (B 1891), was in every physical respect Chaucer the man, whom one can imagine reading his work to a courtly audience, as in the portrait appearing in one of the MSS. of *Troilus*. One can imagine also the delight of the audience which heard the Prologue read in this way, and which was aware of the similarities and dissimilarities between Chaucer, the man before them, and Chaucer the pilgrim, both of whom they could see with simultaneous vision. The Chaucer they knew was physically, one gathers, a little ludicrous; a bourgeois, but one who was known as a practical and successful man of the court; possessed perhaps of a certain diffidence of manner, reserved, deferential to the socially imposing persons with whom he was associated; a bit absent-minded, but affable and, one supposes, very good company—a good fellow; sagacious and highly perceptive. This Chaucer was telling them of another who, lacking some of his chief qualities, nevertheless possessed many of his characteristics, though in a different state of balance, and each one probably distorted just enough to become laughable without becoming unrecognizable: deference into a kind of snobbishness, affability into an over-readiness to please, practicality into Babbittry, perception into inspection, absence of mind into dimness of wit; a Chaucer acting in some respects just as Chaucer himself might have acted but unlike his creator the kind of man, withal, who could mistake a group of stock satirical types for living persons endowed with all sorts [936] of superlative qualities. The constant interplay of these two Chaucers must have produced an exquisite and most ingratiating humor—as, to be sure, it still does. This comedy reaches its superb climax when Chaucer the pilgrim, resembling in so many ways Chaucer the poet, can answer the Host's demand for a story only with a rhyme he "lerned longe agoon" (B 1899)—*Sir Thopas*, which bears the same complex relation to the kind of romance it satirizes and to Chaucer's own poetry as Chaucer the pilgrim does to the pilgrims he describes and to Chaucer the poet.

Earlier in this paper I proved myself no gentleman (though I hope a scholar) by being rude to the Prioress, and hence to the many who like her and think that Chaucer liked her too. It is now necessary to retract. Undoubtedly Chaucer the man would, like his fictional representative, have found her charming and looked on her with affection. To have got on so well in so changeable a world Chaucer must have got on well with the people in it, and it is doubtful that one may get on with people merely by pretending to like them: one's heart has to be in it. But the third entity, Chaucer the poet, operates in a realm which is above and subsumes those in which Chaucer the man and Chaucer the pilgrim have their being. In this realm prioresses may be simultaneously evaluated as marvelously amiable ladies and as prioresses. In his poem the poet arranges for the moralist to define austerely what ought to be and for his fictional representative—who, as the representative of all mankind, is no mere fiction—to go on affirming affectionately what is. The two points of view, in strict moral logic diametrically opposed, are somehow made harmonious in Chaucer's wonderfully comic attitude, that double vision that is his ironical essence. The mere critic performs his etymological function by taking the Prioress apart and clumsily separating her good parts from her bad; but the poet's function is to build her incongruous and inharmonious parts into an inseparable whole which is infinitely greater than its parts. In this complex structure both the latent moralist and the naïve reporter have important positions, but I am not persuaded that in every case it is possible to determine which of them has the last word.[1]

Note

1 Quotations from Chaucer in this paper are made from F. N. Robinson's text (Cambridge, Mass., n.d.). Books referred to or cited are G. L. Kittredge, *Chaucer and His Poetry* (Cambridge, Mass., 1915), p. 45; Eileen Power, *Medieval People* (London, 1924), pp. 59–84. Robinson's note to A 650 records the opinion that *a good felawe* means a "rascal." The medieval reader's expectation that the first person in a work of fiction would represent mankind generally and at the same time would physically resemble the author is commented on by Leo Spitzer in an interesting note in *Traditio*, IV (1946), 414–422.

9 The unity of the *Canterbury Tales*

RALPH BALDWIN

Originally published as part of the Introduction to Ralph Baldwin, *The Unity of the Canterbury Tales* (*Anglistica* 5; Copenhagen: Rosenkilde & Bagger, 1955, pp. 15–16). The original pagination is recorded within square brackets. A very brief passage from p. 15 has been omitted. The endnotes originally appeared as footnotes and are here renumbered.

This study proposes a stylistic analysis of the narrative art of *The Canterbury Tales*. Its scope is the beginning and the ending of the *Tales*, with such transitions as are necessary to yield wholeness and aesthetic pattern to the idea of pilgrimage ...

It is accepted that *The Canterbury Tales* is not a whole, not an achieved work of art, but rather a truncated and aborted congeries of tales woven about a frame, the Pilgrimage from London to Canterbury. Although there is a closely articulated beginning, the *General Prologue*, and this beginning has, in turn, a beginning, a middle, and an end, the middle of the entire work reveals that the plan as presented by the Host is not even one-half realized on the outward journey, and as this study should demonstrate, no return talefest is even attempted. The ending seems to be a hastily subjoined recantation, tonally consorting with the *Parson's Tale* to which it is suffixed. It has been regarded as an anomalous and merely conventional appendage. It would appear then that an ending is nonexistent, because the pilgrimage is never brought back to the Tabard, the fund of stories never equates with the explicit number ordained by Harry Bailey, and the *motifs* released at the outset are never artistically concluded, never resolved.

It is true that the formal circularity that would have given the work that englobed and polished *ratio* lauded by the mediaeval literary theorists is lacking. "Whatever in the Middle Ages is not a long-rhymed story like Chrétien's *romans courtois*, has an additive and tell-as-you-go composition, not a shaded and circular or global composition. This certainly springs from the medieval *artes poeticae* and the medieval mind in general. What is elaborate in such works is the detailed *lexis*, the linguistic style, but not the larger *taxis*; the balanced composition is only found in works important in meaning, but not in trifling *faits divers*."[1]

But this apparent lack of balanced composition in the *Tales* would appear to result not from the surface tell-as-you-go tone, nor yet because it is a medley of "trifling faits divers," but rather because it is incomplete. In this respect it resembles in its building the mediaeval church. The master plan before them, its builders undertook work from the center outward, so to speak, and having provided walls and roof enough to shelter the sacrifice, they were sometimes content to leave the labor and expense of the rest of the building to posterity.

An examination of the beginning and the ending of the *Tales*, the only [16] masonry of our edifice on which Chaucer labored without the help of his editors, reveals that they fulfill an architectonic function, hitherto overlooked, and that they sustain the story as they reinforce each other. They make the pilgrimage not a frame, but a dynamic entity. By avoiding the "in-formal" advance through the text, and by surveying the *Tales* from the vantage points of beginning and ending, the reader may see *The Canterbury Tales* from another perspective.

That the mediaeval poem may without distortion invite an analysis which sees through the *cortex* to the *nucleus* and thus lays open the *sententia*, has been adequately asserted already as follows: "It (the mediaeval poem) had a lying surface meaning (*cortex*) covering an inner truth (*nucleus*). The surface meaning (*cortex* or *sensus*) might be interpreted to reveal a doctrinal truth (*sententia*) which was, in Christian poetry, always an aspect of Charity."[2]

The Canterbury Tales, a mediaeval poem, seen in *formal* focus displays a unity and a nuclear meaning which develop out of the theme or *cortex* of pilgrimage. This is the central point of the narrative, the altar stone, if you will. A consideration of the whole nature of pilgrimage and the season for the journey, gives to *The Canterbury Tales* the dignity, the unity, the "balanced composition only found in works important in meaning."

Notes

1 Helmut A. Hatzfeld, "Esthetic Criticism Applied to Medieval Romance Literature," RPh., I (1948), 324.
2 D. W. Robertson, Jr., "Some Medieval Literary Terminology, with Special Reference to Chrétien de Troyes," SP, XLVIII (1951), 691.

10 | The mixed style

CHARLES MUSCATINE

Originally published as the beginning of the final section of chapter 6 in Charles Muscatine, *Chaucer and the French Tradition: A Study in Style and Meaning* (Berkeley and Los Angeles: University of California Press, 1957, pp. 222–30). Reprinted by permission of the University of California Press. The original pagination is recorded within square brackets. The square brackets that originally enclosed line references in the text have been changed to round brackets. The endnotes originally appeared on pp. 270–71 and are here renumbered. In the rest of this section of chapter 6, Muscatine discusses the *Merchant's Tale* and the *Nun's Priest's Tale*.

The *Canterbury Tales* as a whole is an example of the mixed style. Each of the tales, by analogy and by contrast, takes meaning from others. The effect of the larger form, a structure of juxtapositions and tensions, is to place and control the attitudes evoked separately by its parts, to reveal their virtues and limitations in context. Some of this manipulation of attitudes is announced dramatically by rivalries among the pilgrims. The Miller and Reeve, the Summoner and Friar, are at overt personal debate. The Clerk recognizes in his envoy a relationship to the Wife of Bath. The Cook promises a comment on an innkeeper.[1] These dramatic relationships are in turn supported, and nondramatic ones are established mutely but no less powerfully, by the choice and disposition of the literary materials themselves. Thus the Miller's dramatic announcement of

> "a noble tale for the nones
> With which I wol now quite the Knyghtes tale,"
>
> (*MillProl* 3126–27)

is underscored in his tale by a resemblance to the Knight's in plot and in character grouping. The Reeve's rivalry with the Miller has similar literary support. The Host's implied comparison of the Nun's Priest with the Monk is followed by the Priest's recitation of a "tragedy" which comments on the Monk's collection of tragedies.[2] Criticism has detected (or suspected) a whole web of such relationships among the tales, in genre, subject, plot, characterization, and so on.[3]

It is hard to know where to draw the line between art and algebra in these correspondences. The work is so great as to begin to generate its own relationships. Does the description of the clerk Nicholas in the *Miller's Tale*, with its verbal reminiscences of the Clerk's portrait in the *General Prologue*, announce a comparative study of clerkships? Is Chaucer's Clerk to be compared to the Wife of Bath's fifth husband? Is there a "Marriage Group"?[4] Had Chaucer extended his poem, would the Merchant or the Monk have replied to the *Shipman's Tale*? There are provocative resemblances between the *Miller's Tale* and the *Merchant's*: do they support a philosophical comparison? One could not begin to describe the relational possibilities suggested by Chaucer's language, by phrases repeated—"pitee renneth soone in gentil herte," "allone, withouten any compaignye,"[5]—and by such repeated figures as the rhetorical *comparatio* on the death of Priam, which is used to describe both Constance's departure from Rome and Chauntecleer's abduction from a chicken yard.[6] We need not pause to evaluate all these possibilities. Even what is announced in the gross [223] stylistics of the *Canterbury Tales* shows Chaucer's tireless capacity for definition and comparison. He has a passion for relationships, and the over-all structure of the work, the linear sequence of discrete stories in various styles, meets this passion perfectly.

We are not surprised to find something of the same structure within the individual tales. Many of them can richly stand alone as containing significant measurement within themselves. The dominant attitudes they convey are habitually conjoined with other attitudes, idiosyncrasies with norms, norms with idiosyncrasies or other norms. The perspective is created variously; it is inserted, appended, implied, disguised, or worked plainly into the main pattern of the story. Sometimes it is a matter of plot and circumstance, the irony of a wrong turning that exposes an ignorance and prepares for a defeat.[7] Often it comes with an internal shift of style.

Virtually all the *Canterbury Tales* have some mixture of styles. The poems of dominantly religious inspiration have a realism which, if the poem is successful, as I think the *Prioress' Tale* is, melts symbolically into the conventional frame without conflict or irony. This peaceful stylistic mixture has some of the quality of the religious paradox itself; naturalism and the supernatural make peace in miracle. But in other poems the shifting style brings in whole shifts of assumptions. In poems where one style is heavily dominant, the mixture is enough to comment on, but not enough to rival the dominant attitude; thus the touches of commonsensical humor in the *Knight's Tale*, the scrap of lyricism in the *Reeve's Tale*, and the formal rhetoric in the *Canon's Yeoman's Tale* are relatively minor in effect. The *Wife of Bath's Prologue* swallows up a great mass of learned doctrine without losing its dominantly naturalistic shape. But there are a number of tales in which, as in the *Parliament of Fowls* and the *Troilus*, the mixed style is on display and becomes part of the subject of the poem. These are the tales which seem most "Chaucerian," comprehending in small space, as they do, so much of Chaucer's range.

The *Miller's Tale*

In the *Miller's Tale* the alien style contributes importantly to the realization of the theme, but it is not a central feature of the poem. That it is not accounts partly for the mixture's broadly comic effect. The tale does not have the pathos of a *Troilus* nor the bitterness of a *Merchant's Tale*, because the views it presents are so outrageously unbalanced. The courtliness in the *Miller's Tale* is never given full, traditional value. It is never a norm, always an idiosyncrasy; and it is juxtaposed to a naturalism of exceptional force and vitality.

[224] The normal view is perhaps best apprehended in the fact that the Miller's "noble tale" is fabliau at the stage of richest elaboration. All the fabliau features are here so completely realized that the genre is virtually made philosophical. The simple, sequential fabliau plot has become, in the lucidity of this complicated plot's arrangement, an assertion of the binding, practical sequentiality of all events. The pragmatic, prosaically solid imagery of fabliau is here built into an unbroken, unbreakable wall of accepted fact. The fabliau's preference for physical action becomes an ethical imperative. Even the stock triangle of fabliau—the lecherous young wife, the jealous husband, and the clever clerk (here two clerks)—is a self-assertive vehicle for the purest fabliau doctrine, the sovereignty of animal nature. So fully does the tale fulfill its fabliau entelechy that its working-out is attended, as Tillyard says, by "feelings akin to those of religious wonder."[8]

The poem's dominant style is of great intrinsic interest, and, having passed it by in my discussion of naturalism *per se*,[9] I must notice it here in a rather elaborate preface to the main topic. Let me observe, then, that in no other naturalistic poem of Chaucer is practical circumstance so closely tended, and practical detail so closely accounted for. We are given the name of the town and of the neighboring town, the names of all the characters (Nicholas, Absolon, Alisoun, John, Robyn, Gille, Gerveys) save one (the cloisterer, 3661), a close knowledge of the architecture and plan of the house:

> And broke an hole an heigh, upon the gable,   (3571)
> Unto the gardyn-ward, over the stable . . .

We have a scrupulous accounting of days of the week and of the hours of the crucial day. The description is rich with an expressive superfluity of specification:

> "Clepe at his dore, or knokke *with a stoon*."   (3432)
>
> hente hym *by the sholdres* myghtily . . .   (3475)
>
> *His owene hand* he made laddres thre,   (3624)
> To clymben *by the ronges and the stalkes*
> Unto the tubbes *hangynge in the balkes* . . .

The great mass of such given detail achieves an extraordinary solidity—beyond that of the *Reeve's Tale* or the *Wife of Bath's Prologue*—because so much of it is given specific antecedents or consequences. Where the typical fabliau brings in properties and explanations only as needed, the *Miller's Tale* seems to explain everything. That the town is Oxford explains—overpoweringly ex[225]plains—the presence of a clever clerk. That Absolon is named Absolon "explains" his blond beauty and his femininity.[10] That John the carpenter is made a "riche gnof" in the very first statement explains his securing a pretty, young wife. That Absolon offers her rich gifts, later on, is a link in this chain of explanations. That the carpenter "gestes heeld to bord" in the second verse prepares for the boarder Nicholas in verse four. The boarder's two days' self-confinement is silently prepared for in the eighteenth verse (3204); he rooms "allone, withouten any compaignye." Before Robyn the knave can peek in through Nicholas' door we are told that

> An hole he foond, ful lowe upon a bord,   (3440)
> Ther as the cat was wont in for to crepe . . .

Besides generally poetic consequence on the one hand (the board and the cat for solidity and animality), and practical consequence on the other (the hole for Robyn to peek through), many details through sheer recurrence achieve what I can only call a psychological consequence. Nicholas' door is not only peeked through; it is first cried and knocked at, then heaved off its hinges, then prayed by, then shut fast. That this door is at best only a minor factor in the action is symptomatic of the care with which the "naturalness" of the poem is contrived. The very smallest scraps of image and action are handled thus consequentially, even where they are entirely unnecessary to the gross plot. The cat image cited above is already the second such image in the poem. The hole image twice reappears later. The kinesthetic effect of its lowness is repeated with the carpenter's window (3696). The whole denouement, coming when it does, is by virtue of a mass recurrence of images given an air of utter probability. The nocturnal visit of Absolon to the carpenter's house has first a dress rehearsal that seems inconsequential—"This passeth forth; what wol ye bet than weel?" (3370)—except to familiarize us with this action, with such details as the wall and the hinged window, and with such minute facts as that the window can be heard through (cf. 3744). Similarly, the cockcrow, the knocking, the (sweet-smelling) mouth, the stone (I am citing items consecutively from verse 3675), the coal, the forge, the nobles, the cough, the knocking again, the haunch bone, the flatulence, bread and ale, the cry of "out" and "harrow," the neighbors, the carpenter's arm, the gaping and staring, the carpenter's madness—are all prepared for beforehand.[11] The breathtaking effect of the poem's climax surely owes much to this process. The focal images—the flood, the carpenter in his tub, the axe and cord—are suddenly brought to our conscious attention, not from nowhere (with an effect of mere surprise and chance), but from the semi-[226]conscious storage of previous acceptance, unanticipated, perhaps, but inevitable. It is this solidity of detail, along with the characterization interlaced intimately with it, that gives the ingenious plotting its overpowering substantiality.

In this remarkably self-contained world of facts, no room is left for abstract, *a priori* formulations. The humor of the poem arises from the unequal conflict between fact and the few illusions that unhappily insist on themselves. The devastating victory of the norm is supported, in the manner of comedy, by reducing the "errors" to caricature. The error of religion—to pass over the error of not wedding one's "simylitude" (3228)—is represented by the credulous, illiterate carpenter. His knowledge of Scripture is from mystery plays, seen "ful yoore ago" (3537). Noe (Noah) for him is "Nowel." His piety is all spells and asseverations; he is of that self-satisfied, unthinking persuasion that expresses itself in saws and goes by precedents:

> "This world is now ful tikel, sikerly.   (3428)
> I saugh to-day a cors yborn to chirche
> That now, on Monday last, I saugh hym wirche."

> "Help us, seinte Frydeswyde!   (3449)
> A man woot litel what hym shal bityde.
> This man is falle, with his astromye,
> In som woodnesse or in som agonye.
> I thoghte ay wel how that it sholde be!
> Men sholde nat knowe of Goddes pryvetee.
> Ye, blessed be alwey a lewed man
> That noght but oonly his bileve kan!
> So ferde another clerk with astromye;
> He walked in the feeldes, for to prye
> Upon the sterres, what ther sholde bifalle,
> Til he was in a marle-pit yfalle;
> He saugh nat that."

He is gulled by a clerk, and by his belief in "Goddes pryvetee."
The error of clerk Nicholas is faith in intellect and in the sufficiency of wit:

> "A clerk hadde litherly biset his whyle,   (3299)
> But if he koude a carpenter bigyle."

His quite enormous sufficiency, conveyed in the opening description (3199 ff.), is already touched with irony in the epithet "hende." It is fascinating to watch this term, which means "gracious" and "ready-handed" and "clever" and [227] "comely" and "near at hand," sharpen as the poem progresses.[12] It becomes a signal of his defeat. He has already solved the ethic of the poem, assault, when his cleverness elaborately overextends itself and leads to Absolon's assault on him.

Faith in Love is the heresy most elaborately dealt with in the poem, and it is most elaborately caricatured. Linguistic analysis has shown how much the Oxford idiom of love is the idiom of English rather than of French romance.[13] It is the native version of the imported heresy that is parodied here. More congenial to the setting, it is also funnier than Continental love would have been, for it is exposed to the laughter of the sophisticated, who know better, as well as of the Miller's kind, who know worse. But it remains crushingly conventional, and the stylistic vehicle for the comedy of love is the farrago of convention and naked instinct that is Absolon's courtship of Alisoun:

> "I wol go slepe an houre or tweye,   (3685)
>   And al the nyght thanne wol I wake and pleye."
> Whan that the firste cok hath crowe, anon
> Up rist this joly lovere Absolon,
> And hym arraieth gay, at poynt-devys.
> But first he cheweth greyn and lycorys,
> To smellen sweete, er he hadde kembd his heer.
> Under his tonge a trewe-love he beer,
> For therby wende he to ben gracious.
> He rometh to the carpenteres hous,
> And stille he stant under the shot-wyndowe—
> Unto his brest it raughte, it was so lowe—
> And softe he cougheth with a semysoun:
> "What do ye, hony-comb, sweete Alisoun,
> My faire bryd, my sweete cynamome?
> Awaketh, lemman myn, and speketh to me!
> Wel litel thynken ye upon my wo,
> That for youre love I swete ther I go.
> No wonder is thogh that I swelte and swete;
> I moorne as dooth a lamb after the tete.
> Ywis, lemman, I have swich love-longynge,
> That lik a turtel trewe is my moornynge.
> I may nat ete na moore than a mayde."
> "Go fro the wyndow, Jakke fool," she sayde.

[228] The French lover "rometh" perhaps, but he does not "swelte and swete," nor does he catch up on his sleep before a sleepless night. The courtly delicacy of speech and of toilette[14] have become in this small-town, provincial version the anal-retentive, squeamish spotlessness registered in Absolon's portrait (3312 ff.) and punished with terrible aptness at the end.

The delectable Alisoun sets in motion the lovemaking of the poem, and her celebrated portrait answers to several versions:

> Fair was this yonge wyf, and therwithal   (3233)
> As any wezele hir body gent and smal.
> A ceynt she werede, barred al of silk,
> A barmclooth eek as whit as morne milk
> Upon hir lendes, ful of many a goore.
> Whit was hir smok, and broyden al bifoore
> And eek bihynde, on hir coler aboute,
> Of col-blak silk, withinne and eek withoute.
> The tapes of hir white voluper
> Were of the same suyte of hir coler;

Hir filet brood of silk, and set ful hye.
And sikerly she hadde a likerous ye;
Ful smale ypulled were hire browes two,
And tho were bent and blake as any sloo.
She was ful moore blisful on to see
Than is the newe pere-jonette tree,
And softer than the wolle is of a wether.
And by hir girdel heeng a purs of lether,
Tasseled with silk, and perled with latoun.
In al this world, to seken up and doun,
There nys no man so wys that koude thenche
So gay a popelote or swich a wenche.
Ful brighter was the shynyng of hir hewe
Than in the tour the noble yforged newe.
But of hir song, it was as loude and yerne
As any swalwe sittynge on a berne.
Therto she koude skippe and make game,
As any kyde or calf folwynge his dame.
Hir mouth was sweete as bragot or the meeth,
Or hoord of apples leyd in hey or heeth.
Wynsynge she was, as is a joly colt,

[229]   Long as a mast, and upright as a bolt.
A brooch she baar upon hir lowe coler,
As brood as is the boos of a bokeler.
Hir shoes were laced on hir legges hye.
She was a prymerole, a piggesnye,
For any lord to leggen in his bedde,
Or yet for any good yeman to wedde.

This is not merely a dead convention vivified.[15] So much has been said of the naturalness and realism of it that I may here speak one-sidedly for the effect of the convention itself. The form is still rhetorical *effictio*, and still preserves the convention of the inventory, disarrayed indeed, but listing at every turn the categories of the archetype: the fairness, the eye, the bent brows, the hue, the voice, the mouth, the carriage, the silken costume, the jewelry, the accomplishments. And each category is filled by a superlative. The similes are the similes that apply in the Oxford context, just as Absolon's gifts of spiced ale and piping hot waffles apply. In Oxford it is a brunette rather than a blonde, plucked brows rather than natural, embroidery of black silk rather than of gold, pearls of latten, not precious stones. The convention domesticated carries still some of its original idealizing power. Its function is manifold. I feel in this description, especially where it deals with such unsuspicious images as the "newe pere-jonette tree," an outright, unqualified sympathy with the character, a response in the poet himself similar in some respects to his sympathy with the Wife of Bath. The literary effect is as if to present Alisoun as the one precious illusion in the poem. Here the milleresque philosophy finds its one ideal, and allows itself its one large formulation:

In al this world, to seken up and doun,   (3252)
There nys no man so wys that koude thenche
So gay a popelote or swich a wenche.

She was a prymerole, a piggesnye,   (3268)
For any lord to leggen in his bedde,
Or yet for any good yeman to wedde.

On another level the portrait is comic in the way that Absolon is comic. It matches perfectly (to the sophisticated audience) the gaucherie of his "love-longynge." This is a small-town heroine, whose brows *are* plucked, whose eye *is* lecherous, whose forehead shines—from washing after work (3310 f.). Finally, on the level of terms like "weasel," "loins," "gore," "colt," and "pig's-eye," the [230] portrait describes the delectable little animal who is not to be won by a protracted, artificial wooing.

The strands of imagery that I have rather painfully disentangled are of course twisted solidly together in the poetry. Images like "morne milk," "wolle ... of a wether," "hoord of apples," contribute to more than one strand. The silky black and white of Alisoun's ensemble, if it is not piquantly noncommittal, may contribute to all. "Loins" and "gore" in this context have literary-parodic as well as sexual associations.[16] The humor of Absolon's discovery of the animal is prepared by his misguided attention to the ideal. For the Miller (whose views are presumably being reflected here, though the feeling is possibly too fine for him) the animalism and the ideality must be intertwined. As it does with the Carpenter's religion and Nicholas' cleverness, however, the poem's lusty naturalism bluntly triumphs over the illusion of Love, leaving Alisoun unscathed, perhaps, but not undiscovered.

There is nothing in the fabliau tradition that dictated the introduction of courtly conventionalism in the *Miller's Tale*. Chaucer had no need to encumber himself with the "dreary," "artificial," "hackneyed" form, save the need of meaning. Here he actually realized a potency of the fabliau that is not quite realized in any fabliau of the French tradition. In *Du Clerc qui fu repus*, in *D'Aloul*, in the *Dit de la gageure*, the fragments of courtly convention are inoperative.[17] In the *Miller's Tale* they serve perspective, affording the fabliau a mordantly pointed comment, from below, on the futility of love *paramours*.

Notes

1 *CookProl* 4360.
2 See sec. 4, iii, *post*. [Muscatine refers here to his subsequent discussion of the *Nun's Priest's Tale* – ed.]
3 See, e.g., C. Hugh Holman, "Courtly Love in the Merchant's and the Franklin's Tales," *ELH*, XVIII (1951), 241–252; Wayne Shumaker, "Chaucer's *Manciple's Tale* as Part of a Canterbury Group," *UTQ*, XXII (1953), 147–156; on *2NT* and *CYT*, sec. 3, iii, *supra*.
4 The term was apparently coined by Eleanor P. Hammond, *Chaucer: A Bibliographical Manual* (New York, 1908), p. 256, to describe a small "class of narratives"; its prominence in criticism is owing to G. L. Kittredge, "Chaucer's Discussion of Marriage," *MP*, IX (1912), 435–467 [see above – ed.], and his *Chaucer*, chaps. v

and vi. The existence of the group has since been questioned and defended. A bibliography of the problem is contained in the notes of Lawrence, *Chaucer*, pp. 121–144.

5 See, respectively, *KnT* 1761, *MerchT* 1986, *SqT* 479 (cf. *LGW* F503); and *KnT* 2779, *MillT* 3204.

6 *MLT* 288–94; *NPT* 3355–61.

7 See Germaine Dempster, *Dramatic Irony in Chaucer* (Stanford, 1932), and Charles A. Owen, Jr., "The Crucial Passages in Five of the *Canterbury Tales*," *JEGP*, LII (1953), 294–311 [see above – ed.], where this and other sources of irony are taken up.

8 E. M. W. Tillyard, *Poetry Direct and Oblique*, rev. ed. (London, 1948), p. 92, in one of the few requisitely serious discussions of the poem.

9 [In an earlier section of the chapter – ed.]

10 See Paul E. Beichner, "Absolon's Hair," *Mediaeval Studies*, XII (1950), 222–233. Fr. Beichner provides a virtual history of "Absolon" in the Middle Ages.

11 The interested reader may verify these recurrences in John S. P. Tatlock and A. G. Kennedy, *A Concordance to . . . Chaucer* (Washington, 1927).

12 See Paul E. Beichner, "Chaucer's Hende Nicholas," *Mediaeval Studies*, XIV (1952), 151–153.

13 See E. T. Donaldson, "Idiom of Popular Poetry in the *Miller's Tale*," in *English Institute Essays, 1950* (New York, 1951), pp. 116–140.

14 Expounded in the *Roman de la Rose* 2099–2174 (*Romaunt* 2223–88); but the whole of the God of Love's lecture is of more than passing interest in connection with Absolon.

15 So Lowes, *Convention and Revolt* [Boston, 1919], pp. 98–100.

16 Donaldson, "Idiom," pp. 131–132.

17 See chap. iii, sec. 2, *supra*.

11 | Concepts of pilgrimage and marriage

D. W. ROBERTSON, Jr

Originally published as part of chapter 4 in D. W. Robertson, Jr,
A Preface to Chaucer: Studies in Medieval Perspectives (Princeton, NJ:
Princeton University Press, 1962, pp. 373–7). Reprinted by
permission of Princeton University Press. The original pagination
is recorded within square brackets. A reference to an illustration in
the original has been omitted. The endnotes originally appeared as
footnotes and are here renumbered.

Iconographic materials from the Bible ... abound in Chaucer's poetry,
where they afford a richness and depth of meaning which could not have
been achieved in any other way. Among scriptural concepts which appear in
The Canterbury Tales, the most important is the idea of pilgrimage. Any
pilgrimage during the Middle Ages, whether it was made on the knees in a
labyrinth set in a cathedral floor, or, more strenuously, to the Holy Land,
was ideally a figure for the pilgrimage of the Christian soul through the
world's wilderness toward the celestial Jerusalem. The pilgrimage of the soul
was not in itself a journey from place to place, but an inner movement
between the two cities so vividly described by St. Augustine, one founded on
charity, and the other on cupidity. Love moved the pilgrim's feet and
determined the direction of his journey. The *Tales* are set in a framework
which emphasizes this journey and its implications. The opening in April,
the month of Venus, under the sign of Taurus, the house of Venus, with its
showers and singing birds, suggests the love which may move the pilgrims
to Canterbury toward either one spiritual city or the other.... And as the
journey draws to a close, with Libra's scales of justice hanging in the sky in a
curious but irrelevant echo of Homer, the parson offers to show

> the wey in this viage
> Of thilke parfit glorious pilgrimage
> That highte Jerusalem celestial.
>
> [*ParsP* x (I) 49–51]

[374] The idea is reinforced from time to time in the prologue and tales. Thus
the wife of Bath "koude muchel of wandrynge by the weye" [*GP* I (A) 467]
both in the flesh and in the spirit; old Egeus in the Knight's Tale observes

that "we been pilgrymes passynge to and fro" [I (A) 2848]; Custance in the Man of Law's Tale undergoes a long pilgrimage from home; in the Pardoner's Tale the pilgrimage is seen as a quest for the death of death; and so on. The concept of the pilgrim and of the love which moves him "up a croked wey" [cf. *PardT* VI (C) 761], or more directly to his home, provides a thematic background against which both Chaucer's pilgrims and the characters in their tales may be clearly seen and properly evaluated. The idea needed only to be suggested in the fourteenth century, when one of the most popular subjects for wall paintings, even in remote villages, was St. Christopher, the guide to man's spiritual voyage. As we visualize Chaucer's "folk" moving toward Canterbury, not winding through the soft intricacies of a landscape by Constable, but outlined against a background of gold leaf, we should do well to let the old words of St. Augustine echo in our ears: "Thus in this mortal life, wandering from God, if we wish to return to our native country where we can be blessed we should use this world and not enjoy it, so that the 'invisible things' of God 'being understood by the things that are made' may be seen, that is, so that by means of corporal and temporal things, we may comprehend the eternal and spiritual."

The solution to the problem of love, the force which directs the will, which is in turn the source of moral action, is, figuratively, marriage. The concept of marriage plays a large part in *The Canterbury Tales*, but to understand its significance it is necessary to know something of its wider implications. In the first place, every Christian of whatever condition should be "married." As Thomas Brinton put it, "Every soul is either an adulteress with the Devil or a spouse of Christ."[1] A man either preserves the marriage contracted at baptism,[2] or abuses it. When a man is properly "married" in this way, the "marriage" between the spirit and the flesh, or the reason and the sensuality within him, is preserved intact, and he is also a part of the "marriage" between Christ and the [375] Church. In the Church, a bishop was solemnly "married" to his diocese, and a priest was regarded as the "husband" of his flock; for both inherited in the Apostolic tradition the place of Christ with reference to the Church. In the twelfth century, the Duke of Aquitaine "married" the church of Aquitaine.[3] Similarly, the idea that a prince should be a "husband" to his people gradually acquired the force of law in France during the later middle ages. A fourteenth-century commentator on Justinian wrote that "there is contracted a moral and political marriage between the prince and the *respublica*. Also, just as there is contracted a spiritual and divine marriage between a church and its prelate, so there is contracted a temporal and terrestrial marriage between the Prince and the State."[4] Jehan le Bel compares the "signerie" that a husband enjoys over his wife with that of a feudal lord over his subjects.[5] Marriage is thus a principle of order in the individual, in the church, and in lay society; in medieval terms, a well-ordered hierarchy of almost any kind may be thought of as a "marriage." It follows that there are various kinds of "adultery." When the sensuality or the lower reason rebels, the result is conventionally termed "adultery." As Berchorius puts it, any mortal sin is a kind of "adultery."

Again, a prelate who abuses his office for personal gain is an "adulterer," and so on.[6] "Adultery" implies generally what Chaucer's parson describes as an "up-so-doun" condition in a hierarchy.

The theme of marriage is developed first in the Knight's Tale, where order is represented initially by the marriage of Theseus and finally by the marriage of Palamon. Specifically, it appears here as a solution to the problems raised by the misdirected concupiscent passions, represented by Venus, and by the misdirected irascible passions, represented by Mars. The Miller's Tale which follows is a story of adultery in which a lecherous clerk, a vain clerk, and an avaricious old husband are amusingly shown to suffer the consequences of their abuses of "marriage," which include, incidentally, Nicolas' interest in judicial astrology and Absalon's refusal to accept offerings from the ladies, as well as the actions of [376] both with reference to Alisoun. In the Reeve's Tale we meet an "adulterous" priest, who neglects the "lineage" of the Apostolic succession in favor of his literal lineage—

> he wolde his hooly blood honoure,
> Though that he hooly chirche sholde devoure.
>
> [*RvT* I (A) 3985–86]

This "hooly blood" is pretty thoroughly put in jeopardy in the tale which follows. In the Man of Law's Tale Custance escapes marriage with a pagan Sultan whose mother scorns "this newe lawe" [II (B¹) 337], but she achieves a more proper marriage which she succeeds in preserving in the face of adversity. The wife exerts every effort to turn marriage "up-so-doun," and we meet the results of this kind of inversion in society in the persons of the blind summoner and the hypocritical friar, who abuse their offices in "adulterous" fashion. The clerk systematically restores the order inverted by the wife, calling attention specifically to the duties of the Christian soul as it is tested by its Spouse. There are, however, as he says, few "Grisilids," and in the Merchant's Tale the fool's paradise advocated by the wife in her tale is fully exposed for what it is when an old man seeks to make of marriage a lecherous paradise on earth. Although the theme of the Franklin's Tale is "gentilesse" rather than marriage specifically, the dangers of the kind of "headless" marriage dear to the Epicurean ideals of the middle class are fully revealed. Adultery appears again in three separate guises in the Shipman's Tale. In the Second Nun's Tale there is a literally chaste marriage which is a type of spiritual virginity under Christ. Again, in the Nun's Priest's Tale, the dangers of the service of Venus in marriage are once more shown, and in this instance the idea is applied by implication to the relationship between a priest and his flock. Finally, the pastoral theology of marriage is treated by the parson. Closely related to the theme of marriage is the theme of "multiplying," which is introduced by the wife and vividly developed in the character of the pardoner, in his prologue, and in the Canon's Yeoman's Tale, where a technical term in alchemy is so used that its wider implications in other contexts become unmistakable. If we look back over these developments—and I have mentioned only the more obvious of them—it is not difficult to see that Chaucer sets the marriage theme in humanistic terms in the Knight's Tale, suggesting the proper function of marriage as an [377] ordering principle in the individual and in society, and develops its manifold implications in the subsequent tales. Once it is seen that the elaboration of the theme of marriage in the *Tales* is thematic rather than dramatic, the false problems raised by the old theory of the "marriage group" disappear.

Notes

1 Ed. [Sister Mary Aquinas] Devlin, [O. P. (London, 1954)] i, 36.
2 Cf. Odo Tusculanus, in [Jean Baptiste] Pitra, [ed., *Analecta novissima Spicilegii Solesmensis* (Paris, 1885–88)], ii, 247: "Licet animae omnium christianorum in baptismo desponsetur Christo, et cum eo contrahant matrimonium spirituale."
3 See [Émile] Mâle, *L'art rel[igieux] du XIIe siècle* (Paris, 1924), p. 198.
4 Quoted by E. H. Kantorowicz, "Mysteries of State," *Harvard Theol[ogical] Rev[iew]*, xlviii (1955), 78.
5 *Li ars d'amour*, [ed. J. Petit (Brussels, 1867–69)] ii, 92.
6 *Opera* [Cologne, 1731–32], iii, 97–98.

12 | The range of the middle

PAUL G. RUGGIERS

Originally published as the final section of part 1 in Paul G.
Ruggiers, *The Art of the Canterbury Tales* (Madison: University of
Wisconsin Press, 1965, pp. 42–9). Reprinted by permission of the
University of Wisconsin Press. The original pagination is recorded
within square brackets. The endnotes originally appeared as
footnotes, and extended to p. 50. A reference to discussion
elsewhere in Ruggiers' book has been omitted from footnote 4.

In retrospect we can see that the ironical detachment of the persona-poet and
his withdrawal from functions other than critical and prudential do not
prevent the depiction of his Christian world. On the contrary his detachment
enables the world to be spread out before us in all its multiplicity and
complexity in the great middle of the *Canterbury Tales*. This middle we now
proceed to examine in terms of literary types, of the modes of experience
underlying them, and the themes which subtly shape their final form. From
the vantage of literary genre we may determine the limitations which are
inherent in genre; from the vantage of theme we may determine the shaping
power of thought over type.

Chaucer himself not only gives evidence of his awareness of the range of
literary forms, but also, in terms of content, makes the distinction between
serious and non-serious literature. The reading from the dream of Scipio in
the *Parliament of Fowls* hints at the subject. The *Prologue to the Legend of Good
Women* (F 414 ff.) makes a precise distinction between entertainment and
edification. The *Miller's Prologue* distinguishes low comedy ("cherles tale")
from "storial thyng that toucheth gentillesse,/And eek moralitee and
hoolynesse" (ll. 3179–80). This familiar distinction between works dealing
with the love of this world and those directing our eyes beyond it has its
final statement in the Retraction itself.

In the links on either side of the *Monk's Tale* Chaucer displays both
theoretical and practical knowledge of comedy and tragedy, dealing both
with the "shape" of these forms and with the effect upon the audience. He is
equally cognizant of varieties of romance: stories of love, battle, chivalry, of
elf-queens and enchantments, and of virtue achieved. He knows these
by name as well as by subject, and the effects of his intimate acquaintance

are to be seen everywhere in the *Tales*, even to the extent of parody or burlesque.

[43] If we needed further proof of Chaucer's precise knowledge of the range of types, we see it in the casual ease with which he conflates the attributes of comedy, romance, and tragedy in the *Nun's Priest's Tale*, leavens the moral romance with comedy in the *Wife of Bath's Tale*, and deepens the tone of comedy towards satire in the *Merchant's Tale*.

We may go so far as to say that Chaucer is a plastic poet who exploits all the genres which provide vehicles for his themes. His proclivity is in the main for ironic comedy and romance; they prevail at the heart of his genius. Each is involved with the other, deepened or widened to make way for the more serious and elevated or for the more farcial and satiric attitudes. The same commingling of romance and comedy which we note in the *Troilus* we remark in the *Canterbury Tales*. Even in the predominantly sober *Knight's Tale* or the *Man of Law's Tale*, realism intrudes to deflate the tone and subtly change the point of view.

This special apposition of religio-romantic and comic attitudes to each other is the goal upon which much of Chaucer's intelligence finally bears. The delicate balance between man as God-created yet self-asserting, as God-seeking yet self-loving provides him with his essential materials; the antagonism between the poles of man's nature he spells out from the very beginning in the mixture of springtime joy and penitence and works out in the opposition between the goal of Canterbury/Jerusalem and the desire to reach the goal on terms wilfully defined.

The two terms which we have now isolated to describe the classes into which the tales fall need definition. When we use the term romance to describe the secular literary type, we mean a long form, usually of French origin, in which the hero ideally passes through a succession of adventures, conquers his enemy or enemies, frees a woman, attains her love, and achieves some measure of virtue and acceptance in the process. The most usual form assumed is that of the quest-pilgrimage, with a departure and an arrival at a goal, with the strong possibility of a return. The subject matter is the familiar triad of love, adventure, religion. The hero, by his bravery or daring, and by his ability to overcome obstacles, is raised above the level of ordinary men, and tends by his example to bring about in the audience some idealized vision of experience or a confirmation of their hopes. The most serious and elevated form of romance in the Christian tradi[44]tion has been hagiographic: the saint is shown attesting, in the life of grace, an endurance and perseverance beyond that of other mortals and reaching through suffering the goal of reconciliation with his God. The demonstration of the hero's more-than-human qualities necessitates, in the more naive secular and religious treatments, a world of marvels in which there is assistance (or hindrance) from otherworldly creatures and a beneficent nature.

In its most systematic form, romance is best exemplified by the purgatorial process in the *Divine Comedy*, where life is viewed as a meaningful progress towards an attainable goal and where the *débat* between the vices and virtues is carried out point by point by various devices like the bridle and the whip, the beatitudes, and the loss of the sign of the purged sin. In its serener aspects it sees art as serving the useful function of pointing the way to truth, and of bringing into clear focus a restored natural perfection in which man is crowned priest and emperor over himself. In the Dantean view the total meaning of romance in this sense has to do with learning about charity, or about dealing charitably with others, or with transforming eroticism into something else; in short with setting the soul in order.

Below the purgatorial world of aspiration and hope lies Dante's frozen center of Hell representing the paralysis of the best human motives; and above the center he locates varying degrees of overt and conscious resistance to the good of others and to that of the self, up to the least offensive carnal appetites. The horror of non-commitment to the good in the situation of the trimmers and neutrals indicates something of the medieval fondness for polarity: whoever is not with me is against me. In Chaucer the range of tone is from playful, even joyful, to satirical and serious; humanity is viewed from the vantage of the all-too-human at one extreme, as in the *Miller's Tale* and that of the Reeve, where the audience is apt to see the sexual fulfillment serving as a valid retribution to stupidity or pride, and at the other a wholehearted allegiance to evil, as in the *Pardoner's Tale* in which the upside-down values of the protagonists test or deny order and law. The tragic tends to be an aspect of this range of experience, as the pathetic tends to be an aspect of romance; noise, confusion, and riot are apt to be its dominant note, as a note of hopeful and serene expectation is apt to be that of romance.

As Aristotle pointed out in the opening chapters of the *Poetics*—with acuteness, I feel—literary types are preceded by attitudes to[45]wards experience which the poet holds by personal disposition, and we may add, by convention. Chaucer's views include the notions that man is a significant part of creation, that suffering is meaningful, that life is a process, that aspiration is the inner life of achievement, that the soul has an ultimate destiny, that the upper air is, so to speak, peopled with guardian spirits, and that in the mysterious "below" lie forces of destruction. We need not wonder that Chaucer's specialty is romance.

Aristotle also pointed out what was for him the great dichotomy of classes into which men fall: men better or worse than average. If we add to the first the suggestion of men as they ought to be and to the second men as they are or as they are thought to be, we do not change the division, but rather begin to account for the great variety of experience and types of plot available to the poet. The division was for Aristotle a matter of the broadest kind of morality, and is in the Greek terms a division into the serious and the laughable or absurd. This consideration of the degree of seriousness in the subject matter and in the disposition of the poet we confront in Chaucer, in whom the word "worthy," for example, used in a variety of contexts, points up the distinction in clearly moral contexts between persons striving after virtue and those indifferent to it. For the moral Christian poet, for Dante and for Chaucer to be specific, the view of men as better or worse than the average yields the familiar purgatorial and infernal levels of human actions where the agents are depicted on the one hand as seriously involved in the process of making themselves acceptable to God, and on the other, as arrested at some chosen level less than the Good.

The polarity I am suggesting of two classes of literary experiences was noted long ago by Saintsbury, who recognized that the opposition between them was nearly as sharp as that of Greek tragedy to Greek comedy or satiric play, and who suggested that in Chaucer it may have been studied. The question that is immediately raised is that of tragedy. Chaucer's distinction, made on the basis of a somewhat shadowy literary tradition, has to do with a sad end to the affairs of men. But Chaucer's disposition is sunny alongside Dante's, and he does not specialize in the unhappy tale. Even those which deal with the destruction of the agents are carefully contrived to corroborate the values of the audience; they assume a stance of righteousness and become moral tales; in particular they become what Northrop Frye [46] calls comedies without humor in which the audience does not have to take the villainy seriously.[1]

The *Monk's Tale*, with its series of vignettes, is in the view I have been offering, an anomaly in the *Canterbury Tales*.[2] (Even in the series the tale of Nebuchadnezzar must be seen as a tragedy with a happy ending.) But the anomaly has a function within the larger thematic frame, serving by juxtaposition with the *Nun's Priest's Tale* to point up beyond the fall of princes, beyond an empty contempt of the world, the power of men to escape the operations of mere destiny and to control, up to a point, their progress through the world of accident and chance. Like the good ironist, Chaucer recognizes the role of luck, of canniness, of expedience, but like the good moralist he seriously ponders the mystery of responsibility and the working of the human will. Governance, self-possession, self-control become for him central considerations in both the serious and the non-serious tales. For Chaucer the distinction between a happy or a sad ending becomes a matter of the retention or loss of these. It is instructive to look to Dante where the so-called tragic or sad end of the agent does not preclude his ultimate salvation unless the end is couched in terms of an incorrigible use of the self and others without regard to the larger concerns of human responsibility. If the agent has not lost sight of his eternal goals, nor of the value of hope and repentance, his suffering becomes meaningful and his so-called tragic end is of no consequence in the larger pattern of Divine Comedy, but is rather merely an episode in it. Even in Chaucer's *Troilus*, where it is perhaps useless to talk of grace and perdition, the action ends with a laugh in a Neo-Platonic heaven.

There are other ways by which to classify the tales, and there have been many attempts to classify them.[3] Taxonomy of the tales would, of course, be in a vastly better plight if Chaucer had written the full quota promised in his first plan. With the twenty-four performances [47] of the pilgrimage one always feels strong demurrals about *any* system because of Chaucer's own eclectic handling of the literary types, and because of the small number of examples from which to generalize. One such classification which does not go quite beyond the consideration of types, but which indicates the difficulties of classification is as follows:

1. *Tales mainly realistic*: Miller, Reeve, Cook, Shipman. (Shall we add Friar, Summoner, Pardoner, Canon's Yeoman, Part II? What of the fabliau tone in the *Wife of Bath's Tale* and that of the Merchant?)
2. *Tales of chivalry*: Knight and Squire. (Shall we include Chaucer's parody here? Shall we include here the tales of the Wife of Bath and the Franklin?)
3. *Religious tales about saints*: the Prioress's miracle, and the tale of the Second Nun. (Shall we include the Clerk and the Man of Law in this general classification?)
4. *Pious tales about saintly persons*: Clerk and Man of Law. (Shall we consider these allegories? What about the *Physician's Tale?*)
5. *Moral treatises*: *Melibee*, Parson. (Shall we call them both treatises? Is the *Melibee* also a poem? an allegory? a sermon buried in an artificially contrived frame?)
6. *Fables with moral comment*: Manciple. (Shall we group the *Physician's Tale* here as a legend with moral comment? What of the beast fable in the *Nun's Priest's Tale?*)
7. *Confessions*: *Wife of Bath's Prologue*, *Pardoner's Introduction* and conclusion to his sermon (moral tale? exemplum? fabliau?), the *Canon's Yeoman's Tale*, Part I.
8. *Preacher's exempla*: *Friar's Tale*, *Pardoner's Tale*, *Nun's Priest's Tale?*
9. *Breton lai*: Franklin, and Wife of Bath?
10. *Tales of whatever sort with added didactic elements*: Merchant, Wife of Bath, Nun's Priest, Franklin. (Also Manciple, Physician, Man of Law, Pardoner, Canon's Yeoman, Summoner, Monk? Is the *Merchant's Tale* a parody of romance? Should it be included with Group 1?)
11. *Tragedy*: Monk's tales. (Are they, like the *Physician's Tale*, merely history in a moral context?)

It is not a classification I should care to defend at length, but it does point up a number of difficulties which confront the classifier. One [48] conclusion that is possible from any attempt at grouping is that Chaucer was an experimenter and that the tales individually reflect a constant concern with the forms of art as well as an indifference to their built-in limitations.

In classifying the tales as either comedies or romances I have kept in mind, within the two main categories, the broadest possible correspondence to Chaucer's own distinction between literature for edification and literature for pleasure, recognizing that the tales within each group span the range from serious to non-serious, and attempting to assess the degree to which the tales function as serious statements in the total theme. Such a division is based upon human character as capable or incapable of regeneration and yields the familiar poles of comedy and romance.

Wherever the tales deal with the unwillingness of the agents to surrender their instinctual incorrigibility, with the determined assertion of their appetites over social convention, they belong to the world of comedy, ironic, melodramatic, even exemplary. With such agents we can never feel more than a sneaking and even despairing admiration for their invincible folly. This group includes the tales of the Miller, Reeve, Shipman, Friar, Summoner, Merchant, Pardoner, and Canon's Yeoman.

Wherever the agents manifest powers of growth, submit themselves to a learning process, are in some way regenerated, they belong to the world of romance. We pin our hopes upon these heroes and heroines because they corroborate our inner convictions about human freedom. When they err and fall, in a sense we err and fall with them, but with them we also rise. I see the tales of the Knight, Man of Law, Prioress, Nun's Priest, Wife of Bath, Clerk, and Franklin as romances.

This dichotomy between despair and hope, between corrigibility and incorrigibility, tends to make clear Chaucer's own recognition of the spiritual death that lurks in the one camp and the spiritual life that thrives in the other, and marks him yet again, as he chose once to be remembered, a religious as well as a comic poet. The purgatorial basis of romance and the infernal basis of comedy are not, after all, different for him from what they were for Dante.

The division suggested can lend itself to oversimplification; yet it by-passes the temptation to see the tales of the secular agents and those of the religious as providing a workable scheme of classifica[49]tion.[4] It is not simple for the reason that Chaucer's attitudes and intentions are not simple, either as artist or as a moral commentator. Both the comedies and the romances show variety of treatment, variety of mood. In some the form is freighted with *exempla*, overt statement; in others theme is subtly linked with style, implication, oblique suggestion. The multileveled view of experience which comprises the great middle of the *Canterbury Tales* is not, obviously, any simple alternation of one overt view with another. It is an interaction of worlds in the mind of the poet, presented to us in particular manipulations of literary forms, the manipulations themselves being the result of the thought or meaning each form supports and conveys. Thus the focus of what follows is the thematic range of the comic and romantic forms, the deepening and widening of their scope to allow for the bitter and sardonic as well as the lyrical and spiritual. By such an examination we come to see how, in the most ancient sense, Chaucer reveals himself as the plastic poet in his grasp of the whole range of experience, the world of wish-and-wonder as well as the world of the all-too-real.

Aside from the varying degrees of success and failure in the artistic endeavor which we all feel, there lies over the great bulk of the *Canterbury Tales* what someone has called an incorruptible sincerity of expression reflecting the concern of the poet for the truth of experience.[5] It is this which, more than any other factor, justifies the patient examination of their thematic statement.

Notes

1 *Anatomy of Criticism* (Princeton University Press, 1957), p. 40.
2 A theory of Chaucerian tragedy is coming more and more into being. Cf. D. W. Robertson, Jr., "Chaucerian Tragedy," *ELH*, XIX (1952), 1–37; R. E. Kaske, "The Knight's Interruption of the *Monk's Tale*," *ELH*, XXIV (1957), 249–68; Robert A. Pratt, " 'Joye after Wo' in the *Knight's Tale*," *JEGP*, LVII (1958), 416–23; John F. Mahoney, "Chaucerian Tragedy and the Christian Tradition," *Annuale Mediaevale*, III (1962), 81–99; and George B. Pace, "Adam's Hell," *PMLA*, LXXVIII (1963), 25–35. See too D. W. Robertson, Jr., *A Preface to Chaucer*, pp. 346, 473.
3 Cf. the attempts at classification in Robert O. Payne, *The Key of Remembrance: A Study of Chaucer's Poetics* (Yale University Press, 1963), pp. 147–70, with which I am in substantial agreement on the matter of types, and in which the author is fully aware of the limitations in any system of categories.
4 The decision to omit certain of the tales reflects my own taste and judgment. Much of the *Canterbury Tales* is of varying quality; two tales (Manciple and Physician) are successful on terms other than purely artistic and I recognize the possibility that Chaucer's intention may have included the overt didactic utterances. The Cook's and Squire's fragments cannot yield in their incomplete state a coherent interpretation until we know that Chaucer intended them to be fragments. The *Monk's Tale* belongs, properly, in an appendix, unless we care to place the tale of Nebuchadnezzar in one camp and the others on the opposing side. . . .
5 In 1936, C. S. Lewis, in *The Allegory of Love: A Study in Medieval Tradition* (Oxford University Press, 1936), pp. 163–64, offered the view that Chaucer is mainly a poet of courtly love, that his fourteenth-century audience thought of him as the poet of the dream-allegory and romance written in the high style and imbued with doctrine. To shift emphasis from such matters, Mr. Lewis writes, is to deal falsely, in a sense, with his work. "We have heard a little too much of the 'mocking' Chaucer. Not many will agree with the critic who supposed that the laughter of Troilus in heaven was 'ironical'; but I am afraid that many of us now read into Chaucer all manner of ironies, slynesses, and archnesses, which are not there, and praise him for his humour where he is really writing with 'ful devout corage.' "

In 1948, George R. Coffman, in a footnote to his essay "Chaucer and Courtly Love Once More—The *Wife of Bath's Tale*," *Speculum*, XX (1948), 49–50, defended by way of answer a "prevailing Comic Spirit" in Chaucer and called for not only an interpretation of his "prevailing intent," but also a comprehensive review of the whole problem of terminology as an essential part of repeated attempts "to probe the heart of Chaucer's philosophic and aesthetic concept." Relying upon Lowell's dictum that the main consideration in Dante is the saving of the soul, and in Chaucer, the conduct of life, he offers a prefatory definition of satire drawn from W. F. Thrall and Addison Hibbard, *A Handbook to Literature* (New York, 1936), p. 386: "A literary manner which blends a critical attitude with wit and humor to the end that human institutions may be improved."

Both points of view have their value. The first has been deepened to the point where we have been persuaded to see Chaucer as an allegorist par excellence, using courtly love as an instrument of doctrine, carrying a somewhat wearying freight of Biblical exegesis and Augustinian aesthetic. The other has been widened to include a range of experience that is deeply serious, even "tragic," "psychological," and the like. We have become conscious of stringent attitudes in fabliaux and romances alike, of criticisms implied of the aristocratic milieu, of a sensitivity to profoundly important human problems. We have come to recognize that the Chaucerian manner can be extremely detached, objective, that the audience can, with the poet, have the sense of "looking down" like Troilus from an exalted vantage upon agents vastly inferior in power of action, we feel, to ourselves. The two points of view do not cancel each other out, as both the Bible and Boethius attest, but it should be stated that the term satire for the distancing of poet and audience from subject represents only one face of the coin; as the subject increases in seriousness, the term irony serves us better.

13 Chaucerian "game"–"ernest" and the "argument of herbergage" in *The Canterbury Tales*

GERHARD JOSEPH

Originally published in *ChauR* 5 (1970):83–96. Reprinted by permission of the Pennsylvania State University Press. The original pagination is recorded within square brackets. The square brackets used in the text from p. 92 are the author's. The endnotes originally appeared as footnotes. The text and notes incorporate several minor corrections and alterations, made by the author.

While apologizing for the inclusion of the Miller's narrative in *The Canterbury Tales* (I 3170–86),[1] Chaucer the pilgrim makes a distinction that reverberates through the entire sequence. He invites the reader to "Turne over the leef and chese another tale" if such a "cherles tale" as he is about to encounter should wound his sensibilities. Elsewhere among the tales the fastidious reader may find many a "storial thyng that toucheth gentilesse,/And eek moralitee and hoolynesse." Above all, the audience must not mistake the intention behind the more frivolous stories: "men shal nat maken ernest of game." The Chaucerian narrator here presents a fourteenth-century version of the *ludicra-seria* topos that Ernst Curtius has traced through classical and medieval literature.[2] Because the relationship of jest and seriousness is crucial in Chaucer's art, a preliminary exploration of its implications should prove useful. But I should like to undertake such a tentative examination indirectly—by measuring the "game"–"ernest" collocation against a division which sometimes parallels it: Chaucer's differentiation of human space. I will argue that Tales informed by the spirit of "ernest" have at times another conception of space, the "herbergage" or lodging of this world, than those told in "game." The most telling illustration of this difference appears in Fragment I. Here one of Chaucer's most beautifully serious stories, the *Knight's Tale*, is followed immediately by three fabliaux, one of which, the *Miller's Tale*, has long been recognized as a fine example of Chaucer at his most playful and bawdy. Because of such a direct confrontation Fragment I may be read as a paradigm of the "game"–"ernest" opposition and the "argument of herbergage" implicit in *The Canterbury Tales* as a whole.

[84]

I

When Chaucer the pilgrim distinguishes "ernest" from "game," he asserts a polarity that many of the tales do not particularly support. One can think of several narratives—and the *Knight's Tale* is one of them—in which "high sentence" is leavened with comic and playful ingredients. Still, for the purpose of analysis, we can grant that Chaucer's narrative sequence does seem to include two kinds of stories, if we allow for a certain amount of overlapping—those which show the fourteenth-century mind largely in a mood of high seriousness and those motivated primarily by a medieval propensity for jest. That on balance the *Knight's Tale* would seem to belong in the former category is confirmed by its serious sense of space.

The *Knight's Tale* moves through four earthly enclosures that give way to one another as the locales of significant action: the prison tower in which Palamon and Arcite contend verbally for the right to Emilye, with whom they have both fallen in love (Part I); the grove in which Palamon and Arcite come upon one another and in which they try to slaughter each other before the intercession of Theseus (Part II); the temples of Venus, Mars, and Diana within the amphitheatre that Theseus has built for the clash of two hundred worthies (Part III); and the arena itself in which the climactic tournament takes place (Part IV). The Tale is thus organized scenically: the division of the narrative into four sections parallels the replacement of one enclosure by another.

There are several qualities to be noticed in the spatial progression. For one thing, while both the prison and the grove are merely functional and neutral spaces unconsecrated by any conscious ritual, Theseus goes to elaborate lengths to dignify the tournament in his amphitheatre, to give it the widest possible metaphysical significance by associating it with a human devotion to Venus, Mars, and Diana. Furthermore, the enclosures of the Tale get progressively larger: we move from the cramped "tour, that was so thikke and stroong" [1056], to a grove in which Palamon and Arcite can maneuver in single combat, to the three temples of the amphitheatre, and finally to the "noble theatre" itself of which "The circuit a myle was aboute,/Walled of stoon, and dyched al withoute" (1887–88). The point of such gradual widening is clear: the larger the arena in which violent passions can play themselves out, the less destructive and the more susceptible to ritual they become. Mere decorative elaboration makes for order, a fact that Theseus surely understands. It is for this reason that he moves the combat from the grove into the massive arena [85] with its temples; it is for this reason that he disperses the single combat between an enraged Palamon and Arcite over a company of two hundred knights.

If spatial expansion becomes a process which can mitigate the fury of the passions, the Tale's insistence upon expansiveness of time reinforces such a movement towards order. Within the prison cell there is no temporal lapse between the first sight of Emilye and the quarrel that breaks out between Palamon and Arcite. When, however, the two knights meet in the grove, they agree to a postponement of their combat because Palamon is unarmed. Arcite would, he insists, have preferred to kill Palamon immediately (1603), but because Palamon is unequipped the two knights separate "til amorwe" at which time Arcite brings two sets of arms to the grove for the fight to the death (1621–35). While the ritual of chivalry whereby an armed knight will not strike an unarmed one is responsible for the day's delay, there is something unpremeditated and grudging in the knight's adherence to that ritual. But after Theseus interrupts the carnage in the grove, he deliberately consecrates time under the aegis of Venus, Mars, and Diana, putting the next clash of the two knights off for a year. The transformation of the day-long delay halfheartedly agreed upon by the knights into Theseus' insistence upon a year's wait indicates the movement from accidental to conscious ritualization of time. It is through such a continuing consecration, via expansion, of both space and time that Theseus attempts to bring a temporary, a limited perfection into the confusion of this life, to sublimate an irrational duel to the death into a magnificent tournament in which no knight will be seriously injured (2538–60).

But if the *Knight's Tale* mediates between extremes of life conceived as cramped prison tower and impressive amphitheatre, we are still left with the question of which metaphorical enclosure essentially captures the Knight's vision of life this side eternity. The Boethian flavor of the *Knight's Tale* has long been recognized. And despite the attempt of Theseus to turn the neutral spaces of this life into consecrated arenas, we are ultimately left with the impression that the *Knight's Tale* is Boethian in nothing so much as in its sense of human space as prison. In the *Consolation of Philosophy* Boethius' enslavement to a worldly vision until he is gradually enlightened by the arguments of Lady Philosophy has its physical extension in the prison cell where she first visits him. As Richard Green has concisely described the trope, "The author's own literal imprisonment becomes a figure of the soul's imprisonment in the [86] body, the bondage imposed by the demands of the passions, the enslavement to Fortune in her deceitful favors."[3]

In the *Knight's Tale* Chaucer uses the prison in which Palamon and Arcite find themselves as a correlative for the larger prisons of this life in somewhat the same way as Boethius. The Theban women at the opening of the narrative announce the theme of man's enslavement to Fortune when they complain to Theseus,

> Now be we caytyves, as it is wel seene,
> Thanked be Fortune and hire false wheel,
> That noon estaat assureth to be weel.

> (924–26)

And the tale contains numerous additional references to man's generalized dependence upon the whims of Fortune. What is as a matter of fact striking about Palamon and Arcite when we are first introduced to the working of their minds is the extent to which they are *unlike* a Boethius chained within his complaint at Fortune's whimsicality. Certainly Theseus' sentence for them—life imprisonment with no possibility of ransom—seems arbitrary and excessively harsh. But when Palamon cries out his "A" at the first sight of Emilye, Arcite thinks he is complaining about their lot and reproves him therefore:

> "... Cosyn myn, what eyleth thee,
> That art so pale and deedly on to see?
> Why cridestow? Who hath thee doon offence?
> For Goddes love, taak al in pacience
> Oure prisoun, for it may noon oother be.
> Fortune hath yeven us this adversitee.
> Som wikke aspect or disposicioun
> Of Saturne, by som constellacioun,
> Hath yeven us this, although we hadde it sworn;
> So stood the hevene whan that we were born.
> We moste endure it; this is the short and playn."
>
> (1081–91)

In reply Palamon explicitly disavows Arcite's inference that it is Fortune's prison which has called forth the cry. Palamon and Arcite, that is, do not come to inhabit the all-inclusive Boethian prison *until* they suffer the fetters of a courtly love. Palamon does not become [87] excessively conscious of his literal imprisonment until, as he puts it, "I was hurt right now thurghout myn ye/Into myn herte, that wol my bane be" in his passion for Emilye. Once the rival lovers are so enslaved, the physical cell widens until the whole world becomes a prison that keeps them from Emilye. When Arcite is released through the intercession of Perotheus, the lifelong exile from Athens to which Theseus commits him is a more terrible confinement than the one Palamon will continue to know. "Thyn is the victorie of this aventure," Arcite apostrophizes. "Ful blisfully in prison maistow dure,—/In prison? certes nay, but in paradys!" (1235–37). Palamon will at least be able to see Emilye daily and a changeable Fortune may permit him to attain her at some time in the future, since, unlike Arcite, he will be near her. Chaucer, that is, splits into the exile of Arcite and the continuing imprisonment of Palamon the single fate of Boethius, who knew both exile and imprisonment.

The ultimate prison of the *Knight's Tale* is a spiritual one, the maze of doubt within which Palamon wanders when he addresses the "crueel goddes that governe/This world with byndying of youre word eterne" (1303–24). Like the Troilus of Book IV whose extended questioning of "predestinatioun devyne, and of the liberte of fre wil" (IV, 953–1085) indicates his exile from the mind of "Jove," Palamon entertains the belief that man is confined in the "table of atthamaunt" of "crueel goddes." He never quite goes as far as Troilus' assertion that God's foreknowledge destroys "oure fre chois every del"; the typically Chaucerian swerving, "The answere of this lete I to dyvynys" [1323], rescues Palamon from the adamantine determinism that paralyzes Troilus. But the metaphysical doubt, the ultimate trap in the Christian attempt to comprehend godhead, is clear enough in Palamon's agonized cry: "What governance is in this prescience/That giltelees tormenteth innocence?" (1313–14). Both the *Troilus* and the *Knight's Tale* thus vividly exemplify a progress from the prison of the senses to the more serious prison of the mind and spirit; enslavement by a courtly passion leads directly to religious despair.

The strong medicine with which Lady Philosophy in Books IV and V of the *Consolation* cures Boethius of his spiritual ills, the *vigour and strengthe of wit* that make it possible for man to surmount the "necessitee of destyne" and to understand the concomitant operation of free will and the providence of God, has its equivalent in the "Firste Moevere" speech of Theseus (2987–3074). Once man has won through to an understanding of the "faire cheyne of love" [88] by which the First Mover binds together an apparently chaotic universe, he can triumph over Fortune in all her guises. He will find it possible

> To maken vertu of necessitee,
> And take it weel that we may nat eschue,
> And namely that to us alle is due.
>
> (3042–44)

The contrary of such serenity is "wilfulnesse," the mental torture that makes "this foule prisoun of this lyf" (3061) all the more palpable as prison.

The accidental death of Arcite suggests that even the consecrated amphitheatre of Theseus cannot completely order the forces of chaos that shatter man's best laid plans. Despite the ceremonial forms by which Theseus attempts to make it possible for us to love our cage, man in the *Knight's Tale* finds it all but impossible to escape the formidable jailer, Fortune. Man carries his prison with him, nor is he out of it until at his death he makes his way to the eighth sphere. Only then will he find a wholly comfortable lodging in the ultimate enclosure of the Tale that Theseus evokes, the ordered cosmos itself which only the First Mover fully comprehends.

The *Miller's Tale* has of course been recognized as a subtle "quiting" of the Knight's performance by a social inferior who finds in the elevated sentiments and sombre nobility of the Knight mere laughable affectation. Specifically, the Nicholas-Absolon-Alisoun triangle has been seen as a veiled parody of the Palamon-Arcite-Emilye triangle, and the absurd love-making manners of Absolon as a very explicit reduction of the courtly love that the Knight praises (reservedly, to be sure) in his Tale.[4] But transcending this critique, which chiefly reflects the inability of one social class to comprehend the values of another, is a more fundamental attack: the Miller, the Reeve, and the Cook advance a radically different conception of human space and the possibility of unrestrained "pley" within that space. In the *Knight's Tale* literal enclosures come to shadow forth the Boethian prison from which none of us can escape until death releases us; in such a prison Fortune's arbitrary sway makes it difficult for Palamon and Arcite to attain the object of their desires. But in the fabliaux such obstacles as do exist when a *senex* tries to fence in a young colt of a wife are easily broken down. John the carpenter in the *Miller's Tale* attempts to keep potential lovers from [89] Alisoun: "Jalous he was, and heeld hire narwe in cage,/For she was wylde and yong, and he was old" (3224–25). But all to no avail. In the fabliaux, enclosures, far from being the prisons that keep lovers from their ladies, actually become the essential arena for the joyous union of man and wench. One of the important meanings of the all-purpose "hende" assigned to Nicholas is that he is "at hand," i.e., that he is actually a boarder in the carpenter's house.[5] It is this proximity that makes it possible for him to be "hende" in other senses of the word. And precisely because Absolon must woo Alisoun from the *outside* of John's house, he does not stand a chance against his rival Nicholas inside:

> Ful sooth is this proverbe, it is no lye,
> Men seyn right thus, "Alwey the nye slye
> Maketh the ferre leeve to be looth."
> For though that Absolon be wood or wrooth,
> By cause that he fer was from hire sight,
> This nye Nicholas stood in his light.
>
> (3391–96)

It may indeed be argued that in such sexual games as the fabliaux describe, spatial arrangements all but triumph over character: the proximity of one player and the distance of the other from Alisoun are almost more important than characterization as an index of who "deserves" her.

The *Reeve's Tale* not only supports the Miller's implication that social enclosures are utterly congenial to human delight but even extends that insight to argue for the infinite expansiveness of space within such enclosures. After the miller of that tale has stolen the half bushel of flour from the students John and Alan, they ask him for "herberwe and ... ese, as for hir peny" [4119] (John the carpenter in the *Miller's Tale* had also been undone by such taking in of boarders). In reply the churlishly anti-intellectual miller mocks the learning of the students in the Tale's crucial passage of dramatic irony as he grants their request:

> "Myn hous is streit, but ye han lerned art;
> Ye konne by argumentes make a place
> A myle brod of twenty foot of space.
> Lat se now if this place may suffise...."
>
> (4122–25)

[90] And of course the students do "make a place" for themselves quite handsomely in the energetic bed-hopping that closes the Tale. The *Knight's Tale* has insisted upon the substitution of the arena for the prison and the grove in order to make more palatable the realization that we do inhabit "this foule prison of this lyf." In the fabliaux there is no need for a progressive enlargement of enclosures; the initial little room will do as the most comfortable of "herberwes" from which we have no desire to escape. Far from being a prison, such enclosures are adaptable to the wishes of the carefree young who make, as the youthful John Donne has said, "one little room an everywhere."

What the Cook's contribution to this *debat* would have been we cannot know: the fragmentary tale of Perkin Revelour does not provide enough evidence for a plausible projection. But the Cook's prologue does suggest that he understands the spatial emphasis of the *Reeve's Tale*. His interpretation, which hints at one direction his own fabliau might have taken, gives a name to the argument I have been describing:

> "Ha! ha!" quod he, "for Cristes passion,
> This millere hadde a sharp conclusion
> Upon his argument of herbergage!
> Wel seyde Salomon in his langage,
> 'Ne bryng nat every man into thyn hous';
> For herberwynge by nyghte is perilous."
>
> (4327–32)

The Cook alludes in his phrase "argument of herbergage" only to the "argumentes" of l. 4123—to the question of whether space is or is not expansible for the miller's overnight boarders in the *Reeve's Tale*.[6] It is my contention that the "argument" transcends that local [91] issue and is a controlling principle in the entire structure of Fragment I. Briefly, the Fragment asserts that the quantity and quality of space is relative to the perspective of the human mind contending with it. For the "ernest" pilgrim who manages to see things from the perspective of eternity, human space is dreadfully narrow, a prison with which we must make do and which we can make bearable through carefully ordered rituals. But for the actor or observer who views the world as "game," a cramped "twenty foot of space" easily widens out to become a room "a myle brood," world enough and time for the acting out of a lighthearted human drama.

Moving beyond Fragment I, we see that Chaucer can make the same point within a single Tale and capture the opposing perspectives within the mind of a single pilgrim. That the Nun's Priest, for instance, responds to life partly in "ernest" and partly in "game" reveals itself in the different conceptions of space that govern the frame of his tale and the tale proper. We hear his official homiletic voice as he describes the poor widow's farm and her mature acceptance of a constricted lot. Everything points to the narrowness of her physical circumstances to which in Christian patience she has come to accustom herself: the cottage itself is "narwe," the yard in which she keeps her few animals is "enclosed al aboute/With stikkes, and a drye dych withoute" (VII 2821–48).

But if the Nun's Priest in his serious cast of mind implies that the world is a hard and straitened place for the widow, the spirit of jest that invades his voice once he moves from the frame into the story of Chauntecleer and Pertolote makes for a very different notion of space. The insular vanity of the one and the wifely self-assurance of the other preclude their awareness that the farmyard might in any way be circumscribed or limited. They act as if their enclosure were a sufficient and elastic arena perfectly suitable to the strutting and domestic bliss of their easy lives. The widow cramped by her [92] poverty and the littleness of her cottage world has come to make virtues of such necessities; when Chauntecleer and Pertolote feel any constraint, they merely move to a more comfortable spot in the farmyard. "Oure perche,"

Chauntecleer complains mildly, "is maad so narwe, allas," a fact that makes the treading of Pertolote somewhat awkward within the henhouse itself. But all that Chauntecleer and Pertolote have to do is to "fley doun fro the beem" and the feathering and treading that they both desire is readily available— "twenty tyme" (3169–77). Like the students of the *Reeve's Tale* they can ignore the limitations of space. The miller's little space and the widow's farmyard are thus containers of hyperbolic sexual energy. The saturnalian release within such little rooms humorously buckles (I intentionally borrow the multiple associations of Hopkins' word) the Boethian doctrine that because all of the world's a prison, moderation of desire is man's wisest course. (Similarly, applying the argument of herbergage to the *Troilus* would involve a discussion of whether its narrator is essentially committed to Pandarus' "litel closet" [III, 663] and the game of love that flourishes therein or to the Boethian denigration of "this litel spot of erthe" [V, 1815] during Troilus's retrospective glance over his life from the perspective of the eighth sphere.)

Of course, such a formulation is too allegorically strict to encompass the multiple uses to which Chaucer puts his space. He certainly does not systematically or inevitably link the "herbergage" theme and the "ernest"– "game" polarity in every Tale. Nor, for that matter, are space and figures of spatial enclosure always to be received in a moral or ontological dimension. All narrative must take place somewhere and a good deal of Chaucerian space is primarily functional; it serves as a realistic social and physical context for action. I am merely trying to suggest that Chaucer's limited spaces frequently approach the condition of metaphor and that, when this occurs, the "game"– "ernest" opposition presents one possible context within which to examine them. One thinks, for example, of such "gameful" places as the garden in the *Merchant's Tale* and such serious ones as the boat upon which Custance travels in the *Man of Law's Tale* or the simple house of Grisilde's father with its nearby oxen stall in the *Clerk's Tale* as additional Chaucerian enclosures whose meanings would be illuminated by the perspective I am advocating.

[93]   II

While the argument of herbergage flourishes among some of the tales and within the temperament of individual pilgrims, at its most resonant it is one of the structural principles of the frame within which the tales are narrated, the pilgrimage from London to Canterbury. We begin at the Tabard Inn, a "herberwe" that is blessed, as the Host assures the assembled pilgrims, with an exceptionally "myrie compaignye"; and the tales are spun out as the pilgrims move towards the shrine of Thomas Becket. These terminal herbergages of the journey are *loci* for the antagonistic attitudes towards life and space I have defined. Even pilgrims of high seriousness cannot but join in the Host's contest, given the convivial spirit that the Tabard encourages; even the most worldly and earthy of churls cannot but be reminded of the last things as the company makes its way toward the serious space of the martyred saint.

The Host is the appropriate governor of the group precisely because the competing narrative ideals of "ernest," associated with the shrine of Becket, and of "game" associated with the Tabard, vie with each other in the directions he gives to the pilgrims. His initial aesthetic standard as he announces it in the *General Prologue* seems morally orthodox enough: he tells the company that the prize meal will go to the pilgrim who fashions "Tales of best sentence and moost solaas" (I 798). But "solaas," while it may refer primarily to the serious consolation of Boethian or Augustinian doctrine can just as well include the merry consolation that a Nicholas finds with his Alisoun. And in the links between the Tales the Host is apt to call for a "myrie tale," a tale told primarily for its capacity to entertain rather than for the sake of any lesson it might be thought to inculcate. The most striking instance of the Host's disavowal of "high sentence" appears in the Prologue to the *Pardoner's Tale* where he calls for "som myrthe or japes" from the Pardoner only to be reproved by the gentils, who insist instead upon "som moral thyng" (VI 318–26).

In his instructions to the pilgrims the Host can most readily be seen as a surrogate of Chaucer, the artist. For we must finally speak of the divergent aims of "ernest" and "game" in Chaucer and of the counterpoint of structures that these aims can help to explain in the *Canterbury Tales* as a whole. In the *General Prologue* Chaucer himself is caught up in the ample sense of time and space that the comfortable "herberwes" of this world encourage: he will [94] have time to write a hundred and sixteen or a hundred and twenty tales. The Host will decide which pilgrim deserves to

> have a soper at oure aller cost
> Heere in this place, sittynge by this post,
> Whan that we come agayn fro Caunterbury.
>
> (I 799–801)

This insistence upon concrete spatial arrangements back at the Tabard and the suggestion that the pilgrimage is a two-way affair—a movement towards the shrine of the martyr but also away from that serious space back towards a "herbergage" of good food and merry company—indicate the worldly self-confidence of Chaucer the artist. But by the time of the *Parson's Prologue* the comfort of an earthly "herberwe" has become a cold one indeed. The original intention of Chaucer may have been to take the pilgrims back to the Tabard, but the *Parson's Prologue* offers no congenial lodging. As the sun sinks the pilgrims are merely entering a nameless "thropes ende" [X 12]. And the confident plan of Chaucer in the *General Prologue* has been seriously constrained by the exigencies of time: he must be satisfied with the illusion rather than the fact that, as the Host puts it, "Now lakketh us no tales mo than oon. / Fulfilled is my sentence and my decree . . ." (X 16–17). The intention of four tales for each pilgrim, two going to and two coming from Canterbury, has been modified by Chaucer's recognition that his own space is more limited than he might at a more expansive time have imagined. "Every man, save thou," the Host tells the Parson, "hath toold his tale"

[X 25]. Even this is not literally true, but at any rate the singular "his tale" indicates a severe scaling down of Chaucer's earlier plan. The closing admonition of the Host to the Parson epitomizes this contraction of the Chaucerian world, the growing sense of temporal and spatial constraint that the pilgrims (and the readers) feel as the pilgrimage draws to its close:

> But hasteth yow, the sonne wole adoun;
> Beth fructuous, and that in litel space,
> And to do wel God sende yow his grace!

(X 70–72)

This climatic awareness of the "litel space" we have for our fruitful creations in this world would seem to suggest that Chaucerian space-time is in an ultimate sense closer to that of the *Knight's Tale* or the Nun's Priest's frame rather than to that of the fabliaux. "Ernest" seems gradually to drown out "game" as the company moves towards [95] the Jerusalem Celestial of the *Parson's Prologue* (not even to consider the extreme asceticism of the Retraction). But such is not entirely the case. We do not read the Tales only as if they were told sequentially on a pilgrimage; we respond to them also as if we were in retrospect to judge them all at once and to decide with the Host which of the pilgrims deserves the prize meal. Our standards, like his, are mixed enough. Like him, we are apt to be torn between "ernest" and "game," between the very different perfections of, say, the *Knight's Tale* and the *Miller's Tale*.

For, finally, we do not take the warning of Chaucer the pilgrim not to "maken ernest of game" at face value either in the local context within which it first appears or in its larger application to the *Canterbury Tales* as a whole. The easy, "proverbial" separation of "ernest" and "game" in the prologue to the *Miller's Tale* is obviously naive. As so often when we hear the conventional sentiments of Chaucer the pilgrim, we suspect that the moral imagination of the poet behind him ranges beyond the convention. It may be going too far to say that the apology for the inclusion of the *Miller's Tale* is a piece of out-and-out mockery, but at the very least Chaucer the pilgrim's facile mouthing of a platitude masks the artist's complex understanding of the aesthetic issues involved. And in the completed *Tales* the reader is struck by a like impression of wise comprehensiveness. As we read we come to know an orthodox Chaucer who, while allowing the play impulse a large measure of freedom, insists in his art upon the ultimate subordination of play to the serious business of life, the pilgrimage to Jerusalem Celestial. But in other moods we sense that for Chaucer "game" is prior to "ernest" in all art,[7] or that at any rate the two impulses are so inextricably interwoven in the human personality that an attempt to unravel them would be the height of folly. Chaucer's greatness lies precisely in [96] such a humane inclusiveness. Germane to that "God's plenty" is a paradoxical vision, his simultaneous recognition that jest and seriousness are antithetical principles and that they are completely inseparable in the human condition and therefore in the highest art.[8]

Notes

1 All references to Chaucer's poetry are to *The Works of Geoffrey Chaucer*, ed. F. N. Robinson, 2nd ed. (Boston, 1957).
2 "Jest and Earnest in Medieval Literature" in *European Literature and the Latin Middle Ages* (New York, 1953), pp. 417–35. The Host also uses this "proverbial" (Robinson, p. 683, note to l. 3152) locution in the *Manciple's Prologue* (IX 100).
3 Introduction to Boethius, *The Consolation of Philosophy* (New York, 1962), p. xxiii.
4 See William Frost, "An Interpretation of Chaucer's *Knight's Tale*," *RES*, 25 (1949), 290–304; and Charles A. Owen, Jr., "Chaucer's *Canterbury Tales*: Aesthetic Design in Stories of the First Day," *English Studies*, 35 (1954), 49–56.
5 Paul E. Beichner develops this point in "Chaucer's Hende Nicholas," *Medieval Studies*, 14 (1952), 151–53 and in "Characterization in *The Miller's Tale*," *Chaucer Criticism: The Canterbury Tales*, ed. Richard Schoeck and Jerome Taylor (Notre Dame, Ind., 1960), pp. 124–25.
6 William C. Stokoe, Jr., "Structure and Intention in the *First Fragment of The Canterbury Tales*," *UTQ*, 21 (1952), 126, has remarked that the miller alluded to in the Cook's Prologue is not the one from the *Reeve's Tale* but rather Chaucer's Robin Miller. In the concluding line of the *Reeve's Tale* (4324), the Reeve exults, "Thus have I quyt the Millere in my tale." It is this line, Stokoe argues, that the Cook picks up in his Prologue as he "awarded the decision to the wrong wrangler" in 4327–38. Charles A. Owen, Jr., "The Design of *The Canterbury Tales*," *Companion to Chaucer Studies* (Toronto, 1968), p. 195, summarizes Stokoe's argument approvingly.

My own feeling is that the miller referred to in 4327–38 must be the one in the *Reeve's Tale* rather than Chaucer's Miller. For one thing, were Roger of Ware alluding to Chaucer's Miller in the lines, "This millere hadde a sharp conclusion/ Upon his argument of herbergage," he would probably have used the present or the present perfect tense to describe an action that has just taken place rather than the past tense of narration; for another, there is no "argument of herbergage" between Chaucer's Miller and Reeve—their stories both support Solomon's warning: "Ne bryng nat every man into thyn hous," while there is, as I have shown, an "argument of herbergage" *within* the *Reeve's Tale*. Finally, the Cook's allusion to the miller in 4335–38 puts the issue beyond dispute:

> I pray to God, so yeve me sorwe and care
> If evere, sitthe I highte Hogge of Ware,
> Herde I a millere bettre yset a-werk.
> He hadde a jape of malice in the derk.

Surely it is only the miller in the *Reeve's Tale* who "hadde a jape of malice in the derk"; the reference cannot possibly be to Robin Miller, the pilgrim.
7 The argument of Johan Huizinga (*Homo Ludens: A Study of the Play Element in Culture* [New York, 1955]) that the opposition of seriousness and play is largely illusory may be relevant to such a reading of *The Canterbury Tales*. According to Huizinga all human cultural activities (certainly all art) involve contests of one sort or another, and play is an, if not *the*, essential element in all such contests. From this perspective—though Huizinga never alludes to Chaucer—the comic rivalry of Nicholas and Absolon for Alisoun, the bitter contest between Palamon and Arcite for Emilye, and the larger competition among the pilgrims for the prize meal would all be different tonal gestures of *homo ludens*, the agonistic animal. And the "little rooms" of the fabliaux, Theseus' amphitheatre, and the Tabard Inn would be

less and more ritualized versions of what Huizinga elaborately defines as "playground" (*Homo Ludens*, pp. 10 ff.).

8 Curtius' summation of what happened to the "jest and earnest" topos in the Middle Ages would seem to suggest that Chaucer's double perspective is representative of his age:

> ... the polarity "jest and earnest" is, from the late antique period onward, a conceptual and formal schema which appears not only in rhetorical theory, in poetry, and in poetics, but also in the circle of the ideal of life established by the panegyric style.... But, having determined this, we can take a further step. The testimony already discussed itself permits the assumption that the mixture of jest and earnest was among the stylistic norms which were known and practiced by the medieval poet, even if he perhaps nowhere found them expressly formulated. We may, then, view the phenomenon as a fresh substantiation of the view that the Middle Ages loved all kinds of crossings and mixtures of stylistic genres.... (*European Literature and the Latin Middle Ages*, p. 424).

14 | Antifeminism and Chaucer's characterization of women

HOPE PHYLLIS WEISSMAN

Originally published in *Geoffrey Chaucer: a collection of original articles*, ed. George D. Economou (New York: McGraw-Hill, 1975, pp. 93–110). Reprinted by permission of the author. The original pagination is recorded within square brackets. The endnotes originally appeared as footnotes.

Antifeminism in literary tradition, defined strictly, refers to those writings which revenge themselves upon woman's failure to conform to male specifications by presenting her as a nagging bully and an avaricious whore. Though the attitude arose in part from certain premises of classical and Judeo-Christian philosophies, by the later Middle Ages it had developed into a tradition of social and personal satire, providing rich opportunities for the deployment of a caricature sometimes mischievous but often sour. Chaucer was the heir and the most versatile manipulator of this literary tradition which, on his knees before Queen Alceste in the literary meadow of the *Legend of Good Women*, he comically—and disingenuously—disavowed.[1]

[94] The literary tradition of antifeminism may, however, be defined in a wider sense to include not simply satirical caricatures of women but any presentation of a woman's nature intended to conform her to male expectations of what she is or ought to be, not her own. By this wider definition, an image of woman need not be ostensibly unflattering to be antifeminist in fact or in potential; indeed, the most insidious of antifeminist images are those which celebrate, with a precision often subtle rather than apparent, the forms a woman's goodness is to take. Chaucer recognized this wider definition of antifeminism too. Writing the *Canterbury Tales*, as he did, to investigate the capacity of received forms of human experience to embody adequately the experience of late medieval man, it is hardly surprising that received forms of woman's experience should come under his close scrutiny.

In accordance with this wider definition of antifeminism, our purpose in the following pages will be twofold: first, briefly to trace the development and indicate the antifeminist implications of the established medieval images of women which continued to exert compelling force on the minds and actions of Chaucer's contemporaries; and second, more extensively to examine the different ways Chaucer himself investigates the implications of the established images and their impress on the human spirit in his *Canterbury Tales*.

Medieval culture by Chaucer's time had distinguished four images of women as primary, primary in the sense that the alternative conceptions of women they defined provided the basic vocabulary of individual character creation. Of these four images, two were secular and two were religious; and to paraphrase the Wife of Bath's assessment of her husbands, two of them were good and two were bad. The "good" and "bad" (ostensibly flattering and unflattering) images of the religious tradition had their origin in the female characterizations of Scriptural narrative as apprehended through the Pauline conception of the Old and the New Man (see I Corinthians 15). The Old Testament Woman, Eve the mate of Adam, like him was bound by the laws of the flesh and the material universe; conversely, the New Testament Woman, Virgin Mary the mother of Christ, was freed by the law of grace to enjoy the pleasures of the spiritual realm.

It took very little "glosynge" of the Creation and Fall myth of Genesis 2–3 to extract the Parson's antifeminist moral lesson that God created Eve to be Adam's servant and so that, when [95] she seizes the mastery, the world is turned "up-so-doun." Eve's gluttonous behavior in the Garden defines her as being the essence of carnality; yet, in addition, her lust for material and intellectual possession is a deliberate act of rebellion against the Maker who created her to be second-rate. In this rebellion against the limitations of her created image, Eve is, we shall see, the direct model for Chaucer's new fleshly protestant, the Wife of Bath.

The medieval Church's conception of the New Woman as an antithesis and a corrective to the Old found its principal literary model in the Infancy Narrative of Luke's Gospel. The antiphonal narrative structure of the Infancy uses Elizabeth's conception of John the Baptist to recreate the Old Testament ethos and highlight its revolutionary ethical theme. Thus whereas Elizabeth, like Sarah and Hannah, considers her barrenness reproachful, Mary learns that perpetual virginity will be the reason for her exaltation. Where Elizabeth's renewed capacity leads to a public celebration, Mary conceives in tranquility and stores God's favor in her heart. And where Elizabeth's husband Zachariah questions God's ordinance, the Virgin Mary, correcting Eve as well as the Old Testament priesthood, obediently kneels in assent. In the later Middle Ages, this obedient kneeling was to become increasingly conspicuous until, with Virginia of the *Physician's Tale*, it suffered a pratfall. By this did the Roman maiden acknowledge her model's compelling power.

The Old Eve and New Mary images of women in religious tradition had their counterparts in the two principal secular literary traditions, the courtly and the bourgeois. The bourgeois image of woman, represented most clearly in the Old French fabliaux, inherits directly from Eve her lust for material possession which, in the marketplace mentality of medieval town and village, becomes a gathering of sex and coin. The fabliau woman gathers these possessions from within but primarily from outside the marriage bond; she ventures outside not simply because her husband is inadequate, though he is often so, but more significantly because her lust of possession is insatiable—and is matched by a correspondingly inexhaustible supply of physical energy and mental craft. There is no evidence, for example, that the merchant husband of the *Shipman's Tale* is either physically unsatisfactory or niggardly; his dame is simply playing the Eve game of testing how much is too much.

Although the origin of the courtly image of woman remains a [96] controversial subject, one important source of the conception, surely, was the worship of the Great Mother goddesses in the cults of pagan antiquity. Indeed, the Early Church was responding directly to these cults when it elevated the Virgin to her seat beside God's throne after the Assumption; from there she reigned as the Mother of an imperfect humanity, the source of its wisdom and love. The courtly image of woman conveyed in the Provençal and Italian stilnovist lyric of the High Middle Ages is as clearly a counterpart of this cult image of the Virgin as it is a parody of the feudal lord. The lyricist's *dompna*, physically chaste if not perfect, is exalted like the Virgin herself because of her spiritual superiority; and her function, similarly, is to allure from her pedestal and lead men to wisdom through love. Whatever Eleanor of Aquitaine and her daughters may have intended by encouraging the celebration of the courtly lady, therefore, the image came to function, as did that of the Virgin, for the benefit of their celebrating men.[2]

Perhaps still more important to the courtly conception of woman in the later Middle Ages is an aspect of the image we may designate the Courtly Damsel. The Damsel is distinguishable from the Lady by a significant shift in emphasis: if the Lady drew men to her tower because of her transcending virtue, the Damsel attracts them by her sympathetic weakness; she is not the star but the trophy who, in the popular romances, was bestowed upon her dragon-slaying men. Like the image of the Courtly Lady proper, the image of the Damsel is paralleled by the image of the helpless Virgin in later medieval devotional art; like the Lady, too, the Damsel is traceable ultimately to conceptions of women in pagan antiquity. Although the Damsel is most frequently seen as a descendant of the helpless-young-thing heroines of the Greek romances, in fact the *locus classicus* of the conception for medieval secular literature was the treatment of Lavinia in Virgil's *Aeneid*.

Virgil's conception of Lavinia may be considered a radicalization of Homer's conception of Briseis, in the *Iliad*, as a pawn in a man's world. Although the importance of Lavinia as bride of Rome's founder is suggested in *Aeneid* Two and established clearly in Seven, it is not until the epic's conclusion that she [97] directly motivates the conflict between Aeneas and Turnus. More significant still, Lavinia motivates the conflict by inadvertence. Her mother Amata, endeavoring to persuade Turnus not to enter a duel with Aeneas, has threatened that if her young hero should die, she will die also. Hearing this, Lavinia's

> hot cheeks were bathed in tears; . . .
> and her blush, a kindled fire, crossed

> her burning face. And just as when a craftsman
> stains Indian ivory with blood-red purple,
> or when white lilies, mixed with many roses,
> blush: even such, the colors of the virgin.
> His love drives Turnus wild; he stares at his
> Lavinia; even keener now for battle.[3]

The lilies mixed with roses, the mingled blushes and tears, above all the inciting power of uncomprehendingly innocent beauty—all these features, in the medieval centuries, become part of the Damsel canon. They are recapitulated almost exactly in the figure of Emily, heroine of the *Knight's Tale*, but with the significant difference that Emily momentarily comprehends, and too well.

For his first Canterbury tale, Chaucer transformed Boccaccio's classicizing romance *Il Teseida* into a sympathetically critical examination of the chivalric life in its aspects of lovemaking and statecraft. It is a man's world his Knight-narrator has made, centering on the courtly love posturings of Arcite and Palamon and, more particularly, the rulership of Theseus; the women of the tale, Hippolyta and Emily, are essentially aspects of the concerns of their men. The Knight's characterizations of the heroines present them as having been mastered at the outset, in this feature contrasting significantly with Boccaccio's, which appear to assert their independence before the author closes in. Boccaccio's Hippolyta, in *Teseida* One, performs the antique virago with spirit, though the romance proceeds to ignore her once she is subjugated by the Athenian men. Boccaccio's Emilia, in *Teseida* Three, operates freely within courtly romance conventions—but this representation soon proves to be the booby trap of a lover's wrath.

[98] The freedom of Boccaccio's Emilia first suggests itself rhetorically when the heroine is ushered in by a catalog of spring's perfections yet, though she weaves the season's roses with her charmingly white hands, is not required to submit her own perfections to the expected catalog enumeration. The rhetorical freedom immediately acquires a psychological dimension when we hear that "beautiful young Emilia, as dawn broke each morning, entered alone into the garden which opened out from her room, drawn there by her own nature, not because she was bound by love" (Canto 8).[4] When the heroine is seen by the two young heroes, her freedom becomes the basis of a thematic contrast; their vision of her from their palace prison instantly subjects them to love bondage while Emilia, overhearing their sighs, plays on with a new toy: "As it seemed to her that she knew that she was indeed liked, she took pleasure in it, and considered herself more beautiful, and now adorned herself the more every time she returned to the garden" (Canto 19). But finally the playful freedom of Emilia becomes the occasion of her author's jealousy as Boccaccio vents his masculine resentment on the tease he has created her to be: "Almost stripped of any other worth, they [women] are satisfied to be praised for beauty, and by contriving to please by their charm, they enslave others while they keep themselves free" (Canto 30).

Chaucer's characterization of Emily implies that he perfectly recognized this authorial self-deception, for the Knight's heroine pretends to no freedom of either rhetorical or psychological design. Rhetorically, the Knight interweaves the formal description of the season and the description of the heroine's person so that, as in contemporary tapestries, she becomes part of patterned Nature itself.[5] Familiar images of the lily and the rose define at once the beauties of May and the beauties of its finest flower:

> Til it fil ones, in a morwe of May,
> That Emelye, that fairer was to sene
> Than is the lylie upon his stalke grene,
> And fressher than the May with floures newe—
> For with the rose colour stroof hire hewe.
>
> (1034–38)

[99] Not only the details of Emily's physical appearance but also her actions, in the Knight's treatment, become part of the seasonal patterning. In contrast to the playful and largely undirected activity of Boccaccio's Emilia, the Knight's arises on a special morning, a holiday, at the direct command of the personified season to "do thyn observaunce" (1045). The careful regularization of the poet's language incorporates the heroine's movements into the seasonal ritual:

> And in the gardyn, at the sonne upriste,
> She walketh up and doun, and as her liste
> She gadereth floures, party white and rede,
> To make a subtil gerland for hire hede;
> And as an aungel hevenysshly she soong.
>
> (1051–55)

Admirers of the Knight's portrait of Emily surely are correct in recognizing its superiority to the usual description of the courtly damsel; no mere portrait, indeed, it is in fact an emblematic realization of the central impulse of the courtly life, to transmute nature into a work of art. Within the portrait this impulse is represented symbolically by a detail not so treated in Boccaccio, Emily's "yelow heer . . . broyded in a tresse/Bihynde her bak, a yerde long, I gesse" (1049–50). From this perception that Emily's portrait is an emblem of the courtly life, however, it follows that the portrait does not function as in Boccaccio to introduce the story's heroine. It serves rather as the object of aristocratic contemplation and, more specifically, as the starting point of an action which physically and psychically concerns the male. The Knight's Emily, in contrast to Boccaccio's, is not simply appealingly unselfconscious in her garden scene; like Lavinia, she is virtually without psychological dimension. Whereas Boccaccio's Emilia was able to overhear the young men's love agonies and used the knowledge as a basis for her own maneuverings, the Knight's heroine—whose portrait is isolated rhetorically from the love-plot action by the ironic framing images of the young men in the prison tower (1030–32, 1056–61)—remains oblivious of the kind of attention her image has elicited.

After Emily's image has been implanted in the lovers' minds, moreover, their love agonies and feud develop, again as with Lavinia, in complete independence of her presence and control. The independence, indeed, reaches a point of virtual absurdity when Arcite and Palamon engage in a duel to the death over the image, years later, without ever having once tested its reality. Theseus, coming upon the lovers in the forest, takes the Olym[100]pian view that it is "yet the beste game of alle" (1806) that Emily "woot namoore of al this hoote fare,/By God, than woot a cokkow or an hare!" (1809–10). The Olympian view means, however, that the Duke's lordly recognition of Emily's predicament by no means entails his interest in resolving it for the sake of a mere cuckoo. Instead of deferring to the decision of the heroine herself, as does Dame Nature in the not dissimilar circumstances of the *Parliament of Fowls*, Theseus, rather, tacitly accepts the premise of the heroes' combat and simply elevates that combat into a public tournament—transforming personal male emotional activity into a public ritual of the male state.

Nothing in the Knight-narrator's account of Theseus's decision suggests his awareness of its ungenerosity to the heroine, but Chaucer's own unease about the decision and its premises is implied in his treatment of Emily in the one scene which represents the *Knight's Tale* heroine as a psychological being. The scene, which takes place in the temple of Diana on the morning before the tournament, shows Emily again performing ritual observances—and praying for deliverance from men. This is certainly not the tenor of the prayer spun out by Boccaccio's heroine in *Teseida* Seven, however much the mere content of the two prayers may seem to run parallel. For what Boccaccio's Emilia finally requests of the hunting goddess—after due acknowledgment of her militant chastity and Emilia's own previous dedication to it (Cantos 79–82)—is help in choosing between two equally appealing young men: "if the Fates have decreed that I be subjected to the law of Juno, you must certainly forgive me for it" (Canto 83) and "grant that the one who loves me more, the one who desires me with greater constancy may come to my arms, for I myself do not know which one to choose, so winsome does each one seem to me" (Canto 85).

The sophisticated familiarity with which Boccaccio's Emilia addresses Diana becomes, in the prayer of the Knight's heroine, an expression of personal terror. Emily's terror, specifically her fear of violation, is presented as an all-pervading anxiety which even colors her perception of the very goddess whose protection she implores: "As keepe me fro thy vengeaunce and thyn ire,/That Attheon aboughte cruelly" (2302–3). The direct source of her anxiety, however, is clearly her perception of the loss of freedom and identity, the exploitation, which in her view the relationship with a man necessarily entails. It is thus the Knight's Emily, not Boccaccio's, who prays unequivocally to remain forever a maid,

[101]   And for to walken in the wodes wilde,
         And noght to ben a wyf and be with childe,
         Noght wol I knowe the compaignye of man,

                                          (2309–11)

and who concludes her prayer by imploring the virgin goddess with whom she identifies to insulate her permanently from the exigencies of the courting life (2328–30).

Emily's prayer of course is not granted; the courting life requires her complete subjugation and requires not only the relinquishing of her body but the elimination of her independent will. In this context, Boccaccio's anti-feminist diatribe against Emilia's prompt inclination toward the victorious Arcite (*Teseida* Eight, 124–28) takes on a new aspect:

> And she agayn hym caste a freendlich ye
> (For wommen, as to speken in comune,
> Thei folwen alle the favour of Fortune)
> And was al his chiere, as in his herte.
>
> (2680–83)

The Knight's Emily has become an automaton: she falls in love to order just as she swoons to order in mourning Arcite (2817–26) and just as she marries Palamon to order in the tale's conclusion, when Theseus presses the courtly image of woman into the service of a state affair:

> Lene me youre hond, for this is oure accord.
> Lat se now of youre wommanly pitee.
> He is a kynges brother sone, pardee.
>
> (3082–84)

Emily's final fate in the *Knight's Tale* thus is to become a work of the art of diplomacy: it is not a Galatea but a scroll of parchment that the chivalric mind has wrought.

When Chaucer arranged for the Miller to "quyt" the Knight's sympathetic critique of the chivalric life with an equally sympathetic critique of the bourgeois, he provided also that an examination of the fabliau image of woman would be a central part of the criticism. In this as in other respects, the method of the Miller's tale is to literalize and caricature features of the Knight's; thus, his heroine Alison, like Emily, is a prisoner of male expectations, but the contours of her prison have become the parlor of a burgher Annunciation and the vat of "Nowelis" flood.[6] Unlike [102] her courtly counterpart, Alison at the beginning of the *Miller's Tale* has already passed under the yoke of marriage. Her *mésalliance* with the "riche gnof" John the Carpenter, in an exuberant parody of the Mary-Joseph domestic situation, quickly admits her to the prison of her husband's bedroom and mind:

> Jalous he was, and heeld her narwe in cage,
> For she was wylde and yong, and he was old,
> And demed hymself been lik a cokewold.
>
> (3224–26)

Within her physical "cage," Alison, more like Boccaccio's than the Knight's heroine, proves adept at satisfying her sexual desires and, beyond them, her need for amusement.[7] Yet if her physical gratification with "hende" Nicholas has a natural vitality which exempts it from criticism, the mental titillation achieved by exploiting "joly" Absolon literally reduces her to an ass. This seamy episode, together with the unmistakable cruelty of John's treatment in the tale's apocalyptic conclusion, requires one to recognize that Alison's "free play" within her physical prison is ultimately insignificant; she will never be released from compulsorily fulfilling the expectations of her husband's fabliau mind.

Alison's final imprisonment in the fabliau image is effectively predicted at her introduction when the Miller ushers in his heroine through a parody of the rhetorical *descriptio* of the romance lady (3233–70). It is sometimes urged that Alison's portrait is a triumphant celebration of late medieval naturalism, but a closer inspection of the natural images reveals that few of them are innocent of innuendo. Even the most wholesome, "as whit as morne milk" (3236), does not grace this dairymaid's neck but rather the "barmcloth" covering her loins. The suggestion is subtly reinforced when her breath is compared to a "hoord of apples leyd in hey or heeth" (3262) and finally trumpeted, for all its tactful line-ordering, by the portrait's sublimely bathetic conclusion:

> She was a prymerole, a piggesnye,
> For any lord to leggen in his bedde,
> Or yet for any good yeman to wedde.
>
> (3268–70)

[103] The Miller's Alison, as a caricature of the Courtly Damsel, is not an earth mother but a sex object; and as a caricature of the courtly art of grace, she is a "wezele" (3234) full of craft. The Knight would have us believe that Emily's art, like Perdita's in *The Winter's Tale*, "is an art/That nature makes" (IV, iv, 91–92), since the only sign of her own contriving is the long gold braid at her back. The gossiping Miller's jovial reply is that Alison acts as her own *Natura*, plucking her perfect brows (3245) and running silk braids around her purse (3250–51). Naturally her highly scrubbed forehead shines like a gold noble, perhaps reflecting the brooch on her collar which, "as brood as is the boos of a bokeler" (3266), marks the order of Alison of Bath. For all the physicality of young Alison's portrait, considerable attention is thus lavished on ornament and, notably in the morning-milk image, on ornamented clothes. Alison's body is overlaid with white cloth and outlined by blackthread embroidery; a girdle bars her waist, laces crosshatch her legs—if this heroine indeed must resemble a barn fowl, the barn fowl is etched in grisaille. Grisaille windows became increasingly fashionable in English churches after the mid-fourteenth century, and in a smallish town like Oxford they might still have appeared newfangled. Set against the grisaille Alison, the Knight's Emily—all green and gold, parti-white and red—presents an image not at all in living color but cut from an earlier mold.

Chaucer's characterizations of Emily and Alison, though offered in the first two Canterbury tales, may be accepted nevertheless as his definitive statements on the courtly and bourgeois images of women. Later tales attempt to match these portraits only under special circumstances; the more interesting are those which show Chaucer extending the techniques of the early characterizations to explore other traditional images of women or indeed to invent new combinations of traditional images. Thus when Chaucer extends the technique of the *Knight's Tale* to the Clerk's tale of patient Griselda, he not only intensifies the saint's legend genre by importing material from the Marian apocrypha. He also intensifies the heroine's cryptic protests against the suffrance required by her holy image by adding critical apostrophes in the narrator's own voice. And when Chaucer reuses the parodic technique of the *Miller's Tale* in the Merchant's tale of May and January, he contrives that the heroine's deflation from courtly into bourgeois image will be recapitulated through reli[104]gious images in the tale's brilliant finale. With January's paradisal garden as her setting, May becomes a caricature of the Virgin Bride in the allegorized Canticles; yet when she climbs into an Augustinian pear tree and the arms of her serpent-lover Damian, after all she fulfills the "plit" of mortal women (2335) to suffer the soiled nature of Eve.[8]

The most significant invention in Chaucer's Canterbury characterizations of women, however, transcends technique altogether because it issues directly from his decision of the mid-1380s to redefine the essence of his art. In his characterizations of the Prioress and the Wife of Bath, both in their *General Prologue* portraits and in their tales, Chaucer confronts his audience with the New and Old Women in the form of living images. His purpose is to focus attention on the difficulty of self-realization in an environment which presses such images on human beings.

The Prioress of the *General Prologue* believes herself to be cooperating with her environment by conforming herself to the New Woman image; she conforms to the wrong one. Studying, with the aid of the *Roman de la Rose*, how to play the courtly lady (127 ff.), Madame Eglantyne has not simply denied the nun's vocation, she has also denied herself. As Chaucer the Pilgrim inadvertently tells us, the Prioress's human nature is too big to be forced into images, "for, hardily, she was nat undergrowe" (156). This vision of the Prioress's self-constriction is heightened in her tale's invocation where, her study now the Virgin's humility, she grovels in the role of a suckling child (1674). The barely suppressed natural energies of the Prioress, finding no other outlet, channel themselves into her characterization of her Virginal exemplar: the Virgin of the invocation, whose purity "ravyshedest doun" the Holy Spirit (1659–60); the Virgin of the miracle story, whose motherly love permanently infantilizes her men. The Prioress thus realizes the New Woman image with a vengeance; but the great avenger, so she would have us believe, is that Old Woman par excellence, the Wife of Bath.

The Wife's characterization is presented in three parts—her *General Prologue* portrait, the self-portrait in her own prologue, and the hag-princess of her fairy tale—in which a special kind of progression may be detected. The sequence moves from a com[105]paratively straightforward confirmation of the Old Woman image in its most negative valuation, through a massive display of propaganda which strategically manipulates the negative image while arguing a newly positive evaluation of it, to climax in an attempted rejection of the Old Woman image whether positively or negatively regarded. The Wife of Bath is most truly the feminist in her effort to dispense with images of women altogether, but the Wife of Bath is also imprisoned by the antifeminism of her culture, for in her tale's conclusion the image becomes her will.

Chaucer the Pilgrim's portrait of the "good Wif ... of biside Bathe" (445), in this interpretation, functions primarily to establish the image of the Wife as an incarnation of the fabliau woman and more especially the Old Eve. With a characteristically late medieval richness of determination, Chaucer summons the materials of both experience and authority to supply the concrete details of the portrait. Thus, the apparently naturalistic detail of the Wife's gap-tooth (468) is lifted from physiognomy manuals to serve as an emblem of her lusty vagrancy; similarly, the documentary-seeming vignette of her social competition during the Church offering (449–52) descends from traditional satire on the prideful womanly estate. Two further details of the Wife's portrait, however, the picture of the Wife as mock-knight (469–73) and the precise localization of her cloth making (445, 447–48), point beyond particular sources to the primary source of the portrait as a whole. Chaucer has conceived the Wife of Bath's portrait not simply as a creative agglomeration of features deriving from Alison and Eve but rather as a very nearly systematic parody of one very popular positive conception of the Old Testament Woman. The portrait is in fact a parody of the Virtuous Woman (*mulier fortis*) of Proverbs 31, who, in the tradition of scriptural exegesis established by the Fathers, was regarded as a figure of the Church and of the New Woman Mary in her most militant aspect.[9]

The picture of the Wife as mock-knight—with hat "brood as is a bokeler or a targe," footmantle around her hips, sharp spurs (470–73)—thus may be recognized as a comic literalization of the proverbial "she girdeth her loins with strength, and strengtheneth her arms.... Strength and honor are her clothing" (31:17,25). And equally the Wife's prominent position in the late-[106]fourteenth-century clothing industry—"Of clooth-makying she hadde swich an haunt,/She passed hem of Ypres and of Gaunt" (447–48)—may be understood as a quite literal capitalization on the Virtuous Woman's traditional office: "She layeth her hands to the spindle, and her hands hold the distaff.... She maketh fine linen, and selleth it; and delivereth girdles unto the merchant" (31:19,24). But it is surely the Wife's extension of her capitalist mentality into the marriage industry that provides the most devastating comment on her "realization" of the Virtuous Woman image. The Woman of Proverbs, fruitful not only of goods but of services, is "prized above rubies" (31:10) because "the heart of her husband doth safely trust in her.... She will do him good and not evil all the days of her life.... Her husband is known in the gates, when he sitteth among the elders of the land" (31:11,12,23). The Wife of Bath's parade of husbands, on the other hand, must have been notorious at the "gates"; she too

> was a worthy womman al hir lyve:
> Housbondes at chirche dore she hadde fyve,
> Withouten oother compaignye in youth . . .
>
> (*Gen Prol*, 459–61)[10]

Alison of Bath's quantification of good wifehood in her successive marriage ceremonies does indeed become the central issue in the self-portraying prologue which precedes her tale.[11] This prologue is full of surprises, reflecting some of the most significant decisions of Chaucer's artistic career, not the least of which is the opening statement, which represents the archwife in a posture of humble submission to the antifeminist clerks:

> Experience, though noon auctoritee
> Were in this world, is right ynogh for me
> To speke of wo that is in mariage . . .
>
> (1–3)

[107] Unexpectedly, the Wife promises to duplicate the Old Woman image of the *General Prologue* portrait, using her sexual experience to confirm the assertion of celibate authority that marriage equals torture by one's wife. Expectedly, she very quickly wanders from her stated promise, like Eve questioning the limitations imposed on her freedom of movement and mind: "But that I axe, why that the fifthe man/Was noon housbonde to the Samaritan?" (21–22). Yet unexpectedly again, the Wife's elaborate apology for sexuality, drawing on a rich store of arguments from Scripture and natural philosophy, deliberately caricatures these arguments so that her ostensible defense of appetite becomes an actual self-indictment. Her central text from Scripture, the Old Testament command from Genesis 1:28 that "God bad us for to wexe and multiplye" (28) the world's population, thus quickly becomes an authorization to increase her own store of bedmates (30–34). New Testament prescriptions for marital conduct, especially the Pauline instructions of I Corinthians 7, are wrested out of context similarly to license deploying her "instrument/As frely as my Makere hath it sent" (149–50) while converting each husband into a "dettour and . . . thral" (155) to one devouring queen bee.

The perversity of the Wife's self-justification usually is read as an artist's joke on both the woman and her detractors; in fact it represents Chaucer's profound and sympathetic insight into the effects of antifeminism on the feminine nature. Chaucer here recognizes that the antifeminist image of Old Eve, a product of the mentality which regards natural appetite as unnatural, by compelling the Wife merely to quantify sexuality has thereby ensured her sterility. He sees that she can have nothing to gain from a defense of sexuality which celebrates its fruitfulness, since there can be no display of children to confirm her fulfillment of the "gentil text." And he therefore arranges for the Wife to triumph in this moment of necessity by turning the sterilizing image itself into an asset—for, by flaunting the image of sexual promiscuity, she "covers" the barrenness which is her reproach. The triumph, significantly, is recognized and celebrated by the eunuch Pardoner, who caricatures physical potency to mask the spiritual impotence he suffers within: "'Now dame,' quod he, 'by God and by seint John!/Ye been a noble prechour in this cas'" (*WB Prol*, 164–65). The great difference between the Wife and the Pardoner, certainly, is that the Wife has refused to accept spiritual sterility as her final suffering; the story of her fifth marriage informs us, on the contrary, that in late middle age she has enlisted her deepest resources in a search for creative love. The [108] search, as Chaucer has profoundly understood, must take the form of a direct confrontation with the antifeminist clergy who created the Wife to be grotesque.

The dream which the Wife uses to win the hand of the young clerk Jankyn indicates that she anticipates the usual violation of her nature from this discordant union of Venus and Mercury, but it also suggests that she seeks to make pain its own charm:

> And eek I seyde I mette of hym al nyght,
> He wolde han slayn me as I lay upright,
> And al my bed was ful of verray blood;
> But yet I hope that he shal do me good,
> For blood bitokeneth gold, as me was taught.
>
> (577–81)

The narrative structure of the fifth marriage account precisely fulfills this expectation. The "slaying" is first effected psychologically by Jankyn's sadistic reading of his golden treasury of antifeminism "for his desport" (670) and her torment. The psychological violation becomes physical when the Wife, to silence this aural rape, slaps his cheek and is boxed on the ear. The moment when the Wife lies on the floor "as I were deed" (796) is the moment of blood in her marriage to antifeminism; and it is one which enables the realization of the gold she has dreamed. In another triumph fabricated of necessity, the Wife exploits her vulnerability by assuming the role of martyr in charity (802), thereby manipulating her husband into the corresponding role of guilty sinner who, wholly at her mercy (807), makes complete restitution for his deed: "He yaf me al the bridel in myn hond,/To han the governance of hous and lond" (813–14). The account makes plain that the redefinition of the marital relationship in which the Wife was both "kynde" and "also trewe, and so was he to me" (823–25) is consequent on her having mastered not only body and property but something far more important. The most precious gold bought by the Wife's blood is the control of her identity, for she also "made him brenne his book anon right tho" (816).

Since the Wife presents her reconciliation with the antifeminists as autobiography, it cannot easily be dismissed as sheer wish fulfillment. Yet Chaucer's use of the "glosynge" Friar to comment on the Wife's discourse at this point (830–31) alerts one to the limitations of the reconciliation. By perpetuating the vocabulary of mastery in marriage, the Wife has failed to articulate the dynamics which move the clerk from complete surrender [109] to the female into a state of mutuality; and she has failed, significantly, to deal directly with the absence of charity which has perverted the nature of her life.

The problem of uncharity is recognized explicitly, if it is not resolved, in the Wife of Bath's fairy tale of the old hag and the young knight. In this third and fullest exploration of the narrative pattern of rape, woman's mastery, and reconciliation, the physical violation—the "lusty bacheler's" rape of the maiden—comes first and is easily dealt with by placing the knight at the mercy of Arthur's queen. The psychological violation which follows—the knight's rejection of the "olde wyf" on their marriage bed—is confronted by the victim herself with the weapon of persuasive rhetoric, a woman's last recourse. The persuasion is embodied in the old wife's bedside lecture on "gentilesse" (1109 ff.) which, with the aid of arguments from Boethius, Jean de Meun, and Dante, argues for an appreciation of one human being by another based on inner qualities, not external worth. In context, the old wife's argument emerges as an assertion of the freedom of self-definition— freedom from all established categories or traditionally imposed criteria such as birth, wealth, and beauty—freedom to be, in the fullest Chaucerian sense, "good":

> And therefore, leeve housbonde, I thus conclude:
> Al were it that myne auncestres were rude,
> Yet may the hye God, and so hope I,
> Grante me grace to lyven vertuously.
>
> (1171–74)

The old wife's ancestors—perhaps, that is, the antifeminist images of Old Eve which have shadowed her identity—indeed have been "rude," and it may seem that the wife's prayer for grace to live well is answered symbolically in the tale's conclusion by her transformation into a fairy princess, young and fair and good. The major difficulty with such a reading, however, is that the old wife herself does not suggest that her attributes are symbolic but in fact distinctly insists on the reverse. At the conclusion of her lecture, the old wife turns to her silenced partner and in effect dismisses its special message: "But natheless, syn I knowe youre delit, /I shal fulfille youre worldly appetit" (1217–18). This promise of imminent gratification becomes the young knight's signal; the moral conundrum which she now presents to him he refers back to her with perfect security, for his gesture of submissiveness is actually the psychological trap which the lonely old wife has prepared for her fall. The knight's guise of relinquish[110]ing the mastery springs the mechanism which maneuvers the wife into using her powers of self-determination against herself. Willingly she uses them to transform into the courtly damsel men most desire—and women only because they most desire men's love. The conclusion of the *Wife of Bath's Tale* reveals the Wife once again undervaluing the "self-justifying" potential of her material. No mere perversity in this instance, yet far from a triumph in necessity, this conclusion is one of the most deeply pathetic moments in Chaucer's poetry: for the Wife, in struggling to free herself from imprisoning images, has merely transferred her cell.[12]

Notes

1 A medieval scholar's bibliography of antifeminist literature is supplied by the Wife of Bath's citation of her husband Jankyn's "book of wikked wyves" (*WB Prol*, 669–81). Its contents include: Theophrastus, *The Golden Book of Marriage*, 3rd century B.C.; Saint Jerome, *Against Jovinian*, 393 A.D.; and Walter Map, *Dissuasion of Valerius from Taking a Wife*, c. 1200. To these works in Latin should certainly be added two in French: Jean de Meun's portion of *The Romance of the Rose*, c. 1275, and Eustache Deschamp's *Mirror of Marriage*, c. 1385. A lengthy bibliography of medieval and Tudor antifeminist writings in English is assembled by Francis Lee Utley, *The Crooked Rib* (Columbus, Ohio: Ohio State University Press, 1944). But for an important investigation of "feminist" tendencies in the writings of the Church Fathers which places the antifeminist tradition in a new perspective, see JoAnn McNamara, "Sexual Equality and the Cult of Virginity in Early Christian Thought," Papers of the Berkshire Conference on the History of Women, II (Radcliffe College, 1974).
2 The most comprehensive treatment of the medieval Marian tradition available in English remains Yrjö Hirn's *The Sacred Shrine* (London: Macmillan, 1912), Part II. For the ethical significance of the feminine image in the courtly love system, see Frederick Goldin, *The Mirror of Narcissus* (Ithaca, N.Y.: Cornell University Press, 1967).
3 *The Aeneid of Virgil*, Allen Mandelbaum, trans. (New York: Bantam Books, 1972), Book XII, ll. 89–96.
4 Citations of Boccaccio are from *The Book of Theseus*, Bernadette Marie McCoy, trans. (New York: Medieval Text Association, 1974). The authoritative edition of the Italian is *Giovanni Boccaccio: Teseida*, S. Battaglia, ed. (Florence: Accademia della Crusca, 1938).
5 For the rhetorical background as well as a discussion of the Emily portrait, see D. S. Brewer, "The Ideal of Feminine Beauty in Medieval Literature," *Modern Language Review*, 50 (1955), 257–69.
6 The biblical parodies are discussed in their relation to medieval drama by Beryl Rowland, "The Play of the *Miller's Tale*: A Game within a Game," *The Chaucer Review*, 5 (1970), 140–46.
7 For the Boethian source of the cage image and its implications, see George Economou, "Chaucer's Use of the Boethian Bird in the Cage Image in the *Canterbury Tales*," forthcoming in *Philological Quarterly* [54 (1975):679–84 – ed.].
8 On Chaucer's use of biblical and apocryphal materials, see further F. L. Utley, "Five Genres in the *Clerk's Tale*," *The Chaucer Review*, 6 (1971–72), 198–228; and Emerson Brown, "Biblical Women in *The Merchant's Tale*: Feminism, Antifeminism, and Beyond," *Viator*, 5 (1974), 387–412.
9 Some important references: Augustine, *Sermo 37*, in *Patrologia Latina* 38, cols. 221–35; Bede, "De muliere forti," in *PL* 91, cols. 1039–52; and Bernard, *Super missus est homilia* 2:5, 11, in *PL* 183, cols. 63, 66.
10 Additional parallels in the portrait: the Wife's "coverchiefs" (453) caricature Proverbs 31:22, her "wandrynge by the weye" (467) misdirects Proverbs 31:27; her five pilgrimages literalize Proverbs 31:14; and, for that matter, her prominence at the church offering (449–50) is a pushy version of Proverbs 31:20, 29.

11 Since there are as many interpretations of the *Wife of Bath's Prologue* and *Tale* as there are Chaucer critics, I merely cite three recent analyses which seem to me particularly stimulating even when I do not agree: Norman N. Holland, "Meaning as Transformation: *The Wife of Bath's Tale*," *College English*, 28 (1967), 279–90; David S. Reid, "Crocodilian Humor: A Discussion of Chaucer's Wife of Bath," *The Chaucer Review*, 4 (1969–70), 73–89; and Beryl Rowland, "Chaucer's Dame Alys: Critics in Blunderland?" *Neuphilologische Mitteilungen*, 73 (1972), 381–95.

12 It has not been possible within the space of this chapter to place Chaucer's characterizations in a broader context of medieval attitudes toward women, but for recent work on the subject, see the papers on "Marriage in the Middle Ages," John Leyerle, ed., *Viator*, 4 (1973), 413–501.

15 | Chaucer's idea of an idea

DONALD R. HOWARD

Originally published in *Essays and Studies*, new series, 29
(1976):39–55. Reprinted by permission of the English Association.
The original pagination is recorded within square brackets. The
endnotes originally appeared as footnotes and are here renumbered.

Every literary work was once an idea in its author's mind: when we read the
work we grasp the idea at least in part, and whatever formal qualities we find
in the work—unity or form or structure—could not exist without that idea.
If we can suppose this, what can we suppose about the idea of *The Canterbury
Tales*? Until recently most critics have supposed that Chaucer's idea of *The
Canterbury Tales* was a simple one: they have said that the work is at base a
realistic description of a four-day journey to Canterbury, that if the author
had lived longer he would have added more tales, described overnight stops
and the journey home, that the heart or backbone of the work is the tales
themselves (especially the bawdy ones), and that in these his great achievement was in breaking with convention and going direct to life. In reaction to
this estimate of *The Canterbury Tales* a more recent trend in Chaucer criticism
has advanced an even simpler idea: that the pilgrimage to Canterbury is a
metaphor for the pilgrimage of human life, that the pilgrimage as a penitential act is the heart or backbone of the work (or the 'fruit'), and that the tales
are therefore 'chaff'—which, however, I am happy to add, no amount of
wind has managed to blow away.

All these opinions assume that *The Canterbury Tales* has a single controlling
idea behind it, one that we can articulate and see executed in the work. If we
politely suppose that each is correct (as Egeus would say) 'in some degree',
then taken together they are 'the' idea of *The Canterbury Tales*. And
this means that the idea is not a simple one at all but ornate, many-faceted,
labyrinthine—may I say Gothic—in its complexity. Nevertheless, it is *an* idea
which existed in *a* poet's mind and is embodied in *a* work. It is composed of
many characteristic ideas of his period; but taken [40] together it is singular,
unique—may I say Chaucerian—in its individual embodiment.

This is the claim I made in my book *The Idea of the Canterbury Tales*;[1] if in
this essay I repeat my claim in a mercifully shorter space I hope the repetition
will verge toward clarity and refinement. I have claimed to have seen inside

the mind of Geoffrey Chaucer and to have described the idea which existed in his mind, which moved him to write *The Canterbury Tales*, which informed its whole and its parts, which is embodied in it and makes it live—an outrageous claim, the daughter of Megalomania and Obsession, as it must seem—but I insist that it is less outrageous than previous claims. When a critic says that Chaucer meant to write over a hundred tales which he never wrote (because one ebullient character proposes that the others tell that many tales), or when a critic says that Chaucer meant to describe a journey home which he never described, in a kind of description no medieval author had written, they have made claims far more outrageous. They have claimed to know a startling, original plan which he had in mind but failed to accomplish. I claim to observe a plan sufficiently characteristic of his age which he had in mind and largely did accomplish.

To my claim there is still an objection which can be raised. The objector might say, 'You are presupposing an idea which existed in the author's mind and informs his work, but isn't this *idea* of an idea a modern one, the sort of conception Coleridge advanced when he spoke of "organic unity", the sort of superstition we hold when we praise a modern book for "tightness" or demote it for "sprawl" or "self-indulgence"?' But my reply is no. The kind of idea I have in mind is a medieval conception, one which was part of medieval aesthetics and rhetoric. It is what Erwin Panofsky[2] called 'the artist's quasi-idea'—a concept not of a transcendent realm like the Platonic ideas, nor yet only of remembered experience, but of a mental image in the artist's mind comparable to, but not the same as nor fully sharing in, the ideas which exist in the [41] mind of God. Panofsky showed how the Middle Ages, though it adopted on the whole a mimetic theory of art, held that the object of that mimesis was not 'nature' but the interior reality which exists in the artist's mind. The painter does not paint a rose; he paints his idea of the rose, and this idea or 'quasi-idea' is of a higher order than any single physical specimen and anterior to any artistic embodiment. Edgar De Bruyne in *The Esthetics of the Middle Ages*[3] describes the doctrine when he writes, 'The material work of art is not necessarily a faithful copy of the visible form (a roof is not a reproduction of a mountain range), but it is inevitably a representation of what the artist conceives in his soul. The form is above all an imitation of this spiritual model'. Dante in *De monarchia* II, 2, refers to the doctrine in what Panofsky calls a lapidary sentence: 'Art is found on three levels: in the mind of the artist, in the tool, and in the material that receives its form from art.'

Such an idea of an idea was present in the rhetorical writings of the Middle Ages and was thus part of the medieval conception of poetical composition. The emphasis was on the experience of the writer rather than of the reader, on the *making* of the poetical work. The best-known expression of the idea is in the opening lines of Geoffrey of Vinsauf's *Poetria Nova*: 'If a man has a house to build, his impetuous hand does not rush into action. The measuring line of his mind first lays out the work, and he mentally outlines the successive steps in a definite order. The mind's hand shapes the entire house before the body's hand builds it. Its mode of being is archetypal before it is actual.'[4] We know Chaucer was familiar with this passage because he translated it in the *Troilus*, assigning it to Pandarus as a thought which occurs to him as he plans to arrange the love affair.

About this medieval conception of a poetical idea there is a question which I side-stepped in *The Idea of the Canterbury Tales* and would like to consider in what follows. If we can fairly assume that Chaucer's idea of a poem squared with the medieval conception, did his understanding of that conception, his personal [42] grasp of it and his private thoughts about it, have an idiosyncratic or individual character? Did his idea of a literary idea in some ways verge from the traditional one which he might have had from Dante or Geoffrey of Vinsauf? I say it did. And it differed in a way which scattered seed throughout the history of English letters. Ezra Pound said that 'no-one will ever gauge or measure English poetry until they know how much of it, how full a gamut of its qualities, is already *there on the page* of Chaucer'. I say that Chaucer's idea of an idea is what at base explains the important place he holds in English literary tradition.

And first: Chaucer seems to have introduced into the notion of rhetorical invention an element of chance. The best evidence of this comes about as a result of a mistranslation. Geoffrey of Vinsauf wrote that the poet is like a builder, that the 'measuring line of his mind first lays out the work'. Chaucer's text seems to have read (or he misread it as) *praemittitur* or *praemittetur* instead of *praemetitur*, for he translated it 'sends out':

> For everi wight that hath an hous to founde
> Ne renneth naught the werk for to bygynne
> With rakel hond, but he wol bide a stounde,
> And sende his hertes line out fro withinne,
> Aldirfirst his purpos for to wynne.[5]

And Chaucer embroidered on Geoffrey by adding 'Aldirfirst his purpos for to wynne'. It appears that Chaucer here makes a sort of philological Freudian slip: he begins with Geoffrey's metaphor (the standard medieval one) about planning and building a house, and without discarding the metaphor—for he returns to it later, in III.530, when he says of Pandarus's ´plan 'This tymbur is al redy up to frame'—he has him *send out* his heart's line to *win his purpose*. The builder's plumbline in his original becomes something much closer to a fisherman's line. The act of planning in his original becomes something much closer to a lucky accident, 'winning'—as we would say, 'getting' or 'catching'—something. And the thing [43] caught is not the *archetypus* of his original but a 'purpose'—as we would say, an 'intention'.

This initial act of 'winning a purpose' seems to have troubled Chaucer enough at least that his anxiety about it found its way into some of his works. In his early poems, as critics have shown in detail,[6] he reveals himself casting about for material, hoping to find or 'win' something out of his dream life or reading or experience which he could use in his poems. In *The*

House of Fame, when the Dantean eagle escorts him to the houses of Fame and Rumor, we find him in search of 'tidings': we learn that the mother of tidings is chance ('Aventure', 1982 f.), and we hear the poet explain his presence in the House of Rumor to an unidentified questioner:

> . . . That wyl y tellen the,
> The cause why y stonde here:
> Somme newe tydynges for to lere,
> Somme newe thinges, y not what—
> Tydynges, other this or that,
> Of love, or suche thynges glade.
> For certeynly, he that me made
> To comen hyder seyde me
> Y shulde bothe here and se
> In this place wonder thynges.
> But these be no suche tydynges
> As I mene of.

> (1884–1895)

These 'things' or 'tidings' he has been promised—tidings of love, it was suggested earlier (675 ff.)—are going to fall into his hands by chance: there is nothing he can do to drum them up. The notion is borne out in all of Chaucer's major poems: he does represent the source of each poetic conception as something found or 'won'—in the dream-visions a dream inspired by a book or story, in the *Troilus* the 'old book' by Lollius, in *The Canterbury Tales* a gathering on a pilgrimage which simply 'befell' and a sequence of [44] tales which begins and seems to proceed 'by aventure or sort or cas'.

This lucky accident, this finding or catching a purpose, happens in an interior or 'mentalistic' realm which exists in time, in history. Poems and poets live and die in the House of Fame; but the raw material of their poems, 'tidings', comes from the House of Rumor. This seems to suggest that poems originate in what one hears but the real locus of a poem is not on pages or in books but in the actual realm in which poems survive, in tradition. The heart's line goes *out*, but with luck it draws something in. The purpose won is not the finished poem but its idea; it will be shaped by and will exist in a tradition. The conception is not the same as Northrop Frye's or Harold Bloom's notion that poems are made of other poems: Chaucer suggests that poems are made of a common basic stuff, 'tidings', and that poets survive or do not survive alongside other poets. A poetic tradition is at base only a grab-bag of verbal tidbits ('tidings'); whatever direction it has is owing to Fame—to prestige or reputation. As there is an element of chance in poetic invention, there is an element of chance in poetic tradition—in the survival and influence of a poem. Poems exist in Fame's house, a mental realm which is a castle in the sky built on ice, and the names of 'famous folks' engraved in the ice are melting on the sunny side. It is perhaps the most astonishing image in Chaucer—an allegory, as it actually is, of the world of consciousness seen diachronically, the intercommunion of mind as an historical entity, where tidings are not necessarily true and survival not necessarily just, where what does survive is to the north and in the shade, protected for a time from the mutability of the natural order. While his predecessors likened the process of making a poem to that of building a house, Chaucer thus represented the realm of poetry as itself a house. And he imagined another kind of house from which we get poems, the House of Rumor, and likened it to 'the Domus Dedaly/That Laboryntus cleped ys' (1920 f.). Daedalus, the mythical builder of the labyrinth, was the architect or builder *par excellence*. And the labyrinth he created, that mythic house, was in the Middle Ages itself a symbol of building. In churches [45] and Gothic cathedrals especially in Italy and France we find a labyrinth or maze inlaid as a mosaic on a wall or pavement. In some cases the architect of a Gothic cathedral inscribed his name in the centre of the labyrinth which stood at the centre of the cathedral floor: the builder symbolized God the creator and the labyrinth symbolized creation. It is widely believed, but not proved, that the pavement labyrinths of Gothic cathedrals were used as substitute pilgrimages—the penitent crawled on his knees along the unicursal way from the entrance of the labyrinth to its centre, which was called *ciel* or *Jérusalem*; in France pavement labyrinths were called *Dédales* or *chemins de Jérusalem*.[7] So while the labyrinth symbolized the created universe, it also symbolized the pilgrimage of human life, the world. In appropriating the figure of the labyrinth to describe the House of Rumor, Chaucer seems to have suggested that the source of poems, this interior or mentalistic realm, is the world itself, whose end is to be subsumed in the timeless universe. A poetical idea ultimately comes out of a remembered or reported experience *of the world*; its meaning is complete only at the end of time, when the world is complete. Poems are by their very nature among the transitory things of this world.

This 'House of Rumor' which is like the labyrinth turns out to be a giant wicker cage whirling about, which both holds and filters tidings. The centrality of tidings in this conception of poetry explains why the House of Rumor has the final and climactic position. These tidings are passed about by word of mouth, they become bloated and distorted in the telling, and some escape through the doors or cracks of the House of Rumor. It might be said that they are to poems what phonemes are to words or morphemes to sentences. So if we want to know Chaucer's idea of a poetical idea we have to know what he meant by tidings. According to the OED a tiding is something that has happened, an event—and more often the announcement of such an event, in other words a piece of news. In Chaucer it seems to mean the announcement of such news by word of mouth or by letter. [46] Tidings don't bear a one-to-one relation to the events they report—you can have more than one tiding for one event, and you can have a tiding for a non-event: Chaucer twice (in *The House of Fame*, line 2098, and the Manciple's Tale, line 360) makes it indisputably clear that a tiding is a tiding whether it is true or false. Thus he finds in the House of Rumor the most notorious kinds of liars—'shipmen and pilgrimes/With scrippes bret-ful of lesinges,/Entremedled with tydynges' (2123 ff.), and he adds, 'many a thousand tymes twelve/Saugh I eke of these pardoners . . .' But a tiding can be true. Chaucer believed poems are made of tidings but you can't say he believed they are made of *lies*—they are made of reports whose objective truth is neither here nor there.

In this Chaucer was taking a radical position. Where medieval rhetoric held that poetry, or the idea of a poem, originates in the interior world of ideas, he held that poetry has its origin in rumour, in spoken language. In Chaucer's uses of the term a tiding can 'befall' or 'come' but otherwise it is something you 'say', 'tell', or (most often) 'hear'. Behind it is something that happened or is said to have happened. Tidings never come from reading: if you are a poet and you are looking for tidings, you put aside your book, as indeed Chaucer does in all his dream-visions. But from the book he goes direct to fantasy, not 'life'; the chitchat he hears can even come from talking birds. In pointing to the basic relation of poetry to the spoken language Chaucer seems to have had in mind not the stream of speech as it exists in objective reality but the stream of speech as it exists in our thoughts—what Vigotsky called 'inner speech'.[8]

The notion is important because in *The House of Fame* Chaucer introduces a theory of speech based on the physics of his day. The eagle who lectures the recalcitrant poet explains that speech is sound, that sound is broken air, and that air is the element which [47] by 'kyndely enclynyng' goes up. The result is that if we are to inquire about tidings or fame we must examine the places in the sky where speech goes: we must observe speech in the abstract. The helter-skelter process we observe is presented in a retrospective structure —we observe Fame first; then the stuff of which Fame is made, Rumor; then the stuff of which Rumor is made, tidings. What we learn is that poems are made of tidings which are compounded of truth and falsehood (2108) and which are given names and durations by Fame (2110–2114). The reputations of poems and poets are made of tidings too. There is no reason or justice to the process by which fame is achieved or not achieved: the goddess Fame is as capricious as the goddess Fortune, who is, we learn, her sister (1547). The fame of former nations and heroes is held up by writers (1429–1519), but the fame of the writers themselves is in their names (for names are engraved on the very foundations of Fame's house) and in oral traditions (for minstrels and such are displayed on its outer walls). The writers in Fame's house are grouped by nation, whereas the purveyors of oral tradition were presented in a jumble (1184–1281). This wondrous world in the sky is really the poet's mind—memory is the preserving principle, and it is true we do remember writers one way and speakers or performers another, for writing preserves but petrifies while oral traditions change with the times.

Chaucer is very explicit in saying that the world he flies to is his mind. He says this in two key places, the proems to Books II and III. In the proem to Book II he figures thought as a writer and dreams as writings preserved in the treasury of his brain:

> O Thought, that wrot al that I mette,
> And in the tresorye hyt shette
> Of my brayn, now shal men se
> Yf any vertu in the be . . .
>
> (523–526)

In the proem to Book III he calls upon 'vertu'—'devyne vertu'—to 'shewe now/That in myn hed ymarked ys' (1101–1102) and says this means 'The Hous of Fame for to descryve' (1105). Even the House of Rumor turns about as 'swyft as thought' (1924). We [48] are to find, 'ymarked' in his head, what Thought has written there, in this very dream which he has now written down: an account of 'art poetical', of its origin and duration in a mentalistic realm. When he says in this same passage 'Nat that I wilne for maistrye/Here art poetical be shewed' (1094–1095), the emphasis is on 'maistrye'. He means he *will* 'show art poetical', but not 'for maistrye'. He means he will show it for what he has to say about it, not to show off his own cleverness: he will 'do no diligence/To shewe craft, but o sentence' (1099–1100). Everything that follows in Book III is in the world of the mind: every speech that finds its way to this place retains the image of its speaker (1070–1083) the uttering mind is not separable from the utterance even if (presumably) that mind has only passed on a 'tiding', for tidings do change in passing from mouth to mouth.

This image of the poet's sense of tradition is a different view from the modern one which holds that the individual poet responds to the burden of the past and wrestles single-handed with the anxiety of influence, and to my mind it comes closer to the truth at least for medieval poets: the individual poet has his niche in a historical structure among other poets of his age and nation, and they will survive as part of the structuring together. Chaucer, living just at the dawn of the classical revival, expresses the idea by naming writers of the ancient cultures.

What this must mean is that poets rise or fall, live or die, on the sheer grounds of whether anyone is reading them and talking about them. The fate of a poem depends on its readers, and on different *kinds* of readers. Chaucer acknowledges this in *The Canterbury Tales* when he makes the famous reference to turning over the leaf and choosing another tale. If you don't like 'harlotrie', you will find enough, he tells us, 'grete and smale', of 'storial thyng that toucheth gentillesse', and 'eek moralitee and hoolynesse'. This sounds like a list of genres—we are going to hear fabliaux, romances, and saints' legends or sermons—but the position implied about the nature of genres, a position which could deserve a modest renaissance in our own time, is that genres are not mere classifications imposed after the fact, nor Platonic ideas or universals, but *kinds* which grow out of a dynamic relationship [49] between tellers and hearers—tales, or for that matter tidings, exist because they appeal to different kinds of readers or hearers, and those readers or hearers naturally fall into social groups. Each of the tales told on the Canterbury pilgrimage is from this point of view a tiding—a bit of *lore*—heard and reported by a pilgrim for those pilgrims who share common attitudes and values with him; and then all the tales are 'rehearsed' in sequences by the narrator for various readerships or for a readership with a taste for various kinds of tales.

Now it is just in these sequences of tidings, re-told by the narrator and re-heard by us, that we see embodied in *The Canterbury Tales* what was foreshadowed in *The House of Fame*. The objective truth of a tiding is of no consequence; when it is reified in a tale or a poem or a book it becomes a *thing*, or part of a thing—and 'thing' was a Middle English word for 'poem'—that exists in the world for a certain time. As part of such a thing, every tiding is true in one way or another. You have to *look* for the truth of a tiding, and not all tidings are true in the same way, but every tiding is authentic: either it has a real event behind it or else it 'wexeth lyk the same wight/Which that the word in erthe spak' (*HF*, 1076 f.). It tells us something but the burden is on us to know what that something is. St Augustine said that if you have an image of a man in a mirror it cannot be a true image without being a false man. And he went on to ask, 'if the fact that they are false in one respect helps certain things to be true in another respect, why do we fear falseness so much and seek truth as such a great good? . . . Will we not admit that these things make up truth itself, that truth is so to speak put together from them?'[9]

In *The Canterbury Tales* Chaucer took this position about the relative truth of fictions. And he made his position clear by setting up the Parson as a foil. The Parson in his Prologue isn't smart enough to see what Chaucer saw. 'Thou getest fable noon ytoold for me,' he barks. He takes the position of naïve realism—he thinks all fables are lies and all lies are bad. He thinks you have to have 'whete' or otherwise you will have 'draf'. Chaucer's idea was the reverse. If you tell a tale, true or false, your choice of the tale [50] and your motive and manner in telling it tells a truth about you. There is a truth somewhere, but it is relative, various—and partial. Chaucer never claims to possess the *whole* truth. The Parson doesn't either, to be sure, for he puts himself 'under correccioun'. But the Parson implies that with 'correccioun' one could at least in theory express the whole truth in a prose treatise. Chaucer makes the opposite implication. He quotes St Paul that all that is written is written for our doctrine and says 'that is my intent'. The question that remains is of course how we *get* the doctrine out of all that is written. And Chaucer's answer, very unlike the Parson's but not unlike St Paul's, is that it is up to us to find it in our own way. We use the foolish things of the world to confound the wise. Part of Chaucer's idea is simply that no literary idea can approach its full potential of 'poetic truth' unless it engages the reader's interest and enlists his participation. It demands of us an act of will, for the truth of a poem is in *our* idea of it.

Now it is undeniable that one way of gaining the truth from a poem was to read it allegorically. This was to an extent true of medieval notions about reading; it was much truer after Chaucer's time and well into the seventeenth century that poems, especially pagan poems, were understood to be 'mysteriously meant'. All of this has been documented by Don Cameron Allen.[10] But there was another notion about poetic truth, in some ways harder for us to grasp because it is more familiar to us—because it has never died and because we take it for granted. And this was Chaucer's idea. But it is not an idea in the usual sense—not something he thought consciously but something he *did*. It was what we would call a feeling: Chaucer seems to have had a feeling that at the heart of any literary work is something that has happened, or at least been told, a 'tiding'. True or false, some tidings catch our fancy and some do not—who knows why? Chaucer followed his instincts and acted on this feeling. We might compare the way most of us would describe our 'idea' of how to teach a class or write a paper: we do what works for us, and what works for us *is* our idea even [51] though often enough we cannot state that idea except by inventing examples or telling anecdotes. I am claiming then that at the heart of Chaucer's idea was a feeling of which he was not perhaps fully conscious but which *I* am able to articulate—a most outrageous claim, as it may seem, the very daughter of Fatuity and Delusion—but I am not alone in thinking it. On the contrary, I am indebted to that scholar who has dealt most penetratingly with Chaucer's use of medieval rhetoric, Robert Payne. As Payne has recently reminded us,[11] Chaucer knew that no artist can provide what he thinks are the necessary and adequate aims for poetry unless he thinks he knows what he is doing. But, Payne adds, Chaucer also knew 'that for even the best of men, what one thinks he is doing is never quite exactly what he is doing'.

Then if the heart of Chaucer's idea was in what he did more than in what he thought, what did he do? It used to be said that what he did was to break with convention and go direct to life; now, for a generation, scholars have been toiling to prove that he broke with life and went direct to convention. This counter-trend has produced a sort of universal rule of thumb that nothing in Chaucer is what it seems. The Pardoner is really Faux-Semblant, Chauntecleer is the friars, Pandarus is the devil, the Wife is La Vieille. If this had been so, how could we explain the enthusiasm of readers in the centuries after Chaucer's death for Chaucer's pilgrims and tales, much the same pilgrims and tales we feel enthusiasm for—the Pardoner, who attracted the anonymous author of the *Tale of Beryn*, or the Wife's tale, which attracted John Milton as a study of 'the discommodities of marriage', as he called it, or the Squire's tale, which attracted Spenser and Milton? Their enthusiasm argues powerfully in favour of Chaucer's idea, whose universal rule of thumb was that everything is *exactly and only what it seems*, that every utterance is *exactly and only what it says*. The Pardoner is only the Pardoner; Chauntecleer, Chauntecleer; Pandarus, Pandarus; the Wife, the Wife. We must practise a rule of abstinence, must do as the Nun's Priest counsels—keep our eyes open and our mouths shut. Chaucer seems to have believed that [52] you can get tidings, can 'tell a tale after a man', can 'rehearse' it in such a way that people will react as Harry Bailly and the pilgrims react, by laughing, by being dumbfounded, by arguing, by calling a halt, by telling another tale. What causes this reaction is the uniqueness and delimitedness, the authenticity, of each personage and utterance. This authenticity is what *we* perceive as Chaucer's irony: Chaucer teases us—or we tease ourselves—into supposing that things are something bigger and the characters something more than what they seem, and the irony is that they are not. They are always and only themselves; it is for us to make of them what we will.

Among those unique and delimited personages the slipperiest of them is Chaucer himself, the gatherer of tidings who appears in his own works as observer, speaker, and writer. In the present century our attitude to him has been shaped by Kittredge's argument that 'a naif Collector of Customs would be a paradoxical monster'.[12] It was a very witty remark, and Kittredge went on to argue that 'naivete is incompatible with a sense of humor'. 'If I am artless,' Kittredge said, 'I may make you laugh; but the sense of humor, in that case, is yours, not mine.' In another mood, and another lecture, Kittredge seems to have acknowledged that Chaucer understood and capitalized on this circumstance.[13] And the most subtle treatments of the 'narrator' have acknowledged this: given all the formalistic distinctions we can make between the man and the artist, or among the man, the pilgrim, and the poet, we never know positively which we are hearing, and are not meant to know. We engage ourselves with a disembodied voice which is written down and which we must pretend to hear. Seen this way Chaucer *is* a 'naif' and therefore *is* a paradoxical monster—we may assume, a very smart and knowing one. There is nothing after all in this poetry except tidings. And Chaucer's irony is not only in the voice: it is the essential irony of all tidings, the irony we experience every time we pick up a newspaper, read the weather report, or the stock market quotations, the latest scandal or emergency or unsolved murder or incipient war: we [53] understand what the tidings are and say, but puzzle over what they mean, what outcome or import they may have. Tidings are news, and the news is by nature ironic: we never understand it until it becomes history, but then it is no longer news, and we have historiography to contend with—itself an ironic circumstance.

Seen from this point of view, the Wife is an ironic figure because she is *not* La Vieille or *die ewige Weibliche* or the 'old dance' or any such thing—she is always and only the Wife. We do not understand her. She does not understand herself. Chaucer does not understand her and does not claim to. When he says she had five husbands 'withouten oother compaignye in youthe', the irony is that he means exactly and only that: 'without other company in youth'. Things are after all not what they seem, but this is because the remark may *seem* to mean 'outside of other company in youth' yet it does not necessarily mean that. It can equally mean 'without having other company in youth'. The OED cites it as an obsolete sense 'intermediate between senses I and III', which I suppose does get at Chaucer's effect. It is a tiding; we may make of it what we can. And perhaps the best we can make of it is that our actual experience of the world is precisely of this kind. If you met the Wife, wouldn't you wonder what she'd been like before that first marriage? Isn't it just that fomenting time of her life which she would not tell you anything about—would probably not fully understand herself, or remember? And isn't one explanation of her complicated marital history the possibility that in her formative youth she *was* without company? What we don't know is what is interesting and important here. The phrase is pregnant with meaning but the only scholarly way to decide that meaning is to follow the OED and create an intermediate category—which is to call it ambiguous. We perceive such ambiguities as ironic, but the irony is *in us*—it is in our response to Chaucer's idea, which was to express accurately those tidings which experience and the world presented to him. If you call it deadpan or tongue-in-cheek or ironic you are only acknowledging, what is surely true, that Chaucer knew he could count on this 'ironic' response in us, or most of us. Irony is an acquired taste, and not everyone acquires it. So Chaucer's idea was risky and theatrical, 'distanced', and [54] highly disciplined. It calls upon a frame of mind in us—anticipates that frame of mind and in part inculcates it. It is not a 'strategy', for strategy by definition manipulates. It is rather a stance which invites and permits.

It was this part of his idea, this stance, which Chaucer bequeathed to English literature. It has been the mainstay of English fiction, the essence of the drama and the novel as they were to develop. The artist effaces or disguises himself, throws attention on the 'realities' of his story, the 'true history' he purports to relate. But the authenticity he offers is not in realities or history or even in tidings. It is in appearances, in the way things *seem*. It is therefore a wholly mentalistic or psychological phenomenon: the tiding reported by the writer and acknowledged by the reader can be true or false. It has its authenticity in inner experience—in the mentalistic world of Rumor and Fame. Fiction in this tradition deflects our attention to *seeming*: to the author's or narrator's mind, or to one character's mind, and always in some measure to the reader's mind. Its verisimilitude resides not in details but in the aura of the unknown and unknowable that pervades details and is the essence of 'tidings'. Chaucer appears to have grasped this principle before anyone else; but others grasped it too and later English writers may have found it elsewhere. Pound stated a precise historical fact when he wrote that what was to characterize English poetry 'is already there on the page of Chaucer', for he did not imply *post hoc ergo propter hoc*; he meant that Chaucer found it first.

Such an estimate of Chaucer's place in English letters, like Dryden's or Arnold's, makes Chaucer stand at the head of modern (as opposed to medieval) literature, and I espouse this view. But there is another side to Chaucer's idea of an idea which makes his abstemious way of putting tidings on paper altogether compatible with medieval thought: he acknowledged that it was all *only an idea*. In the last analysis tidings are noise, and while we may grasp a truth from the total experience of hearing or reading them, from the experience of contemplating *seeming*, the better way is silence. For this reason Chaucer always rejects in the end the very thing he is in search of. The alternative to the jumble of tidings is Troilus's [55] distant laughter, the poet's silent adoration of the Daisy; at the end of *The Canterbury Tales*, before the Parson's loquacious discourse, in the Manciple's Tale, the talking crow is deprived of his ability to 'countrefete the speche of every man ... whan he sholde telle a tale' (134–135), Phebus the god of poetry destroys his harp, and the audience is bombarded with a collection of proverbs on the virtue of silence. Chaucer's idea of a literary idea included the recognition that a work of literature is only one of many things in this world, that it lives in an inner world of ideas and sententiae and memories which alone give duration and authenticity to tidings, and that this inner world too will vanish in the end.

Notes

1 University of California Press, 1975 [actually published in 1976 – ed.].
2 *Idea: A Conception in Art Theory*, trans. Joseph J. S. Peake (rpt. Icon Editions, 1968), esp. chap. 3.
3 trans. Eileen B. Hennessy (New York, 1969), p. 142.
4 trans. Margaret F. Nims (Toronto, 1967), pp. 16–17.
5 *Troilus* I. 1065–1069. Quotations are from *The Works of Geoffrey Chaucer*, ed. F. N. Robinson (Cambridge, Mass., 1957).
6 Notably, for example, J. A. W. Bennett, *Chaucer's* Book of Fame: *An Exposition of 'The House of Fame'* (Oxford, 1968).
7 See W. H. Matthews, *Mazes and Labyrinths: Their History and Development* (rpt. Dover, 1970), esp. chap. 9.
8 See 'Thought and Speech', in *Psycholinguistics*, ed. S. Saporta and J. R. Bastian (New York, 1961), pp. 509–35. On Chaucer's sense of this see my essay 'Experience, Language, and Consciousness: *Troilus and Criseyde*, II, 596–931', in *Medieval Literature and Folklore Studies: Essays in Honor of Francis Lee Utley*, ed. Jerome Mandel and Bruce A. Rosenberg (New Brunswick, N.J., 1970), pp. 173–92.
9 *Soliloquia*, II. 10 (*PL* 32:893), trans. mine.
10 *Mysteriously Meant: The Rediscovery of Pagan Symbolism and Allegorical Interpretation in the Renaissance* (Baltimore and London, 1970).
11 'Chaucer and the Art of Rhetoric', in *Companion to Chaucer Studies*, ed. Beryl Rowland (Oxford Univ. Press, 1968), p. 53.
12 *Chaucer and His Poetry* (Cambridge, Mass., 1915), p. 45 f.
13 E.g., *ibid.*, pp. 75 f., 160 f., 183–5.

<table>
<tr><td>

16

</td><td>

The art of impersonation:
a general prologue to
the *Canterbury Tales*

H. MARSHALL LEICESTER, Jr

</td></tr>
</table>

Originally published in *PMLA* 95 (1980):213–24. Reprinted by
permission of the Modern Language Association of America.
The original pagination is recorded within square brackets. The
endnotes originally appeared on pp. 222–24 and are here partially
renumbered.

Nec illud minus attendendum esse arbitror, utrum . . . magis secundum
aliorum opinionem quam secundum propriam dixerint sententiam, sicut
in plerisque Ecclesiastes dissonas diversorum inducit sententias, imo
ut tumultuator interpretatur, beato in quarto dialogorum attestante
Gregorio.

In my judgment it is no less necessary to decide whether sayings
found [in the sacred writings and the Fathers] are quotations from the
opinions of others rather than the writers' own authoritative pronounce-
ments. On many topics the author of Ecclesiastes brings in so many
conflicting proverbs that we have to take him as impersonating the
tumult of the mob, as Gregory points out in his fourth *Dialogue*.

Abelard

In his much praised book *The Idea of the* Canterbury Tales, Donald R.
Howard has isolated a perennial strand in the Chaucer criticism of the last
thirty years or more—isolated it, defined it clearly, and given it a name.
Discussing the Knight's Tale, he remarks:

Chaucer . . . introduced a jocular and exaggerated element that seems to
call the Knight's convictions into question. For example, while the two
heroes are fighting he says "in this wise I let hem fighting dwelle" and
turns his attention to Theseus:

> The destinee, ministre general,
> That executeth in the world over all
> The purveiaunce that God hath seen biforn,
> So strong it is that, though the world had sworn
> The contrary of a thing by ye or nay,
> Yet sometime it shall fallen on a day
> That falleth nat eft within a thousand yeer.
> For certainly, our appetites here,

Be it of wer, or pees, or hate, or love.
All is this ruled by the sight above.
This mene I now by mighty Theseus,
That for to hunten is so desirous,
And namely at the grete hert in May,
That in his bed there daweth him no day
That he nis clad, and redy for to ride
With hunt and horn and houndes him beside.
For in his hunting hath he swich delit
That it is all his joy and appetit
To been himself the grete hertes bane.
For after Mars he serveth now Diane.

(1663–1682)

All this machinery is intended to let us know that on a certain day
Theseus took it in mind to go hunting. It is impossible not to see a
mock-epic quality in such a passage, and hard not to conclude that its
purpose is ironic, that it is meant to put us at a distance from the
Knight's grandiose ideas of destiny and make us think about them. This
humorous element in the Knight's Tale is the most controversial aspect
of the tale: where one critic writes it off as an "antidote" to tragedy
another puts it at the center of things, but no one denies it is there. It
introduces a feature which we will experience in many a tale: we read
the tale as a dramatic monologue spoken by its teller but understand that
some of Chaucer's attitudes spill into it. This feature gives the tale an
artistry which we cannot realistically attribute to the teller: I am going to
call this *unimpersonated artistry*. In its simplest form it is the contingency
that a tale not memorized but told impromptu is in verse. The artistry
is the author's, though selected features of the pilgrim's dialect, argot, or
manner may still be impersonated. In its more subtle uses it allows a
gross or "low" character to use language, rhetoric, or wit above his
capabilities. (Sometimes it is coupled with an impersonated *lack* of art,
an artlessness or gaucherie which causes a character to tell a bad tale, as
in *Sir Thopas*, or to violate literary conventions or proprieties, as in the
Knight's Tale.) The effect is that of irony or parody, but this effect is
Chaucer's accomplishment, not an impersonated skill for which the
pilgrim who tells the tale deserves any compliments.[1]

Having generated this principle, Howard goes on to apply it, at various
points in the book, to the tales of the Miller, the Summoner, the Merchant,
the Squire, and the Manciple. He is in [214] good and numerous company.
One thinks of Charles Muscatine's characterization of certain central monologues in *Troilus*: "the speeches must be taken as impersonal comments on
the action, Chaucer's formulation, not his characters'"; of Robert M. Jordan,
who, having presented an impressive array of evidence for a complicated
Merchant in the Merchant's Tale, argues from it, like Dryden's Panther,
"that he's not there at all"; of Anne Middleton's exemption of selected

passages of the Physician's Tale from the pilgrim's voicing; of Robert B. Burlin's praise of the Summoner's Tale despite its being "beyond the genius of the Summoner"; and of many other commentators on the Knight's Tale, some of whom I mention later.[2]

Now in my view this "unimpersonated artistry" is a problem, and a useful one. Howard's formulation—an attempt to describe an aspect of Chaucer's general practice—is valuable because it brings into the sharp relief of a critical and theoretical principle something that is more diffusely present in the practical criticism of a great many Chaucerians: the conviction, often unspoken, that at some point it becomes necessary to move beyond or away from the pilgrim narrators of the *Canterbury Tales* and to identify the poet himself as the source of meaning. If the assumption is stated this generally, I probably agree with it myself, but Howard's way of putting it does seem to me to reflect a tendency, common among Chaucer critics, to invoke the poet's authority much too quickly. Howard helps me to focus my own discontent, not with his criticism (much of which I admire), but with a more general situation in the profession at large. If we consider "unimpersonated artistry" as a theoretical proposition, it seems open to question on both general and specific grounds; that is, it seems both to imply a rather peculiar set of assumptions to bring to the reading of any text and, at least to me, to be an inaccurate reflection of the experience of reading Chaucer in particular.

"Unimpersonated artistry" implies a technique, or perhaps an experience, of reading something like this: we assume that the Canterbury tales are, as they say, "fitted to their tellers," that they are potentially dramatic monologues or, to adopt what I hope is a less loaded term, that they are instances of *impersonated* artistry, the utterances of particular pilgrims. After all, we like to read Chaucer this way, to point out the suitability of the tales to their fictional tellers, and most of us, even Robert Jordan, would agree that at least some of the tales, and certainly the Canterbury frame, encourage this sort of interpretation.[3] We read along, then, with this assumption in mind, until it seems to break down, until we come across a passage that we have difficulty reconciling with the sensibility—the temperament or the training or the intelligence—of the pilgrim in question. At that point, alas, I think we too often give up. "This passage," we say, "must be the work of Chaucer the poet, speaking over the head or from behind the mask of the Knight or the Miller or the Physician, creating ironies, setting us straight on doctrine, pointing us 'the righte weye.'" Unfortunately, these occasions are seldom as unequivocal as the one case of genuine broken impersonation I know of in the *Tales*, the general narrator's "quod she" in the middle of a stanza of the Prioress' Tale (VII. 1771). Different critics find the poet in different passages of the same tale and often have great difficulty in deciphering his message once they *have* found him—a difficulty that seems odd if Chaucer thought the message worth a disruption of the fiction.

Thus, Howard, whose observations on the critical disagreement over the humorous element in the Knight's Tale are well taken, offers an interpretation of "The destinee, ministre general ..." that is in fact uncommon. His account of the ironic tone of these lines in context is at least more attentive to the effect of the language than are the numerous readings that take the passage relatively straight. Even within this group, however, the range of proposed answers to the question "Who's talking here?" is sufficiently various to raise the issue I am interested in. To mention only those who discuss this particular passage, Frost, Ruggiers, and Kean are representative of the large body of criticism that remains relatively inattentive to the whole question of voicing in the tale.[4] They share a view of the passage as a piece of "the poem's" doctrine, to be taken seriously as part of an argument about man's place in the cosmos. Of those who, like Howard, find something odd about the passage, Burlin suggests that the speaker is Chaucer, who intends to suggest by it that Theseus is a man superior to Fortune but unaware of Provi[215]dence (p. 108), while Neuse, the only critic to attribute the speech unequivocally to the Knight, maintains that it differentiates the latter's implicitly Christian view of the story from Theseus' more limited vision.[5] Who *is* talking here, and to what end? One might ask what the consequences for interpretation are if one concedes both that the passage makes gentle fun of the machinery of destiny, at least as applied to so trivial an event, and that it is the Knight himself who is interested in obtaining this effect. Howard's suggestion to the contrary, the passage is not really directed at Theseus' hunting but at the improbably fortuitous meeting in the glade of Theseus, Palamon, and Arcite, described in the lines that immediately follow (i. 1683–713). This encounter is one of many features in the first half of the tale that show that most of the plot, far from being the product of portentous cosmic forces (Palamon and Arcite are consistently made to look silly for taking this view), is generated by human actions and choices, not least by those of the narrating Knight in conspicuously rigging events and manipulating coincidences. The Knight, as Neuse points out (p. 300), is adapting an "olde storie" for the present occasion, and the irony here reflects his opinion of the style of those "olde bookes." To him that style embodies a dangerous evasion of human responsibility for maintaining order in self and society by unconsciously projecting the responsibility onto gods and destinies.

The point is that a notion like "unimpersonated artistry," by dividing speakers into parts and denying them the full import of their speaking, puts us in the difficult position of trying to decide which parts of a single narrative are to be assigned to the pilgrim teller and which to the "author," and in these circumstances it is not surprising that different critics make the cut in different places. All such formulations involve finding or creating two speakers (or even more)[6] in a narrative situation where it would appear simpler to deal with only one. The procedure seems to me theoretically questionable because it is unparsimonious or inelegant logically: it creates extra work, and it also tends to lead to distraction. Narrative entities are multiplied to the point where they become subjects of concern in their own right and require some sort of systematic or historical justification such as "unimpersonated artistry" or the deficiency of medieval ideas of personality,[7] and before long we are so busy trying to save the appearances of the epicyclic constructs we ourselves have created that we are no longer attending to the poems that the constructs were originally intended to explain. Therefore, I would like to preface my more detailed opposition to "unimpersonated artistry" with a general caveat. I call it Leicester's razor: *narratores non multiplicandi sunt praeter absolutum necessitatem.*

Naturally I do not intend to let the matter rest with this general and essentially negative formula, though I think its application would clear up a lot of difficulties. I want to use the space my principle gives me to argue that the Canterbury tales are individually voiced, and radically so—that each of the tales is primarily an expression of its teller's personality and outlook as embodied in the unfolding "now" of the telling. I am aware that something like this idea is all too familiar. Going back, in modern times, at least as far as Kittredge's characterization of the *Canterbury Tales* as a "Human Comedy," with the pilgrims as dramatis personae, it reaches its high point in Lumiansky's *Of Sondry Folk*[8] (and apparently its dead end as well, since no one since has attempted to apply the concept systematically to the entire poem). Moreover, as I said before, we are all given to this sort of reading now and then. I think one reason the idea has never been pushed so hard or so far as I would like to take it is that the voicing of individual tales has almost always been interpreted on the basis of something external to them, usually either some aspect of the historical background of the poems (e.g., what we know from other sources about knights, millers, lawyers, nuns, etc.) or the descriptions of the speakers given in the Canterbury frame, especially in the General Prologue. Such materials are combined in various ways to construct an image of a given pilgrim outside his or her tale, and each tale is then read as a product of the figure who tells it, a product whose interpretation is constrained by the limitations we conceive the pilgrim to have. The specific problem of historical presuppositions, the feeling that medieval men *could not* have thought or spoken in certain ways, I would like to postpone until later, because the assumptions involved are often relatively tacit and well [216] hidden and the problems they present are easier to handle in specific instances. It is clear, I hope, how such assumptions can lead to the kind of constraint on interpretation I have just outlined and how such a constraint puts us in danger of arguing from inference back to evidence, in Robert O. Payne's useful phrase,[9] when what is desired is an understanding of the evidence—the text—in front of us.

It is the specific problem of the Canterbury frame, however, that has been the more stubborn obstacle to reading the tales as examples of impersonated artistry. Since I do not mean by this phrase what either the critics or the defenders of similar notions appear to have meant in the past, the topic is worth pausing over. The issue is generally joined over the question of verisimilitude, the consistency with which the fiction of the *Tales* can be felt to sustain a dramatic illusion of real people taking part in real and present interaction with one another. The critic who has most consistently taken this dramatic view of the poem is Lumiansky, who locates both the "reality" of the pilgrims and the "drama" of their relations with one another outside the tales themselves, preeminently in the frame. He ordinarily begins his discussion of a given tale and its dramatic context with a character sketch of the pilgrim drawn from the General Prologue (and from any relevant links) and then treats the tale itself as an exemplification and extension of the traits and situations in the frame. He is attentive to such details as direct addresses to the pilgrim audience within a tale (such as the Knight's "lat se now who shal the soper wynne") and to a degree to the ways tales respond to one another, as in Fragment III, or the Marriage Group. This approach leads to an account of the poem as a whole that doubles the overt narrative of the frame and, in effect, allows the frame to tyrannize the individual tales: what does not fit the model of actual, preexisting pilgrims really present to one another is not relevant to the enterprise and is variously ignored or dismissed. Other critics have not been slow to point out that this procedure neglects a great deal.[10]

The objection to this "dramatic" model that I would particularly like to single out is its disregard for the poem's insistent, though perhaps intermittent, *textuality*, for the way the work repeatedly breaks the fiction of spoken discourse and the illusion of the frame to call attention to itself as a written thing. The injunction in the Miller's Prologue to "turne over the leef and chese another tale" (I. 3177), the more interesting moment in the Knight's Tale when the supposedly oral narrator remarks, "But of that storie list me nat to write" (I. 1201)[11]—such interruptions not only destroy "verisimilitude" but call attention to what Howard has named the "bookness" of the poem (*Idea*, pp. 63–67), as do, less vibrantly, incipits and explicits, the patently incomplete state of the text, or "the contingency that a tale not memorized but told impromptu is in verse." Now this conspicuous textuality (by which I mean that Chaucer not only produces written texts but does so self-consciously and calls attention to his writing) certainly militates strongly against the illusion of drama as living presence. It is no doubt this realization, coupled with the counterperception that some tales do seem "fitted to the teller," that has led Howard and others to adopt formulations like "unimpersonated artistry" in order to stay responsive to the apparent range of the poem's effects. Such a notion allows the critic to hover between "bookness," which the French have taught us always implies *absence*, and what Howard calls "voiceness": the *presence* we feel when "the author addresses us directly and himself rehearses tales told aloud by others: we seem to hear his and the pilgrim's voices, we presume oral delivery" (*Idea*, p. 66). If we cannot have presence fully, we can at least have it partly. But when and where exactly and, above all, *whose*? As I have tried to suggest, a phenomenon like "unimpersonated artistry"—which is, remember, an *intermittent* phenomenon—tries to save the feeling that someone is present at the cost of rendering us permanently uncertain about who is speaking at any given moment in (or of) the text: the pilgrim, the poet, or that interesting mediate entity Chaucer the pilgrim.

It seems to me that the "roadside-drama" approach, the critiques of this approach, *and* compromise positions (whether explicitly worked out like Howard's or more intuitive) have in common a central confusion: the confusion of *voice* with *presence*.[12] All these views demand that the voice in a text be traceable to a person, a subject, *behind* the language, an individual [217] controlling and limiting, and thereby guaranteeing, the meaning of what is expressed. The language of a given tale, or indeed of a given moment in a tale, is thus the end point of the speaker's activity, the point at which the speaker delivers a self that existed prior to the text. For this reason all these approaches keep circling back to the ambiguous traces of such an external subject—in the frame, in the poet, in the facts of history, or in the "medieval mind." But what I mean by "impersonated artistry" does not involve an external subject.

In maintaining that the *Canterbury Tales* is a collection of individually voiced texts, I want rather to *begin* with the fact of their textuality, to insist that there is nobody there, that there is only the text. But if a written text implies and enforces the absence of the subject, the real living person outside the text who may or may not have "expressed himself" in producing it, the same absence is emphatically *not* true of the voice *in* the text, the voice *of* the text. In writing, voice is first of all a function not of persons but of language, of the linguistic codes and conventions that make it *possible* for an "I" to appear.[13] But this possibility means that we can assign an "I" to any statement. Language is positional. It always states or implies a first person in potential dramatic relation to the other grammatical persons, and it does so structurally—qua language—and regardless of the presence or absence of any actual speaking person. Thus, by its nature as a linguistic phenomenon, any text generates what it is conventional to call its speaker. The speaker is created by the text itself as a structure of linguistic relationships, and the character of the speaker is a function of the specific deployment of those relationships in a particular case to produce the voice of the text.

This kind of "voiceness" is a property of any text, and it is therefore theoretically possible to read any text in a way that elicits its particular voice, its individual first person. Such a reading would, for example, try to attend consistently to the "I" of the text, expressed or implied, and would make the referential aspects of the discourse functions of the "I." To put it another way, a voice-oriented reading would treat the second and third persons of a discourse (respectively, the audience and the world), expressed or implied, primarily as indications of what the speaker *maintains* about audience and world and would examine the way these elements are reflexively constituted as evidence of the speaker's character. We would ask what sort of person notices these particular details rather than others, what sort of person conceives of an audience in such a way that he or she addresses it in this particular tone, and so forth.

One might conceive of a study that undertook to work out a poetics of the speaker in literature. It would be a classic structuralist enterprise, moving from linguistic structures to a systematic demonstration of how it is possible for literary speakers to have the meanings they do. But since I do not believe, for reasons I will not go into here,[14] that such an enterprise would succeed, and since in any case it is not where my interests lie, I would like to move back to Chaucer by way of a further distinction. While any text can be read in a way that elicits its voice, some texts actively engage the phenomenon of voice, exploit it, make it the center of their discourse—make it their content. A text of this sort can be said to be *about* its speaker, and this is the sort of text I contend that the *Canterbury Tales* is and especially the sort that the individual tales are. The tales are examples of impersonated artistry because they concentrate not on the way preexisting people create language but on the way language creates people.[15] They detail how what someone says "im-personates" him or her, that is, turns the speaker into a person, or better, a personality (I prefer this word to "person" because "personality" suggests something that acts like, rather than "is," a person). What this implies for the concrete interpretation of the poem is that the relation that I have been questioning between the tales and the frame, or between the tales and their historical or social background, needs to be reversed. The voicing of any tale, the personality of any pilgrim, is not *given* in advance by the prologue portrait or the facts of history, nor is it dependent on them. The personality has to be worked out by analyzing and defining the voice created by each tale. It is this personality in the foreground, in his or her intensive and detailed textual life, that supplies a guide to the weighting of details and emphasis, the *interpretation*, of the background, whether portrait or history. To say, for example, that the Miller's Tale is not "fitted to its teller" because it is "too [218] good" for him, because a miller or the Miller would not be educated enough or intelligent enough to produce it, is to move in exactly the wrong direction. In fact, it is just this sort of social typing that irritates and troubles the Miller himself, especially since both the Host and the general narrator social-typed him long before any Chaucer critic did (I. 3128–31, 3167–69, 3182). The characters in his tale repeatedly indulge in social typing, and the Miller types several of them in this way.[16] The Miller's handling of this practice makes it an issue in the tale, something he has opinions and feelings about. The end of the tale makes it quite clear how the maimed, uncomfortably sympathetic carpenter is sacrificed to the mirth of the towns-folk and the pilgrims; he is shouted down by the class solidarity of Nicholas' brethren: "For every clerk anonright heeld with oother" (I. 3847). One could go on to show how the Miller's sensibility in the tale retrospectively and decisively inflects the portrait of him in the General Prologue, making it something quite different from what it appears to be in prospect, but the same point can be suggested more economically with the Physician. When we read in the Prologue that "His studie was but litel on the Bible" (I. 438), the line sounds condemnatory in an absolute, moral way. Reconsidered from the perspective of the tale, however, the detail takes on a new and more intensive individual life in the light of the Physician's singularly inept use of the exemplum of Jephthah's daughter (VI. 238–50). Retrospectively the poet's comment characterizes a man of irreproachable if conventional morality whose profession channels his reading into medical texts rather than sacred ones and who uses such biblical knowledge as he has for pathetic effect at the expense of narrative consistency: he forgets, or at any rate suppresses, that Jephthah's daughter asked for time to bewail her virginity, whereas Virginia is being killed to preserve hers. The situation in the tale is a good deal more complex than this, but I think the general point is clear enough: it is the tale that specifies the portrait, not the other way around.

The technique of impersonation as I am considering it here has no necessary connection whatever with the question of the integration of a given tale in the Canterbury frame. The Knight's mention of writing in his tale is indeed an anomalous detail in the context of the pilgrimage. It is often regarded as a sign of the incomplete revision of the (hypothetical) "Palamon and Arcite," supposedly written before Chaucer had the idea of the *Tales* and afterward inserted in its present position in Fragment I. The reference to writing is taken as evidence that the Knight was not the "original" speaker and, in a reading like Howard's, that he is still not always the speaker.[17] As far as it goes, the argument about the chronology of composition is doubtless valid, but it has nothing to do with the question of whether or not the tale is impersonated, a question that can, and ought to, be separated, at least initially, from the fiction of the pilgrimage. Details like the Knight's "write" are not immediately relevant because they do not affect the intention to create a speaker (they may become relevant at a different level of analysis later). Impersonation, the controlled use of voicing to direct us to what a narrative tells us about its narrator, *precedes dramatization of the Canterbury sort* in Chaucer, analytically and no doubt sometimes chronologically. The proper method is to ascribe the entire narration in all its details to a *single* speaker (on the authority of Leicester's razor) and to use it as evidence in constructing that speaker's consciousness, keeping the question of the speaker's "identity" open until the analysis is complete. It is convenient and harmless to accept the frame's statement that the Knight's Tale is "the tale the Knight tells" as long as we recognize that it merely gives us something to call the speaker and tells us nothing reliable about him in advance.

I want to conclude an already perverse argument with a further perversity. I have argued that we ought to reverse the ordinary commonsense approach to the relations between foreground and background in the poem and see the pilgrims as the products rather than as the producers of their tales. I have suggested further that Chaucer's fiction may explain, rather than be explained by, the facts of fourteenth-century social history. I now want to maintain that the poet is the creation rather than the creator of his poem. More perversely still, I want to put a nick in my own razor and reintroduce a version of the double narrator in Chaucer. I do this in order to question a notion more widespread and [219] apparently more durable than the various versions of "unimpersonated artistry," the notion of Chaucer the pilgrim. I must admit to being less sure of my ground here. For one thing, I am challenging an idea first put forward by E. Talbot Donaldson,[18] who has for years been producing the best line-by-line interpretations of Chaucer that I know, using what amounts to the very technique of reading I have been urging here.

Nevertheless, it seems clear on the face of it that issues of the sort I have been discussing are raised by the notion of Chaucer the pilgrim, the naïve narrator of the General Prologue and the links, who so often misses the point of the complex phenomena he describes in order that Chaucer the satirist or the poet or the man can make sure *we* see how very complex they are. The idea leads to a multiplication of speakers of the same text, not serially (though some critics have considered this possibility too),[19] but simultaneously. It requires that in any given passage we first decide what Chaucer the pilgrim means by what he says and then what Chaucer the poet means by what the pilgrim means. Here, too, there is often confusion about the distinction between the voice of the text and a presence behind and beyond it who somehow guarantees the meaning we find there.[20] Descriptions of Chaucer the poet sometimes take on a distinctly metaphysical cast, as in this passage from Donaldson's *Speaking of Chaucer*:

> Undoubtedly Chaucer the man would, like his fictional representative, have found [the Prioress] charming and looked on her with affection. To have got on so well in so changeable a world Chaucer must have got on well with the people in it, and it is doubtful that one may get on with people merely by pretending to like them: one's heart has to be in it. But the third entity, Chaucer the poet, operates in a realm which is above and subsumes those in which Chaucer the man and Chaucer the pilgrim have their being. In this realm prioresses may be simultaneously evaluated as marvellously amiable ladies and as prioresses.
>
> (p. 11)[21]

But the "higher realm" Donaldson is talking about is and can only be the *poem*, the text—as he himself knows perfectly well—and Chaucer the poet can only be what I have been calling the voice of the text. Donaldson is, as always, attentive to what the text *says* here, in particular to the tensions among social, human, and moral elements that the General Prologue undeniably displays. The division of the speaker into pilgrim, man, and poet is a way of registering these tensions and their complexity, of suggesting "a vision of the social world imposed on one of the moral world" (p. 9),[22] and I can have no objection to this aim. I do not see the need, however, to reify these tensions into separate personalities of the same speaker, and I think this way of talking about the narrator of the General Prologue is misleading because it encourages us to treat him *as if we knew who he was* apart from his utterances. The general personality traits of Chaucer the pilgrim have themselves become reified in the Chaucer criticism of the last twenty years, and this frozen concept of the character has fostered a carelessness in reading that Donaldson himself rarely commits.

If I were going to try to characterize the speaker of the General Prologue myself, I would follow the lead of John M. Major in calling him, not naïve, but extraordinarily sophisticated.[23] I doubt, however, that this characterization, even if accepted, would go very far toward solving the problems of the poem, because it still does not tell us much about who the speaker is, and that is what we want to know. The notion of Chaucer the pilgrim at least offers us an *homme moyen sensuel* with whom we can feel we know where we are, but I think that it is just this sense of knowing where we are, with whom we are dealing, that the General Prologue deliberately and calculatedly denies us. For a brief suggestion of this intention—which is all I can offer here—consider these lines from the Monk's portrait, a notorious locus for the naïveté of the narrator:

> He yaf nat of that text a pulled hen,
> That seith that hunters ben nat hooly men,
> Ne that a monk, whan he is recchelees,
> Is likned til a fissh that is waterlees,—
> This is to seyn, a monk out of his cloystre.
> But thilke texte heeld he nat worth an oystre;
> And I seyde his opinion was good.
> What sholde he studie and make hymselven wood,
> Upon a book in cloystre alwey to poure,
> Or swynken with his handes, and laboure,
> As Austyn bit? How shal the world be served?
> [220] Lat Austyn have his swynk to hym reserved!
> Therfore he was a prikasour aright . . .
>
> (i. 177–89)

The Monk's own bluff manner is present in these lines. I agree with most commentators that he is being half-quoted, that we hear his style, for example, in the turn of a phrase like "nat worth an oystre!" Present too are the standards of his calling, against which, if we will, he may be measured. The social and moral worlds do indeed display their tension here, but who brought these issues up? Who is responsible for the slightly suspended enjambment that turns "As Austyn bit?" into a small firecracker? For the wicked specificity with which, at the beginning of the portrait, the Monk's bridle is said to jingle "as dooth the *chapel* belle"? Who goes to such pains to explain the precise application of the proverb about the fish, "This is to seyn . . ."? Who if not the speaker? But these observations do not permit us to say that he is *only* making a moral judgment or only making fun of the Monk (the two are not quite the same, and both are going on). A sense of the positive claims made by the pilgrim's vitality, his "manliness," is also registered by the portrait.[24] The speaker's amused enjoyment of the Monk's forthright humanity is too patent to let us see him as just a moralist. The way his voice evokes complex possibilities of attitude is neatly caught by "And I seyde his opinion was good": that's what he said when he and the Monk had their conversation, but is he saying the same thing now in this portrait? Did he really mean it at the time? Does he now? In what sense?

The point of this exercise is not merely to show that the speaker's attitude is complex and sophisticated but also to stress how obliquely expressed it is, all in ironic juxtapositions and loaded words whose precise heft is hard to weigh. What we have, in fact, is a speaker who is not giving too much of himself away, who is not telling us, any more than he told the Monk, his whole mind in plain terms. The tensions among social, moral, and existential worlds are embodied in a single voice here, and they are embodied precisely *as tensions*, not as a resolution or a synthesis, for we cannot tell exactly what the speaker thinks either of the Monk or of conventional morality. What we *can* tell is that we are dealing with a speaker who withholds himself from us, with the traces of a presence that asserts its simultaneous absence. The speaker is present as uncomprehended, as not to be seized all at once in his totality. He *displays his difference* from his externalizations, his speaking, in the very act of externalizing himself. It is this effect, I think, that creates the feeling of "reality" in the text, the sense that there is somebody there. In literature (as in life) the reality of characters is a function of their mystery, of the extent to which we are made to feel that there is more going on in regard to them than we know or can predict. Criseyde is a well-known and well-analyzed example in Chaucer,[25] and I suggest that the general narrator of the *Canterbury Tales* is another. His lack of definition may also explain why he can be taken for Chaucer the pilgrim. Because his identity is a function of what he leaves unspoken—because it is derived from implication, irony, innuendo, the potentialities of meaning and intention that occur in the gaps between observations drawn from radically different realms of discourse[26]—there is a temptation to reduce his uncomfortable indeterminacy by forcing the gaps shut, by spelling out the connections. But suppressing the indeterminacy in this way involves reducing complex meanings to simpler ones. One infers "Chaucer the pilgrim" by ignoring the things the speaker "does not say" (since, after all, he does not *say* them—only suggests) and by insisting that he "means" his statements in only the plainest, most literal sense. Such an interpretation does not fail to recognize that the complexities of meaning are there; it simply assigns them to "the poem" or to "Chaucer the poet," thus producing what I am arguing is a contradiction: the simple and naïve narrator of a complex and sophisticated narration.

In fact, however, not only the General Prologue but the whole of the *Canterbury Tales* works against a quick or easy comprehension of the speaker. It is to suggest how it does so that I am going to reintroduce a sort of double narration. First of all, though, it should be clear that there is only one speaker of the entire poem and that he is also the poem's maker. The conspicuous textuality of the work makes this fact inescapable. It may be that Chaucer would have "corrected" anomalies like the Knight's "But of [221] that storie list me nat to write" and that he would have supplied a complete and self-consistent set of links between the present fragments to round out the Canterbury fiction. It seems much less likely that he would have revised the Man of Law's promise to tell his rime-royal tale in prose or the "quod she" in the middle of the Prioress' Tale or the "turne over the leef" passage in the Miller's Prologue or the inordinate and undramatic length of the Melibee. And I am quite certain that he would not have altered the fundamental "contingency that a tale not memorized but told impromptu is in verse." What is at issue here is not simply a neutral medium that we are entitled to ignore. If pentameter couplets are the *koiné* of the poem, stanzaic verse (especially rime royal but also the Monk's stanza and even Sir Thopas' tail rhyme) functions as a formal equivalent, a translation into writing, of a different level of diction: it identifies a speaker with pretensions to an elevated style, in life as well as in storytelling. If it is functional in the poem that one kind of verse be sensed as verse, why not other kinds, and prose as well? The poem's insistence on these distinctions has interesting implications for the problem of oral delivery. The *Canterbury Tales* is not written to be spoken as if it were a play. It is written to be read, but read *as if* it were spoken. The poem is a literary imitation of oral performance.[27]

One effect of this fundamental textuality is to keep us constantly aware that the frame, the reportage, is a patent fiction. There is no pilgrimage, there are no pilgrims. Whether or not Chaucer ever went to Canterbury, whether or not the characters in the poem are drawn from "real life," what we have in front of us is the activity of a poet, a maker, giving his own rhythm and pattern, his own shape and voice, his own complex interpretation to the materials of the poem. And that maker *is the speaker of the poem*, the voice of the text. There is no one there but that voice, that text. The narrator of the *Canterbury Tales* is the speaker we call Chaucer the poet, though it would be more accurate—I cannot resist, this once—to call him Chaucer the poem.

This being said, it is also true that one of the first discoveries we make when we try to characterize this maker and speaker on the evidence of his discourse, to begin to specify the voice of the text, is that he is an impersonator in the conventional sense: he puts fictional others between himself and us. This is the sense in which the tales are double-voiced: each of them is Chaucer impersonating a pilgrim, the narrator speaking in the voice of the Knight or the Reeve or the Second Nun. They are his creatures, voices that he assumes; he gives them his life.

But it would be as accurate, from another perspective, to say that he takes his life from them, and the amount of time and effort spent on making the pilgrims independent, the sheer labor of consistent, unbroken impersonation to which the poem testifies, suggests that this is the more compelling perspective, for Chaucer as for us. The enterprise of the poem involves the continual attempt, continually repeated, to see from another's point of view, to stretch and extend the self by learning to speak in the voices of others; and the poem itself is, among other things, the record of that attempt.

I have tried to evoke, however briefly, the incompleteness—the indeterminacy and the resistance to classification—of the voice that speaks in the General Prologue. One corollary of this quality is the cognate incompleteness of the Prologue itself, one of whose principal themes is the insufficiency of traditional social and moral classifying schemes—estates, hierarchies, and the like—to deal with the complexity of individuals and their relations. The speaker not only embodies this insufficiency, he recognizes it and feels it: "Also I prey yow to foryeve it me, / Al have I nat set folk in hir degree / Heere in this tale, as that they sholde stonde" (I. 743–45). From this insufficiency he turns to the pilgrims. He sets them free to speak in part to free himself from the constraints and uncertainties generated by his own attempt to classify them—an attempt that, however universal and impersonal it may look at the beginning of the Prologue, is always only his view and one too complex for him to speak by himself. The Prologue does not do justice to the pilgrims. By the same token and for the same reasons it does not do justice to the narrator and his understanding of his world. In the tales, therefore, he slows us down, keeps us from grasping him too quickly and easily, by directing our attention to the variety and complexity of the roles he plays, the voices he assumes. He is, we know, each of the pilgrims [222] and all of them, but he seems to insist that we can only discover him by discovering for ourselves who the Knight is, who the Parson, who the Pardoner and the Wife of Bath.

We may be impatient to know the speaker of the General Prologue, but as the voice of the poem as a whole, he is the last of the pilgrims we may hope to comprehend, and then only by grasping each of the others individually and in turn and in all the complexity of their relationships to one another. The relation of the voice that speaks in the General Prologue to the personality of the poet is like that of an individual portrait to its tale and that of the Prologue itself to all the tales. It is a prologal voice, a voice that is only beginning to speak. Chaucer's Prologue, like this prologue of mine, needs the tales to fulfill itself in the gradual and measured but always contingent and uncertain activity of impersonation, in both senses. The speaker of the *Canterbury Tales*—Chaucer—is indeed as fictional as the pilgrims, in the sense that like them he is a self-constructing voice. He practices what I have called the art of impersonation, finally, to impersonate himself, to create himself as fully as he can in his work.[28]

Notes

1 Howard, *The Idea of the* Canterbury Tales (Berkeley: Univ. of California Press, 1976), pp. 230–31.
2 Muscatine, *Chaucer and the French Tradition* (Berkeley: Univ. of California Press, 1957), pp. 264–65. In a more general statement on the *Canterbury Tales*, on pp. 171–72, Muscatine observes: "No medieval poet would have sacrificed all the rich technical means at his disposal merely to make a story sound as if such and such a character were actually telling it. The *Miller's Tale*, to name but one of many, would have been thus impossible." See also John Lawlor, *Chaucer* (New York: Harper, 1968), Ch. v. Jordan, *Chaucer and the Shape of Creation* (Cambridge: Harvard Univ. Press, 1967), Ch. vi. Jordan is, on theoretical and historical grounds, the most thoroughgoing and principled opponent of the notion of consistent impersonation in Chaucer's work. In this connection the book just cited deserves to be read in its entirety, as does Jordan's "Chaucer's Sense of Illusion: Roadside Drama Reconsidered," *Journal of English and Germanic Philology*, 29 (1962), 19–33. Middleton, "The *Physician's Tale* and Love's Martyrs: 'Ensamples Mo than Ten' in the *Canterbury Tales*," *Chaucer Review*, 8 (1973), 9–32. Burlin, *Chaucerian Fiction* (Princeton: Princeton Univ. Press, 1977), p. 165. Elizabeth Salter's reading of the Knight's Tale, in *Chaucer: The Knight's Tale and the Clerk's Tale* (London: Edwin Arnold, 1962), pp. 7–36, is perhaps the most consistently developed in terms of the "two voices" of the poet. See also Paul T. Thurston, *Artistic Ambivalence in Chaucer's Knight's Tale* (Gainesville: Univ. of Florida Press, 1968).
3 Howard states the position admirably (pp. 123–24). I suppose no one would

question that the Wife of Bath's and Pardoner's tales virtually demand this approach.

4 William Frost, "An Interpretation of Chaucer's Knight's Tale," *Review of English Studies*, 25 (1949), 290–304; Paul Ruggiers, "Some Philosophical Aspects of *The Knight's Tale*," *College English*, 14 (1958), 296–302; P. M. Kean, "The *Knight's Tale*," in her *Chaucer and the Making of English Poetry* (London: Routledge and Kegan Paul, 1972), II, 1–52.

5 Richard Neuse, "The Knight: The First Mover in Chaucer's Human Comedy," *University of Toronto Quarterly*, 31 (1962), 312–13.

6 See, e.g., Jordan, *Shape of Creation*, p. 181, where what is apparently envisioned is Chaucer the poet projecting Chaucer the pilgrim as the (intermittent?) narrator of the Knight's story. For an instance of how far this sort of thing can go, see A. P. Campbell, "Chaucer's 'Retraction': Who Retracted What?" *Humanities Association Bulletin*, 16, No. 1 (1965), 75–87.

7 Jordan once again provides the clearest example of this historicist form of argument, but D. W. Robertson also uses it, e.g., in the Introduction to his *Chaucer's London* (New York: Wiley, 1968), pp. 1–11, where he both specifies and generalizes such statements in his *A Preface to Chaucer* (Princeton: Princeton Univ. Press, 1962) as the following: "The actions of Duke Theseus in the Knight's Tale are thus, like the actions of the figures we see in the visual arts of the fourteenth century, symbolic actions. They are directed toward the establishment and maintenance of those traditional hierarchies which were dear to the medieval mind. They have nothing to do with "psychology" or with "character" in the modern sense, but are instead functions of attributes which are, in this instance, inherited from the traditions of medieval humanistic culture" (pp. 265–66; see also the discussion of the Friar's Tale that immediately follows). This whole line of argument probably originated with Leo Spitzer's "A Note on the Poetic and the Empirical 'I' in Medieval Authors," *Traditio*, 4 (1946), 414–22. Spitzer's argument is drawn from particular textual investigations and is relatively tentative about its conclusions. Judging from his remarks on Boccaccio, I am not at all sure that Spitzer would see Chaucer as a representative user of the "poetic 'I,'" but in any case I think his successors, unlike him, are arguing from "history" to texts, not the other way around. Spitzer's formulation has become fossilized in these Chaucerians.

8 G. L. Kittredge, *Chaucer and His Poetry* (Cambridge: Harvard Univ. Press, 1915), Ch. v; the famous phrases are on pp. 154–55. R. M. Lumiansky, *Of Sondry Folk: The Dramatic Principle of the* Canterbury Tales (Austin: Univ. of Texas Press, 1955).

9 Payne, *The Key of Remembrance: A Study of Chaucer's Poetics* (New Haven: Yale Univ. Press, 1963), p. 3.

10 Jordan is particularly good at evoking the element of "the girlhood of Shakespeare's heroines" that often finds its way into this sort of interpretation; see "Roadside Drama," esp. pp. 24–26.

11 Quotations from Chaucer are from F. N. Robinson, ed., *The Works of Geoffrey Chaucer*, 2nd ed. (Boston: Houghton, 1957).

12 In what follows I ought to acknowledge a general obligation to the work of Jacques Derrida, perhaps more to its spirit than to any specific essay or formulation. For a representative discussion of the problem of presence and a typical critique of "logocentric metaphysics" see "Writing before the Letter," Pt. I of *Of Grammatology*, trans. Gayatri Chakravorty Spivak (Baltimore: Johns Hopkins Univ. Press, 1976), pp. 1–93.

13 See Emile Benveniste, *Problems in General Linguistics*, trans. Mary Elizabeth Meek,

Miami Linguistics Series, No. 8 (Coral Gables, Fla.: Univ. of Miami Press, 1971). Chapters xviii and xx are especially helpful, but the whole section (Chs. xviii–xxiii, pp. 195–248) is of value.

14 One might observe in passing that many "structuralist" discussions of voice in literature seem plagued by the same confusions as Chaucerian ones. See, e.g., Roland Barthes, "To Write: An Intransitive Verb?" in Richard Macksey and Eugenio Donato, eds., *The Structuralist Controversy: The Languages of Criticism and the Sciences of Man* (Baltimore: Johns Hopkins Univ. Press, 1970), where he remarks of the discourse of the traditional novel that it "alternates the personal and the impersonal very rapidly, often even in the course of the same sentence, so as to produce, if we can speak thus, a proprietary consciousness which retains the mastery of what it states without participating in it" (p. 140). There is not space here to deal with this extraordinary idea, but see Jonathan Culler's sympathetic and skeptical discussion of this notion and related ideas in *Structuralist Poetics* (Ithaca: Cornell Univ. Press, 1975), pp. 189–205.

15 There are a number of tales—the Prioress' is one and the Shipman's another—that suggest how this happens whether the speaker intends it or not.

16 E.g., "A clerk hadde litherly biset his whyle, / But if he koude a carpenter bigyle"; "What! thynk on God, as we doon, men that swynke"; "She was a prymerole, a piggesnye, / For any lord to leggen in his bedde, / Or yet for any good yeman to wedde" (I. 3299–300, 3491, 3268–70).

17 See Alfred David, *The Strumpet Muse* (Bloomington: Indiana Univ. Press, 1976), pp. 77–89.

18 Donaldson, "Chaucer the Pilgrim," *PMLA*, 69 (1954), 928–36; rpt. in his *Speaking of Chaucer* (London: Athlone, 1970). Howard discusses the topic in his "Chaucer the Man," *PMLA*, 80 (1965), 337–43.

19 See Rosemary Woolf, "Chaucer as a Satirist in the General Prologue to the *Canterbury Tales*," *Critical Quarterly*, 1 (1959), 150–57.

20 I suspect that this confusion has to do with a natural desire on the part of critics to evade the feelings of contingency and responsibility that haunt the act of interpretation. If the voice of the text is assumed to be that of an external subject, one justifies what one reads out of the text on the authority of a poet who must have "meant" to put it in. See Donaldson's brilliant and humane critique of stemma editing on similar grounds in "The Psychology of Editors of Middle English Texts," *Speaking of Chaucer*, pp. 102–18.

21 [Originally published in Donaldson's "Chaucer the Pilgrim" (1954), p. 936: see above – ed.]

22 [Also in Donaldson 1954, p. 934 – ed.]

23 See Major's valuable and neglected article "The Personality of Chaucer the Pilgrim," *PMLA*, 75 (1960), 160–62.

24 See Jill Mann's excellent discussion in *Chaucer and Medieval Estates Satire* (Cambridge: Cambridge Univ. Press, 1973), pp. 17–37, esp. p. 20.

25 See Arthur Mizener, "Character and Action in the Case of Criseyde," *PMLA*, 54 (1939), 65–81, and Robert P. apRoberts, "The Central Episode in Chaucer's *Troilus*," *PMLA*, 77 (1962), 373–85.

26 This observation suggests that a paratactic style is particularly conducive to producing the kind of effect I am describing, because the information (syntax) that would *specify* the connection between statements is left out. See Erich Auerbach, "Roland against Ganelon," in his *Mimesis: The Representation of Reality in Western Literature* (Garden City, N.Y.: Anchor-Doubleday, 1953), pp. 83–107. Parataxis is one of the main descriptive techniques of the General Prologue, particularly noticeable in the three central portraits of the Shipman, the Physician, and the

Wife of Bath, but widely employed throughout. Further, the structure of the Prologue itself is paratactic (composed of juxtaposed independent portraits), and so is that of the poem as a whole (composed of juxtaposed independent tales).

27 I have neglected B. H. Bronson's criticisms of Chaucer the pilgrim and related matters (see esp. his *In Search of Chaucer* [Toronto: Univ. of Toronto Press, 1960], pp. 25–33), because my assumptions about the relations between literary and oral cultures in Chaucer's poetry start from a position very nearly opposite to his. I agree with him, however, that the problem of performance in Chaucer is worth further study; in fact, I think it is a central theme throughout the poet's career. In the *Canterbury Tales*, the frame exists precisely to provide a literary representation of the ordinarily extratextual and tacit dimensions of storytelling in writing. The poem presents not merely stories but stories told to an audience that is part of the fiction, and this circumstance allows Chaucer to register the effects of a range of conditions of performance.

28 In preparing this article, I was assisted by a grant from the Research Committee of the Academic Senate of the University of California, Santa Cruz; I am grateful for this support.

17 | Chaucer and Boccaccio: *The Knight's Tale*

ELIZABETH SALTER

Originally published as chapter 4 of Elizabeth Salter, *Fourteenth-Century English Poetry: Contexts and Readings* (Oxford: Clarendon Press, 1983, pp. 142–81). © The Estate of Elizabeth Salter 1983. Reprinted by permission of Oxford University Press. The first one and a half pages of the chapter have been omitted. The original pagination is recorded within square brackets. The endnotes originally appeared on pp. 205–6.

Every study of the *Knight's Tale* tells us that Chaucer reduced the immense length of the *Teseida* to roughly a quarter of its size, and that out of a romantic epic with pseudo-classical machinery he produced a medieval romance. Taking into account the possibility that an earlier translation was pressed into service as the Knight's "Canterbury Tale",[1] part of what he did to the Italian may have been suggested by the framework for which the English was intended. The Canterbury-pilgrimage setting, and the semi-dramatic link-up with a chivalric narrator would have made a good deal of the *Teseida* unusable. There are, however, reasons for thinking that the allocation of the story of Palemone and Arcita to the Knight of the *Canterbury Tales* could never have been more than an initial and, after that, intermittent motive force in Chaucer's treatment of the *Teseida*. One of the most significant areas in which change is worked is that which concerns the subject of Gods and men. As a broad generalization, it would be true to say that what is mainly a narrative element in Boccaccio's poem [143] becomes a thematic element in Chaucer's *Knight's Tale*. Chaucer grows interested in the *idea* of man and his subjection to the dictates of the Gods, whereas Boccaccio is content to enrich the story of that subjection with rhetorical and descriptive colour. Where Boccaccio deals in the lament, Chaucer sometimes deals in the protest; where Boccaccio proposes little more than an outlet to sorrow in renewed action, Chaucer attempts a philosophical justification of man's suffering. Predictably, the *Knight's Tale* gains in pathetic, dramatic, and imaginative appeal, but this in itself frequently amounts to a painful commentary upon Boccaccio's narrative and makes heavy demands of Chaucer when he comes finally to the point of resolution and reconciliation.

It is easy to see, on the one hand, how the *Teseida* provided Chaucer with materials and motifs for development, and, on the other, how he altered their significance—sometimes setting them in new contexts and groupings, sometimes angling and supporting them quite differently. The motifs of the instability of Fortune and the enmity of the Gods are already present in the Italian—the first running throughout the poem, referred to often by the principal characters and by the poet himself, and the second accepted as a premiss, a main-spring of part, at least, of the action. Thus Juno's hatred of Thebes—an illogical consequence of Jove's infidelities in that city—is seen to be instrumental in its destruction, and in the wretched afflictions of the two Theban captives, Palemone and Arcita; the third book opens with

> Poi che alquanto il furor de Iunone
> fu per Tebe distrutta temperato . . .

> The anger of Juno was somewhat lessened after the destruction of Thebes . . .

> *(Teseida,* III, st. 1)

And Arcita, banished from Athens, takes a pessimistic view of Juno's continual intervention in his life and that of Palemone:

> E oltre a ciò l'iddii ne sono avversi:
> come tu sai, antica nimistate
> serva Giunon ver noi, e diè perversi
> mali a color che passar questa etate;
> [144]   e noi ancor perseguendo ha somersi,
> come tu vedi, in infelicitate
> estrema; e Ercul né Bacco n'aiuta,
> per che io tengo mia vita perduta.

> *(Teseida,* III, st. 66)

Besides, the gods are unfriendly: As you know, Juno nurses an ancient grudge against us, and has inflicted spiteful injuries on those who went before us. She persecutes us still, and has overwhelmed us with utmost misfortune. Hercules, Bacchus help her—and for this reason, I consider my life lost.

The relationship between the persecutions of the Gods and the unpredictable acts of the 'alta ministra', Fortune (VI, st. 1), is not very clearly articulated; Arcita and Palemone feel themselves to be tormented by both kinds of power, and it could be assumed, if rather loosely from the poetry, that Fortune is envisaged as the instrument of divine pleasure and displeasure. Palemone and Arcita curse 'la malizia / dello' nfortunio loro', 'the spite of their misfortune' (III, st. 3); Arcita, when he is freed but banished from Athens by Teseo, sees his life driven forward by 'l'adirata fortuna', 'angry fortune' (III, st. 76); and Boccaccio himself, in one memorable sequence, meditates on the dramatic vicissitudes in the history of his two heroes, all brought about by Fortune:

> L'alta ministra del mondo Fortuna,
> con volubile moto permutando

di questo in quel più volte ciascheduna
cosa togliendo e tal volta donando,
or mostrandosi chiara e ora bruna
secondo le pareva e come e quando,
avea co' suoi effetti a' due Tebani
mostrato ciò che può ne' ben mondani.

                                        (*Teseida*, VI, st. 1)

Fortune, that lofty governess of the world, who changes one thing into
another over and over, with her inconstant movements, giving and
taking away, now showing bright and now dark, as and how and when
it suits her, had showed what power she had over worldly things
through her treatment of the two Thebans.

His conclusions, after reviewing their capture, imprisonment, falling in love,
their deprivations, the one banished, the other a [145] captive, their illegal
duel, their condemnation by Teseo and their eventual pardon, are full of
amazement and uncertainty: what can be said in the face of such power?

Deh, chi fia qui che dica che'mondani
provvedimenti a' moti di costei
possan mai porger argomenti sani?
Se non fosse mal detto, io dicerei
certo che fosser tutti quanti vani,
questo mirando e ciò ch'ancor di lei
si legge e ode e vede ognora aperto,
ben che ne sia come ciò fa coverto.

                                        (*Teseida*, VI, st. 5)

Now who would say here that worldly prudence can explain her movements with sound arguments? I would say, if it were proper to speak so,
that all such attempts were entirely worthless, considering this case and
others that we read and hear of and see continually, even though the
way she works is hidden.

It is interesting to notice, however, that Boccaccio handles these materials
with a measure of detachment: they are not allowed to assume more than a
limited importance in the poem as a whole. They serve to draw out our
sympathy for the miserable Arcita and Palemone, they stimulate our awareness of the predicament of man's life, set between the Gods and Fate. But
there is always a sense that Boccaccio resists their power to involve him, his
characters, and his readers in deep concern. They do not ever move us
strongly, or absorb our interest totally. So, for instance, the poet can cover,
in one single-toned stanza (III, st. 1), the pleasure taken by Juno in the fall of
Thebes, the subsequent retreat of Mars to his Thracian stronghold, and his
own intention to celebrate, now, the battles of Cupid. And as, in the account
of the temples of Mars and Venus, the authority of the Gods, expressed in
images of great descriptive richness, commands the attention without invoking the passions, so, through the poem, the authority of Fate asks for sad
recognition without invoking despair.

Chaucer's reaction to what he found in the Italian may, in the initial stages, appear tentative: in the light of the completed work, however, even the smallest change is full of significance. So when Arcite attempts to reconcile Palamon to their unhappy [146] imprisonment, and associates, for the first time, the influence of the malign planet Saturn with that of Fortune as twin causes of 'adversitee' (l. 1086), we have a clear instance of Chaucer's desire to benefit from his original, but also to widen and deepen its implications. The choice of Saturn is not, in itself, startling: the orbit of Saturn was the most extensive of any planet known to the fourteenth century, its 'aspect', or position, most hostile:

> So stood the hevene whan that we were born . . .
>
> (l. 1090)

But the introduction of planetary influences, absent in the *Teseida* at this point, argues not only that Chaucer, with his scientific interests, was eager to give his readers a more varied range of reference:

> A 'fortunat ascendent' clepen they whan that no wicked planete, as Saturne or Mars . . . is in the hous of the ascendent, ne that no wicked planete have noon aspect of enemyte upon the ascendent . . .[2]

Nor does it only argue that he wished to increase the immediate pathos of the human situation—two young men assailed by all kinds of invincible forces. It must also mean that he was preparing to strengthen the motif, already briefly announced by the Italian references to Juno and her "furor" directed against Thebes (III, st. 1), of absolute power wielded by the Gods. While Saturn is called up first as a 'wicke aspect of disposicioun . . .' (l. 1087), it must have been in Chaucer's mind that, as father of Jove, he stood in close relationship to Juno, wife of Jove—and, further, to Venus, daughter of Jove. Astrological patterns, always vividly present to Chaucer, suggested a way of enlarging and vitalizing that which, in the *Teseida*, is an effective but subordinate narrative device. Once Saturn, in whatever guise, has entered the poem, the serious, even sinister potential of the narrative can begin to be realized. Palamon's response to the words of Arcite hints at this: nothing in the *Teseida* prompts his prayer to Venus, with its allusions to 'destiny', 'everlasting decree', and 'tyranny':

> And if so be my destynee be shapen
> By eterne word to dyen in prisoun,
> Of oure lynage have som compassioun,
> That is so lowe ybroght by tirannye . . .
>
> (ll. 1108–11)

[147] It might be possible to forecast, from those lines, something of Palamon's next address to the Gods, with its contempt for their 'word eterne' (l. 1304). At least they indicate a growing preoccupation with the frailty of human life, faced not only by the evidence of man-made disaster but also by the thought of unalterable and incomprehensible destiny.

And if this subject of men and Gods is beginning to hold promise of a stronger dramatic tension than it ever developed in the *Teseida*, the related, but not identical, subject of men and Fortune is being given a new weight of philosophical reference. This makes itself clear in Arcite's reaction to his release from prison by Theseus. The irony of his situation—free, but banished from all he loves—calls for some comment, and on the whole the theme of Boccaccio's comment is 'Fortune is changeable' (IV, st. 11), an observation which may be used to raise hope as well as to console for the loss of hope. Chaucer also allows Arcite that sentiment initially:

> Wel hath Fortune yturned thee the dys . . .
> For possible is . . .
> That by som cas, syn Fortune is chaungeable,
> Thow maist to thy desir somtyme atteyne . . .
>
> (ll. 1238–43)

But only here is it given a recognizably Boethian development. Chaucer's own translation of the *Consolatio Philosophiae* conveniently 'places' the content of Arcite's speech, which uses Boethian ideas in a limited way, with purely local point, but not in a totally improper or untruthful way. Following the line taken by Boccaccio's characters, Arcite still sets store by the thought that Fortune may eventually reward the unbanished Palamon. If, of course, he were well advanced along the path of Boethian consolation he would not only accept that 'alle fortune (is) good, the whiche fortune is certeyn that it be either ryghtful or elles profitable . . .',[3] but he would also have a different concept of what constitutes ultimate happiness, seeing that

> the unstablenesse of fortune may nat atayne to resceyven verray blisful-
> nesse . . .
>
> (*Boece*, Bk. II, pr. 4, ll. 148–9)

[148] He is, however, a character involved in a romance of love and war, and such insights could hardly by expected at that stage of the narrative. His lament over the wilful discontent of man, and his ill-judged efforts to change the appointed course of events are Boethian in expression:

> Allas! why pleynen folk so in commune
> On purveiaunce of God, or of Fortune,
> That yeveth hem ful ofte in many a gyse
> Wel bettre than they kan hemself devyse?
>
> (*K. T.*, ll. 1251–4)

> Men weren wont to maken questiouns of the symplicite of the pur-
> veaunce of God, and of the ordre of destyne, and of sodeyn hap . . . Yif
> we wisten the causes why that swiche thinges bytyden, certes thei sholde
> cesen to seme wondres . . .
>
> (*Boece*, Bk. IV, pr. 6, ll. 25–7; IV, met. 5, ll. 32–6)

It is true that his applications are sometimes narrow; he is very much concerned with the recent loss and the possible restitution of creaturely happiness, and his definition of 'felicitee' remains obstinately centred upon human fulfilment. Where the lady Philosophy describes the stumbling path of the 'drunkard', man, towards 'the soverayn good' (III, pr. 2, ll. 79, 86), Arcite uses the same metaphor for man reaching out towards all kinds of lesser joys.

But the model is Boethian: Arcite's speech touches lightly and reminiscent-ly upon a whole problematic area of thought, relating to man's pursuit of false happiness, his resilience to adversity, and his difficult acceptance of divine purpose. If it does not press for exact Boethian equivalences or for identical resolutions, it associates itself unmistakeably with rich philosophic argument, and illustrates a seriousness of intent which Arcita lacks in the *Teseida*:

> Infinite harmes been in this mateere.
> We witen nat what thing we preyen heere:
> We faren as he that dronke is as a mous.
> A dronke man woot wel he hath an hous,
> But he noot which the righte wey is thider,
> And to a dronke man the wey is slider.
> [149]   And certes in this world so faren we;
> We seken faste after felicitee,
> But we goon wrong ful often, trewely.
>
> (*K. T.*, ll. 1259–67)

In strict Boethian terms, Arcite is only partially in command of the truth: in terms of the character which Chaucer received from Boccaccio, he is im-pressively and newly aware of significances, echoing the Lady Philosophy in some of her best statements:

> God, whan he hath byholden from the hye tour of his purveaunce . . .
> dooth swich thing, of which thing unknowynge folk ben astonyd . . .
>
> (*Boece*, Bk. IV, pr. 6, ll. 217–24)

Such an enlargement of the original subject of 'Fortune' was no doubt suggested to Chaucer by his imaginative sense of Arcite's pressing need for more help than that subject could give him in his predicament. But this introduction of the concept of divine providence may have a relevance beyond that of the local and dramatic. Chaucer was to use the *Consolatio* increasingly as the *Knight's Tale* proceeded towards its complex denouement, and here, perhaps, we have the first intimation of one special and important reason for that use. The *Consolatio* offered a wealth of materials and methods for coping with those human dilemmas of pain and belief which were beginning, even so early in Chaucer's dealings with the *Teseida*, to claim his attention. A stronger interest in the quality and causes of human suffering seems to have led him, characteristically, in two directions, neither of which, characteristically, had been fully explored by Boccaccio: towards the dra-matic presentation of bewilderment and anger in those who suffer, and towards the provision of good reason for the ending of that drama in reconciliation. What we might expect is some correlation between the lively conduct of the first, and the grave conduct of the second: as the picture of perplexed human beings and enigmatic Gods is laid in with darker, more vivid strokes, so the recourse to philosophic comment and explanation must become more urgent. Chaucer would not have had such need to augment Boccaccio's scattered and somewhat formal references to the power and operation of Fortune if he had not already committed himself to heightening Boccaccio's description of the [150] wretched and persecuted life of man on earth. And as far as the whole poem is concerned, 'correlation' will be of over-riding importance: the power of the human drama should be adjusted to the power of the philosophical solution, and just as the first should not raise unanswerable questions so the second should not uncomfortably suggest answers that undermine the very nature of the narrative.

It is easy to see that a poet of Chaucer's particular talent might well be tempted to exploit the dramatic at the expense of other elements less responsive to imaginative treatment. What is also important to recognize is that there could be dangers in an enthusiastic plundering of the *Consolatio*, a treatise ultimately designed to aid in the rejection of worldly preoccupations and values, for a story which was so focused upon success and failure of a worldly kind. Nothing could, in terms of the medieval contract between poet and source-narrative, prevent the final rededication of the *Knight's Tale* to mundane happiness: it must end in a wedding, not in a death. Chaucer's introduction of Boethian materials of consolation into his version of Boccaccio's poem took, therefore, certain risks: it risked their being found inadequate to deal with newly dominant themes, and unsuitable to comment upon the basic and unalterable narrative.

There are also, however, the Boethian materials of complaint to consider: the *Consolatio* offered a model for the expression of human scepticism and anger as well as for the expression of magisterial wisdom and penitent acceptance. Chaucer availed himself of both, using the Boethian complaint as a means of reinforcing and extending that which he received from Boccaccio as a narrative motif, and had already begun to shape anew: the exercise of absolute authority by the gods, and the pattern of justice and injustice meted out to men. If Arcite was given some of Lady Philosophy's words to re-express, Palamon was given in his turn those of Boethius himself, culpable, and impassioned:

O thou governour, governynge alle thynges by certein ende, whi refusestow oonly to governe the werkes of men by duwe manere? Why suffrestow that slydynge Fortune turneth so grete enterchaungynges of thynges; so that anoyous peyne, that scholde duweliche punysche felons, punysscheth innocentz? ...

[151] O thou, what so evere thou be that knyttest all boondes of thynges, loke on thise wrecchide erthes.

(*Boece*, Bk. I, metre 5, ll. 31–7, 49–52)

But while it is true that Palamon's outburst—'... O crueel goddes that governe / This world with byndying of youre word eterne ...' (ll. 1303–4)

—is loosely based upon this passage from the *Consolatio*, it is altered very considerably, both in direction and in content. Whereas the *Consolatio*, by its very debate-structure, is able to control the effect of such a complaint, and reveal it clearly and immediately as an error of human understanding,

> Whan I hadde, with a contynuel sorwe, sobbyd or borken out thise thynges, sche, with her cheere pesible, and nothyng amoeved with my compleyntes, seide thus . . .
>
> (*Boece*, Bk. I, pr. 5, ll. 1–4)

the English poem, already diversely inclined to attitudes both sympathetic and bracing, has no similar power. Palamon's speech, with some of its materials Boethian, takes some colouring from the straightforward statements of the Italian about the 'ancient enmity' of the gods. The tone of Boethius in his appeal is sad, regretful: the tone of Palamon in his is angry, resentful—a heightening of emotions intimated, at least, in the *Teseida's* phrases, 'la malizia / dello' nfortunio', 'antica nimistate / serva Giunon ver noi', 'il furor di Iunone' (III, st. 3, 66, 1). The new note is struck in 'O crueel goddes', as compared with 'O thou governour', and sustained in the far more emphatic and concrete line 'that governe / This world with byndyng of youre worde eterne'. The vocabulary is bitter and pungent—'table of atthamaunt', 'rouketh', 'slayn', 'prisoun', 'siknesse'—where that of the treatise is melancholy—'slydynge Fortune', 'anoyous peyne', 'fraude', 'fals colour', 'dreden'. The questions asked are direct and desperate with their new application of the Boethian concept of man as a 'divyne beest' to the sickening image of man as not more than butcher's victim—but a victim called upon perversely to suffer more than once.

> What is mankynde moore unto you holde
> Than is the sheep that rouketh in the folde?
> For slayn is man right as another beest,
> [152]   And dwelleth eek in prison and arreest . . .
> And whan a beest is deed, he hath no peyne;
> But man after his deeth moot wepe and pleyne . . .
>
> (ll. 1307–20)

No doubt Chaucer was remembering the lament of Boethius, 'we men, that ben noght a foul partie, but a faire partie of so greet a werk, we ben turmented in this see of fortune' (Bk. I, metre 5, ll. 52–4). His telling compression of the original ideas, however, and his weighted, emphatic language make Palamon's challenge much more difficult to dispose of in a context which is, in any case, morally ambiguous:

> What governance is in this prescience,
> That giltelees tormenteth innocence?
>
> (ll. 1313–14)

Just how potent such 'ambiguity' is in our judgement of the nature of the speech may be illustrated simply by those lines which refer to the divine powers. Chaucer's substitution of 'crueel goddes' for 'governour' has always been noticed as an adaptation of the *Consolatio* to the 'classical setting of the tale.'[4] The 'cruel gods', addressed generally in the opening words, are then specified at the close of the speech as Saturn, Juno, and Venus:

> But I moot been in prisoun thurgh Saturne
> And eek thurgh Juno, jalous and eek wood . . .
> And Venus sleeth me on that other syde
> For jalousie and fere of hym Arcite.

(ll. 1328–33)

Boethius has been merged with Boccaccio, to provide an attack upon the pagan deities, with their wanton malice—an attitude which also inspires Chaucer's dismissive stanza at the end of another poem, based upon Boccaccio's work—*Troilus and Criseyde*:

> Lo here, of payens corsed olde rites,
> Lo here, what alle hire goddes may availle . . .

(v. 1849–50)

But in the very centre of the speech, Chaucer allows Palamon to mention 'God' in terms that would be generally acceptable [153] as Boethian or Christian:

> And yet encresseth this al my penaunce,
> That man is bounden to his observaunce,
> *For Goddes sake,* to letten of his wille
> Ther as a beest may al his lust fulfille . . .

(ll. 1315–18)

In other words, man, in obedience to God, is bound to observe moral laws, and restrain the promptings of his will. Are we, then to accept Palamon's protests as legitimate in their literary-historical setting but illegitimate in the sense that their Boethian model is designed to be self-evidently fallible? The inconsistency of reference to the 'deities' or the 'Deity' makes, on the one hand, for uncertainty about this; on the other, it makes for an interesting 'open-ended' situation, in which we may begin to think that the poet is motivated less by moral considerations than by the desire to give a favoured theme full, dramatic, and imaginative scope. Palamon's protest reaches for the most effective weapons of vocabulary and argument, without precisely imitating them in their original context, and without hesitating to barb them further. Thus Boccaccio's description of Juno's 'long-harboured enmity', 'antica nimistate', of her 'perverse wrongs', 'perversi mali' done to Thebes (III, st. 66), is given a new seriousness as an accusation against a formidable triad, Saturn, Juno, and Venus. The cruelty of the gods, frequently stated but not lengthily dwelt upon in the Italian, is expounded with the help of persuasive rhetoric and concepts drawn powerfully, if rather ruthlessly, from a distinguished philosophical treatise.

And at the same time the incomplete transposition of materials into a 'classical' format guarantees that the problems are not sealed off as parts of a historically distanced narrative. Subtler ingredients, of a medieval Christian flavour, are suggested in the lines which speak of man impelled 'for Goddes sake' to the control of his basic instincts. It is not only the play of fear and anger which we notice in this passage, as Palamon confronts the effective actions of Juno and Saturn: it is also the working, though from an orthodox Christian viewpoint the imperfect working, of the reason and the conscience. This juxtaposition of widely differing motives and emotions within one [154] loosely-structured whole makes Palamon's 'arguments' so difficult to judge, but so easy to admire. He cannot be condemned out of hand on 'Boethian', or medieval Christian grounds, for his wilful misunderstanding of divine purpose: the firmness of his ground for complaint against the gods is only too well substantiated by the narrative, and by Chaucer's own decisive highlighting of that narrative. On the other hand, Palamon cannot be set aside, as one quite limited by his historical circumstances to nothing but stoic acceptance of the irrational and often cruel interventions of deities such as Juno, Venus, and Saturn in the lives of men. The speech is as forthcoming in dramatic appeal as it is resistant to logical analysis.

And although Chaucer, in the guise of his pilgrim-narrator, agrees to 'stynte of Palamon a lite' (l. 1334), drawing back somewhat from this painful contact with his indignation and misery, even to the extent of inviting the listener or reader to pronounce judiciously upon 'who hath the worse, Arcite or Palamoun?' (l. 1348), the poem never really manages to shrug off the consequences of its full involvement in the theme of 'prescience / that giltelees tormenteth innocence'. Nor are there many signs that Chaucer struggled hard to do so: indeed, he continued to increase the part played by the gods in the story—introducing 'the wynged god Mercurie' to direct Arcite back to Athens and ultimately to his death:

> ... To Atthenes shaltou wende,
> Ther is thee shapen of thy wo an ende ...
>
> (*K. T.*, ll. 1391–2)

Arcite's response is humanly courageous, and, in spite of its brave rhetoric, humanly unsuspecting of the deeper ironies of the god's words:

> ... to Atthenes right now wol I fare,
> Ne for the drede of deeth shal I nat spare
> To se my lady, that I love and serve.
> In hire presence I recche nat to sterve ...
>
> (*K. T.*, ll. 1395–8)

Similarly, the soliloquy of Arcite which Palamon, escaped from prison, overhears is shaped afresh, with special emphasis, not present in the equivalent Italian,[5] upon the malicious role of [155] the gods in the fortunes of the two knights:

How longe, Juno, thurgh thy crueltee,
Woltow werreyen Thebes the citee? ...
And yet dooth Juno me wel moore shame,
For I dar noght biknowe myn owene name ...
Allas, thou felle Mars! allas Juno!
Thus hath youre ire oure lynage al fordo ...

(K. T., ll. 1543–4; 1555–6; 1559–60)

It is in this general direction that Chaucer's presentation of the temples of the gods, in which the lovers make their separate prayers, differs so crucially from that of Boccaccio. With regard to the temple of Venus, we have already seen how, in the earlier *Parlement of Foules,* Chaucer is capable, even anxious, to preserve as much as possible of the Italian *matiere* and *sens*.[6] Here, the situation is quite different. The temple of love is briskly, almost mechanically described; the nature of the passion inspired by Venus is conveyed solely in terms of formal art—gone is the scented garden, except as a brief reference in a painted landscape, gone are the moving tableaux of beauty, danger, and delight which engaged the poet of the *Parlement*:

And by hymself, under an ok, I gesse,
Saw I Delyt, that stod with Gentilesse.
I saw Beute, withouten any atyr,
And Youthe, ful of game and jolyte,
Foolhardynesse, Flaterye and Desyr ...

(P. F., ll. 223–7)

The zestful poetry of the dream-vision, with its flickering half-lights of pleasure and fear, is replaced by poetic cataloguing which brings out, in the most unambiguous manner, the stark pain of the reign of Venus:

First in the temple of Venus maystow se
Wroght on the wal, ful pitous to biholde,
The broken slepes, and the sikes colde,
The sacred teeris, and the waymentynge,
The firy strokes of the desirynge
That loves servantz in this lyf enduren;
The othes that hir covenantz assuren;
Plesaunce and Hope, Desir, Foolhardynesse,
[156]   Beautee and Youthe, Bauderie, Richesse,
Charmes and Force, Lesynges, Flaterye,
Despense, Bisynesse, and Jalousye.

(K. T., ll. 1918–28)

The summary words in which the garden of love is designated as a landscape-background—

... al the mount of Citheroun ...
Was shewed on the wal in portreyynge,

> With al the gardyn and the lustynesse.
> Nat was foryeten the porter, Ydelnesse ...
>
> (*K. T.*, ll. 1936, 1938–40)

measure the distance between this poem and the *Parlement*. The stress is entirely different: Venus has become a goddess of power only—her forces are drawn up against beauty and riches, she is implacable and inescapable:

> Thus may ye seen that wysdom ne richesse,
> Beautee ne sleighte, strengthe ne hardynesse,
> Ne may with Venus holde champartie ...
>
> (*K. T.*, ll. 1947–9)

In the *Parlement of Foules* Venus and Richesse are at one, 'in disport', while Beauty walks outside, in the garden (ll. 260, 225).

And symptomatic of the changed nature of Chaucer's interests in the *Knight's Tale* is the appearance of the Goddess herself as a statue, not as Boccaccio's half-naked woman:

> ... e vide lei nuda giacere
> Sopr'un gran letto assai bello a vedere.
>
> (*Teseida*, VII, st. 64)

She saw her reclining naked on a huge bed that was very beautiful to see.

The Venus of the *Knight's Tale* is impeccable, from the point of view of medieval iconography: half-risen from the sea, garlanded with the roses of love, attended by doves, and by her blind son, Cupid. She only departs from accepted tradition by carrying a cittern instead of a shell.[7] But nothing disturbs the hard image of glittering dominion:

> The statue of Venus, glorious for to se,
> Was naked fletynge in the large see,
> [157]   And fro the navele doun al covered was
> With wawes grene, and brighte as any glas ...
>
> (ll. 1955–8)

For all her 'glory', Venus here is not unrecognizable as the 'deere doghter' of the vengeful god, Saturn; aggression, not seduction, is the key-note of the passage, which closes with 'arwes brighte and kene', not with the languid fruits of love.

> Biforn hire stood hir sone Cupido;
> Upon his schuldres wynges hadde he two,
> And blynd he was, as it is often seene;
> A bowe he bar and arwes brighte and kene.
>
> (ll. 1963–6)

As might be expected, the temple of Mars is treated with explosive violence. Boccaccio's account, although of a 'cruel place', 'il luogo rio' (VII, st. 32), is dominated to a great extent by the poet's admiration, expressed through the medium of Arcita's Prayer, for the forcefulness of his subject, rather than by his revulsion from its evil implications. The 'lofty struggles of Mars' are as much the theme here as the 'infortune of Marte' (*K. T.*, l. 2021) is the equivalent theme of Chaucer's adaptation. As in the temple of Venus, the expert quality of the painting—'da sottil mano', 'with cunning hand' (VII, st. 36)—recommends itself: more startlingly here, since the pictures are of humanity wasted by war—

> ... e qualunque sforzato
> fu, era quivi in abito musorno ...
>
> (*Teseida*, VII, st. 36)

Whatever was won by force appeared there in sombre form.

The whole temple had been built by 'skilful Mulciber, with (all) his art ...', 'Mulcifero sottil, con la sua arte' (VII, st. 38). Moreover, it is worth noticing that most of the qualities and characteristics of the 'religion' of Mars are expressed as allegorical temple-figures, in gestured tableaux:

> E con gli occulti ferri i Tradimenti
> vide, e le 'nsidie con giusta apparenza;
> lì Discordia sedea e sanguinenti
> ferri avea in mano, e ogni Differenza.
>
> (*Teseida*, VII, st. 34)

[158] And she saw there Betrayals with their hidden weapons, and Plots with honest faces; Discord sat with bloodstained swords in hand, and every kind of Strife.

The epithet 'l'allegro', for 'Furore', 'lively, vivacious Fury' (st. 35), illustrates the easy way in which horror can be temporarily accepted as visually interesting; the altars, burning with the fires of war, are 'luminoso', 'shining, bright' (st. 35), and become even brighter, 'più chiaro' (st. 40), with the arrival of the god himself. The earth gives off wonderful scents, 'e diè la terra mirabile odore', and the armour of the statue of Mars moved 'with a sweet sound', 'le cui armi risonaro / tutte in sé mosse con dolce romore ...' (st. 40). The attitudes of Boccaccio to his materials are, in this whole sequence, from a moral viewpoint, extremely fluid. Pity and revulsion are contributory elements; dominant always, however, is an appreciative sense of the power of the God and of his activities which may not be identified precisely as admiration, but which comes very close to that emotion.

Chaucer's handling of the Italian here seems to be characterized partly by a greater reserve, and partly by a greater determination. On the one hand, he seems reluctant to imitate Boccaccio in his relish for the landscape and the temple of Mars: on the other hand, he seems anxious to channel and direct the description in the service of one particular theme. This becomes very clear in his adaptation of the Martian landscape of Thrace—a landscape real in the *Teseida*, painted in the *Knight's Tale*. It is not only the difference between art and reality which matters here; in any case, for reasons much debated by

Chaucerian commentators, Chaucer appears to hover between the two in the detail of his description. The narrator appears to *visit* the painted forest, *hear* the ominous storm tossing the trees and the angry clangour in the temple itself:

> First on the wal was peynted a forest,
> In which ther dwelleth neither man ne best,
> With knotty, knarry, bareyne trees olde,
> Of stubbes sharpe and hidouse to biholde,
> In which ther ran a rumbel in a swough,
> As though a storm sholde bresten every bough.
> And dounward from an hille, under a bente,
> Ther stood the temple of Mars armypotente,
> [159]   Wroght al of burned steel, of which the entree
> Was long and streit, and gastly for to see.
> And therout came a rage and swich a veze
> That it made al the gate for to rese.
> The northren lyght in at the dores shoon,
> For wyndowe on the wal ne was ther noon,
> Thurgh which men myghten any light discerne.
> The dore was al of adamant eterne,
> Yclenched overthwart and endelong
> With iren tough; and for to make it strong,
> Every pyler, the temple to sustene,
> Was tonne-greet, of iren bright and shene.
>
> (ll. 1975–94)

Boccaccio's text is very systematic here, making precise distinctions between the real landscape outside, the 'insane and violent creatures', 'l'Impeti dementi', Sin, Anger, Treachery, and Deception (st. 33), who inhabit the temple, and the paintings of conquered peoples upon its walls. It would not be wise to conclude too hastily, as some have done,[8] that Chaucer was turning back to the ultimate source of Boccaccio's account in the *Thebaid* of Statius, where there is a more dramatic movement between the phenomena of real-life and art:

> terrarum exuviae circum, et fastigia templi
> captae insignibant gentes, caelataque ferro
> fragmina portarum bellatricesque carinae,
> et vacui currus protritaque curribus ora,
> paene etiam gemitus : adeo vis omnis et omne
> vulnus. ubique ipsum, sed non usquam ore remisso
> cernere erat : talem divina Mulciber arte
> ediderat.[9]

All around were spoils of every land, and captured peoples adorned the temple's high front, and fragments of iron-wrought gates and ships of war and empty chariots and faces ground by chariot-wheels, ay, almost even their groans! truly every form of violence and wounds. Himself was everywhere to behold, but nowhere with softened looks; in such wise had Mulciber with divine skill portrayed him.

His reading of Latin, which was never expert, may not have included the *Thebaid,* and it is far more likely that his presentation is an inconsistent reshaping of Boccaccio's Italian: the decision to transform a real landscape and location into a painting on a temple wall is only intermittently observed. [160] It remains true, however, that Chaucer's rejection of Boccaccio's winter scene in Thrace, which has a severe beauty of its own—

> ne' campi trazii, sotto i cieli iberni,
> da tempesta continua agitati,
> dove schiere di nimbi sempiterni
> da' venti or qua e or là trasmutati
> in varii luoghi ne' guazzosi verni,
> e d'acqua globi per freddo agroppati
> gittati sono, e neve tuttavia
> che 'n ghiaccio a mano a man s'indura e cria . . .
>
> (VII, st. 30)

. . . on the Thracian plains, under wintry skies, torn by continual tempests, where ranks of perpetual cloud are blown here and there in stormy winters, and water-drops freeze as they fall, and snow too, that gradually hardens and turns to ice.

and his concentration, instead, upon the 'selva steril di robusti / cerri', 'forest of barren and massive oaks' (st. 31), which shrouds the temple of Mars, betrays much more than a rather formal taste in landscape-description. There is a terrible grandeur in Boccaccio's snow-swept Thracian plains, just as there is grandeur, too, in his whole concept of Mars and his domain— elements which Chaucer might understandably have found less appropriate to his changed purposes. For it is a narrow, more single-toned interpretation which he offers of all the gods, but in particular, of Mars: not his "lofty struggles", but his ugly omnipotence, to be focused in the temple statue—

> The statue of Mars upon a carte stood
> Armed, and looked grym as he were wood . . .
> A wolf ther stood biforn hym at his feet
> With eyen rede, and of a man he eet.
>
> (*K. T.,* ll. 2041–2, 2047–8)

Predictably, then, the extensive winter-scene is reduced to the 'colde frosty regioun' (l. 1973) and Boccaccio's gnarled forest, cut off significantly from pastoral life, 'né v'era bestia alcuna né pastore . . .' (st. 31), becomes Chaucer's sole exemplar. His alterations are slight, but significant, in that they establish a claustrophobic and threatening sense of evil which is never, afterwards, relieved: Boccaccio's furies, weaving among the [161] trees 'with loud clamour', 'grandissimo romore' (st. 31) are replaced by an undefined,

tempestuous thunder—'As though a storm sholde bresten every bough ...'
(1. 1980). Boccaccio's temple of clear-burnished steel, reflecting the sun,
though indirectly,

> tutta d'acciaio splendido e pulio,
> dal quale era dal sol riverberata
> la luce ...
>
> (st. 32)

shines more darkly in Chaucer's version; the single epithet in 'Wroght al of
burned steel' (1. 1983) does not produce the same effect as the Italian 'splendi-
do e pulio'. Only the iron supporting pillars are 'bright and shene' (1. 1994);
only cold 'northern light' (1. 1987) penetrates, through a tunnel-like entrance.
Even the expansion of Boccaccio's 'la stretta entrata', 'the narrow entrance'
(st. 32), to 'the entree / Was long and streit' (ll. 1983–4) helps to enforce this
impression of a dark cave, or tomb, reached through a cramped passage,
down which the fierce winds of violence desolately blow:

> And therout came a rage and swich a veze
> That it made al the gate for to rese.
>
> (ll. 1985–6)

The extent of Chaucer's involvement with what Mars signifies, in every
part of human life, may perhaps be judged from the vivid and direct use of
the formula 'I saugh' (ll. 1995, 2011, etc.) for the account of the inside of the
temple. Suggested, probably, by the 'videvi' (st. 35, 37, etc.) of the Italian
which introduces the spectacle confronting the personified Prayer of Arcite as
she reaches the goal of her journey, it is likely to be an indication that, in his
excited enlargement of the theme of human disaster, Chaucer loses touch
with the fiction of Knight-narrator (a fiction never particularly strong for
him) and writes more personally. The catalogue, whether of images or of
paintings, is relentlessly thorough, and, where Boccaccio's description had
been vivid, even melodramatic, this is chilling both in its exactness and in its
resonance. The detail, which Chaucer only occasionally remembers as detail
in a *painted* [162] temple, refers in a precise and agile fashion to the conceptual
basis of violence—

> Ther saugh I first the derke ymaginyng
> Of Felonye, and al the compassyng ...
>
> (ll. 1995–6)

to its everyday manifestations in the life of man—

> The careyne in the busk, with throte ycorve;
> A thousand slayn, and nat of qualm ystorve ...
>
> (ll. 2013–14)

to the traditional figures of allegory, which define its component parts—

> The crueel Ire, reed as any gleede ...
> Contek, with blody knyf and sharp manace ...

> Yet saugh I Woodnesse, laughynge in his rage,
> Armed Compleint, Outhees, and fiers Outrage . . .
>
> (ll. 1997, 2003, 2011–12)

and some of its most famous victims in history—

> . . . the slaughtre of Julius,
> Of grete Nero, and of Antonius.
>
> (ll. 2031–2)

This variousness of reference is the key to the nature of the passage: whatever literary, astrological, and iconographical sources Chaucer had for his expansion of the Italian,[10] the final impression is, in one word, disturbing. The impact of the decor of Boccaccio's temple is strong, but distanced slightly by the fact that the aggressive pageant is displayed either in terms of formal allegory—

> Videvi ancora l'allegro Furore,
> e oltre a ciò con volto sanguinoso
> la Morte armata vide e lo Stupore
>
> (VII, st. 35)

She saw quick Fury also, as well as armed Death with bloody face, and Stupefaction

or, when the actors are human, in terms of group-activity—

> [163]
> . . . e qualunque sforzato
> fu, era quivi in abito musorno;
> vedeanvisi le genti incatenate,
> porti di ferro e fortezze spezzate
>
> (VII, st. 36)

Whatever was won by force appeared there in sombre form; there were to be seen people in chains, iron gates, and shattered fortresses.

The stress is on quantity rather than specific quality—'ogni forza con gli aspetti elati', 'every kind of violence with elated looks . . .' (st. 37); 'ognifedita', 'every kind of wound' (st. 37). The image of Mars appears 'everywhere', 'in ogni luogo'. Rarely, in Boccaccio's recital, are we stabbed with any special sense of the pity of violence as it erupts into the life of the individual, nor is our attention invited by the ugliness of death and destruction as it occurs in a personal, even domestic context:

> The shepne brennynge with the blake smoke;
> The tresoun of the mordrynge in the bedde . . .
> The nayl ydryven in the shode a-nyght;
> The colde deeth, with mouth gapyng upright . . .
>
> (ll. 2000–1, 2007–8)

Chaucer's inclusion of so many images of casual horror in this cavalcade dedicated to Mars—the dead hunter, the mauled child, the scalded cook—

juxtaposing them with more conventional images of martial activity—the strewn battlefield, the ravaged city, the victorious tyrant—curiously webs the heroic with the pathetic. The general effect of the passage is to stress, once more, man's helplessness whether he win or lose in the service of Mars. Even the high accolade of triumph in battle may be succeeded by the accolade of death; conquest is always at risk—'With the sharpe swerd over his heed / Hangynge by a soutil twynes threed' (ll. 2029–30). There is, here, a sad and obvious reference to the coming fate of Arcite, who will conquer but die, and who has already expressed the peril of man's situation in a line which owes something to Boethius but much more to the poet's apprehension of a mystery,

> Infinite harmes been in this mateere.
>
> (l. 1259)

Apart from this, there is the more general melancholy conclusion that this desperate review of human affairs, which lays [164] much more stress upon the suffering of victims, is all that can be mustered 'in redoutynge of Mars and of his glorie' (l. 2050). It may be true, indeed, that Chaucer has decided to widen the scope of his Martian panorama by drawing upon the kind of incident associated with the 'children of Mars' in medieval astrological tradition as well as upon the detail of his Italian source.[11] The record of every-day disasters, the listing of the 'trades of Mars'—

> The barbour, and the bocher, and the smyth
>
> (l. 2025)

look forward to the live *genre*-scenes of fifteenth-century art, in which humanity, aggressive, oppressed, industrious, creative, acts out life as dictated by the power of the planetary deities.[12] But this does not explain, in any very simple way, why Chaucer felt the necessity to supplement Boccaccio, obscuring the heroic contours and shading in the misery of the inhabited landscape. Nor does it explain the precise and vivid language in which misery makes itself felt—

> The careyne in the busk, with throte ycorve . . .
>
> (l. 2013)

nor the insistent probing of misery to come at its hidden fibres, its small, painful incongruities:

> The hunte strangled with the wilde beres;
> The sowe freten the child right in the cradel;
> The cook yscalded, for al his longe ladel.
> Noght was foryeten by the infortune of Marte
> The cartere overryden with his carte:
> Under the wheel ful lowe he lay adoun.
>
> (ll. 2018–23)

But it is quite evident, when the statue of Mars comes to be presented, in its full iconographic state—

> This god of armes was arrayed thus:
> A wolf ther stood biforn hym at his feet
> With eyen rede, and of a man he eet . . .
>
> (ll. 2046–8)

that Chaucer felt the need to demonstrate, more strongly than Boccaccio had done, the unmotivated savagery which was an [165] inevitable part of the glory of Mars. When Boccaccio mentions the images of Mars set about his temple, they are, it is true, of 'aspetto fiero', of 'fierce expression' (st. 37): even here, however, Chaucer builds upon the Italian, stressing the unbridled passion of the God—

> Armed, and looked grym as he were wood.
>
> (l. 2042)

It is not surprising that the 'sweet sound' with which the armour of the altar-image of Mars eventually signalled victory to Boccaccio's Arcita—

> . . . le cui armi risonaro
> tutte in sé mosse con dolce romore . . .
>
> (*Teseida*, VII, st. 40)

Whose armour rang with a sweet sound as it moved

finds no place in the sinister reverberation of the English version:

> . . . and atte laste
> The statue of Mars bigan his hauberk rynge;
> And with that soun he herde a murmurynge
> Ful lowe and dym, and seyde thus, 'Victorie!'
>
> (ll. 2430–3)

Even the different ordering of material may be significant here. In the *Teseida*, the prayers of Arcita, Palemone, and Emilia are made to Mars, Venus and Diana in that order, and the temple-descriptions follow suit. Only slight reference is made to the strife in heaven caused by the conflicting claims of the three human beings, and that reference is obscurely placed, between the account of the temple of Venus, and Emilia's sacrifice:

> e sì ne nacque in ciel novella lite
> intra Venere e Marte; ma trovata
> da lor fu via con maestrevol arte
> di far contenti i prieghi d'ogni parte
>
> (VII, st. 67)

and thus once more a new quarrel broke out in heaven between Venus and Mars; but with masterly skill they were to find a way of fulfilling the prayers of both parties.

[166] If there is irony in the Italian, it is faintly heard.

But the sequential changes made by Chaucer reveal more fully, and more ruthlessly, the ironies embedded in this narrative: the whole third section of his poem, dealing with the temples and the petitions, works to a crescendo of emotion, which does not reach its climax until the great concluding speech in heaven by 'pale Saturnus the colde ...' (l. 2443). Twice Chaucer alters Boccaccio's sequence of events. In the first place his account of the temples moves from the 'oratorie' of Venus to those of Mars and Diana, both of which, in their different ways, have the power to realize that violence which is only implied in the worship of love. Violence runs like a thread of variable thickness through the descriptions; if it is the subdued theme of the decorations in the place of love—

> Lo, alle thise folk so caught were in hir las,
> Til they for wo ful ofte seyde 'allas'!
>
> (ll. 1951–2)

it is openly displayed by the murals in the temples of Mars and Diana, the menacing god, the avenging goddess:

> Ther saugh I Attheon an hert ymaked,
> For vengeaunce that he saugh Diane al naked;
> I saugh how that his houndes have hym caught
> And freeten hym, for that they knewe hym naught ...
>
> (ll. 2065–8)

Then further, as if to intensify such a process, the three sacrifices to the gods are made in the order of Palamon to Venus, Emelye to Diana, and Arcite to Mars. The effect of this is to strengthen the impression of growing disaster, as the three human beings go about their votive rites only dimly conscious of how they illustrate the truth of Arcite's earlier comment—

> We witen nat what thing we preyen heere ...
>
> (l. 1260)

As they receive portents, they are pathetically unaware of the doubleness of their significance; only Emelye, now placed importantly between Palamon and Arcite, is given clear intimation that her suit cannot be granted. And whereas Boccaccio's [167] heroine quickly becomes resigned to discovering which of the two knights she is destined to marry—

> e la mia volontà, ch'è ora mista,
> dell' una parte si farà parente! ...
>
> (*Teseida*, VII, st. 87)

for my desire, which is undecided at the moment, will become fixed upon one of them! ...

Chaucer's heroine is presented as a creature terrified before the signs of divine recognition. Drops of blood ooze from the wood on the altar-fires, with a strange whistling noise not mentioned by Boccaccio; the goddess herself appears, bow in hand, not delegating her message to her 'chorus of Virgins' as in the Italian (st. 88); her words, unlike theirs, are stern, unequivocal—

> Among the goddes hye it is affermed,
> And by eterne word writen and confermed,
> Thou shalt ben wedded ...

(K. T., ll. 2349–51)

And she vanishes, not to the sound of barking dogs and hunting-horns, but to the sound of clattering arrows—

> ... the arwes in the caas
> of the goddesse clateren faste and rynge,
> And forth she wente ...

(ll. 2358–60)

The 'aventure of love' which she is promised, and which she does not desire, comes like a harsh conquest.

Conquest is, indeed what Arcite's prayer confirms; he and his god are to use force to win love:

> And wel I woot, er she me mercy heete,
> I moot with strengthe wynne hire in the place.

(ll. 2398–9)

The tension of the episode mounts when Arcite is granted his 'victorie', but in a context far more ominous than Boccaccio had thought necessary. The fact that the Theban does not now seem to suspect that anything but happiness may attend his victory, and goes to his lodging 'as fayn as fowel is of the brighte [168] sonne' (l. 2437), gives no real relief to the situation; it is a grim comment upon the inability of man to deal with the secret workings of the gods, and serves as a tense introduction to the council in heaven which follows. And that council provides the definitive statement to which this whole section of the poem has been tending; Saturn is invoked to expound his nature and his powers in defence of his granddaughter, Venus:

> I am thyn aiel, redy at thy wille;
> Weep now namoore, I wol thy lust fulfille.

(ll. 2477–8)

And so, finally, departing radically from his Italian original, Chaucer shows us the goddess of love sponsored by forces quite as deadly as those appropriate to Mars, the 'stierne god armypotente' (l. 2441); no part of the divine plan, whatever god is concerned, operates without pain for humanity. Saturn, on behalf of Venus, is implacable:

> 'My deere doghter Venus', quod Saturne,
> 'My cours, that hath so wyde for to turne,
> Hath moore power than woot any man.
> Myn is the drenchyng in the see so wan;
> Myn is the prison in the derke cote
> Myn is the stranglyng and hangyng by the throte,
> The murmure and the cherles rebellyng,

> The groynynge, and the pryvee empoysonyng;
> I do vengeance and pleyn correccioun,
> Whil I dwelle in the signe of the leoun.
> Myn is the ruyne of the hye halles,
> The fallynge of the toures and of the walles
> Upon the mynour or the carpenter.
> I slow Sampsoun, shakynge the piler;
> And myne be the maladyes colde,
> The derke tresons, and the castes olde;
> My lookyng is the fader of pestilence.'

(ll. 2453–69)

The crucial positioning of this new speech, and the high finality of its poetic rhetoric make it extremely likely that Chaucer regarded it as the culmination of many processes of thought and action: it sums up, in relentless detail, what we may long have suspected—that the "remedie" for strife will not depend upon any weighing of just dispensation, but only upon the [169] superior craft and executive power of one god over another. Peace is to be restored to Mars and Venus by recourse to the old god Saturn, the purveyor of 'vengeance and pleyn correccioun', and it is already clear that peace will involve a kind of treachery—'the derke tresons and the castes olde ...'—and violent death—'I slow Sampsoun, shakynge the piler ...'. Nothing is admirable about Saturn's recitation of his activities; it is a fearful record of disastrous intervention in human affairs, which leaves out of account, completely, that more benevolent side of Saturn's influence, traditionally exerted upon agriculture and husbandry.[13] But for all that, his proposed solution is acceptable, not only to Mars and Venus, but to his son, Jupiter, who was anxious, it is said, to end the strife—'Juppiter was bisy it to stente' (l. 2442). The stage is now set, darkly, for the concluding section of the poem, which will illustrate the outmanoeuvring of human courage and magnanimity by divine ingenuity.

In many ways, the sweeping changes made by Chaucer in the replacement of Boccaccio's fierce and bloody battle by a tournament—his strict condensation of the Italian, his elimination of divine interference in the lists, and his removal, by edict of Theseus, of battle-to-death—all work towards producing Arcite's accident as a greater shock than it appears to be in the *Teseida*. His is the only fatality, and this insists, again, upon the way in which human compassion and care have no power against the prestige-struggles of the gods. In the *Teseida*, only Venus is responsible for sending an infernal fury to cause Arcita's horse to throw him: here, in the *Knight's Tale*, it is Saturn who operates on behalf of the unhappy Venus, chagrined to see the knight of Mars victor of the tournament—

> Weep now namoore, I wol thy lust fulfille.

(l. 2478)

The fact that Arcite's fall is arranged by Saturn, not Venus, gives his drawn-out sufferings a melancholy sense of inevitability; if he is under the influence of Saturn, already announced as dispenser of disease and death, there can be no hope for him. Moreover, as Chaucer's cold, precise analysis of his internal injuries makes quite certain, the manner of his death is particularly Saturnian: in his planetary role, Saturn [170] reigns over the retentive 'virtue', or force, in man's body, and it is the domination of the retentive virtue over the expulsive which finally prevents any relief of the 'venym and corrupcioun' gathered in Arcite's shattered chest:

> Swelleth the brest of Arcite, and the soore
> Encreesseth at his herte moore and moore.
> The clothered blood, for any lechecraft,
> Corrupteth, and is in his bouk ylaft,
> That neither veyne-blood, ne ventusynge,
> Ne drynke of herbes may ben his helpynge.
> The vertu expulsif, or animal,
> Fro thilke vertu cleped natural
> Ne may the venym voyden ne expelle.
> The pipes of his longes gonne to swelle,
> And every lacerte in his brest adoun
> Is shent with venym and corrupcioun.
> Hym gayneth neither, for to gete his lif,
> Vomyt upward, ne dounward laxatif.
> Al is tobrosten thilke regioun.
>
> (ll. 2743–57)

In providing such clinical detail absent in the Italian, Chaucer enriches his theme of the painfulness of life, and the ruthlessness of divine determination. The prettier triumph for Venus may, indeed, be hinted at in Arcite's recommendation of Palamon to Emelye—

> Foryet nat Palamon, the gentil man . . .
>
> (l. 2797)

But her first dark triumph is the death-bed of Arcite, who ends, as he has begun, in sharper bewilderment than Boccaccio's Arcita at the unresolved enigma of existence:

> What is this world? What asketh men to have?
> Now with his love, now in his colde grave,
> Allone, withouten any compaignye.
>
> (ll. 2777–9)

It is not difficult to understand, at this point in the poem, why Boccaccio's conduct of the last movements of the story was [171] not perfectly satisfying to Chaucer. The tracing of the ascent of Arcita's soul

> Ver la concavità del cielo ottava
>
> (*Teseida*, XI, st. 1)

towards the concavity of the eighth sphere

the austere judgement of the blindness and folly of those who still mourn
upon earth

> e seco rise de' pianti dolenti
> della turba lernea, la vanitate
> forte dannando dell' umane genti,
> li quai, da tenebrosa cechitate . . .
>
> (XI, st. 3)

And he smiled to himself at the dolorous plaints of all the Greeks,
condemning the vanity of humankind, who live in dark and blind
ignorance.

and the long-drawn-out practicalities of the consolatory speech made by
Teseo (XII, st. 6) all presuppose a situation which demands swift acceptance
on both narrative and thematic levels. As no great complexity of issue has
arisen in the Italian, so no great ingenuity has to be expended upon the final
settlement of causes and characters; reconciliations can be achieved with a
certain briskness. Arcita is admitted to a heavenly perspective, regret dis-
solves as his history of suffering is recognized to be trivial; Teseo and his
court are persuaded of the natural propriety, even the desirability of a death
which can be seen as a victor's crown, an escape from old age, disgrace,
infirmity. Who would hesitate when asked to choose one or the other—to be
drawn

> . . . o ad oscura
> vecchiezza piena d'infiniti guai,
> e questa poi da morte più sicura
> è terminata; overo a morte, essendo
> giovani ancora e più lieti vivendo . . .
>
> (XII, st. 8)

. . . either from a dark old age full of an infinity of woes, finally
terminated by a more certain death, or to death being still young, and
living more joyfully . . .

[172] Order swiftly reasserts itself in attitudes of mind, and in rituals of
mourning and marriage. Arcita's gesture of contempt as he passes 'nel loco
che Mercurio li sortio' (XI, st. 3), Teseo's comforting and comfortable sermon on how to live happily with the certainty of death, are not unsuitable in
their context; Boccaccio has never given the reader grounds for thinking that
solutions such as these will not serve his purposes. But Chaucer may not
have been content to minimize the final impression of human suffering by
means of a plain rejection of the importance of worldly affairs: neither may
he have been content to rest his case upon the kind of stoic argument put
forward so confidently by Boccaccio's Teseo. His treatment of the poem had
driven towards a serious confrontation of human and divine; his narrative
had allowed the growth of a theme which could not so easily be disposed
of—

As flies to wanton boys are we to the gods:
They kill us for their sport . . .

The 'crueel goddes', against whose motives and actions Palamon early protests, are revealed as cruel over the course of the poem: that human protest, which should, according to the nature of its source-materials, have emerged as another example of man's 'tenebrosa cechitate', his 'dark blindness' (XI, st. 3), all too positively emerges as an example of man's sombre vision of reality. There is little in Palamon's words which the poem, with its new emphases, does not bear out. Even the bleak substitution of Mars for Mercury as the guide of Arcite's soul to its last home—'Arcite is coold, ther Mars his soule gye' (l. 2815)—reminds us as much of Palamon's first pessimistic comment upon life after death—

But man after his deeth moot wepe and pleyne,
Though in this world he have care and wo . . .

(ll. 1320–1)

as it does of the 'character' of the knightly narrator, brusquely discussing a difficult subject.[14]

In these circumstances, Chaucer may well have realized that his poem demanded more for its conclusion than Boccaccio's had done: as the gods and their intervention in human life had been strongly invoked, so that intervention must be ultimately [173] justified. It would not be enough to show Arcite reconciled to his death: there must be some sense of an over-all coherence, of an over-riding divine purpose which might make all questions either answerable, or irrelevant. And it is, of course, the effort to rise to an occasion newly created by the adaptation of the Italian work which we must wholeheartedly admire in the ending of the *Knight's Tale.* This is not to say that we must admire the method of procedure or the finished product.

Chaucer's recognition of the difficulty of what lay before him, as he reached the death of Arcite, makes itself felt in various ways. Characteristically, he begins by taking some tentative steps towards a possible solution; Arcite's speech is full of unanswered questioning, but he does call twice upon Jupiter as the guide and receiver of his soul—

And Juppiter so wys my soule gye . . .

(l. 2786)

So Juppiter have of my soule part . . .

(l. 2792)

thus anticipating, but very lightly, what Theseus is to say in his final peroration of 'Juppiter the kyng / That is prince and cause of alle thyng' (ll. 3035–6). By contrast, the comment of the narrator upon the fate of Arcite's soul is not only laconic but inconsistent:

. . . ther Mars his soule gye . . .

(l. 2815)

The subsequent account of the grief of Emelye and the Athenians is a curious mixture of sentimental, almost absent-minded writing on the behaviour of bereaved women—

> For in swich cas wommen have swich sorwe,
> Whan that hir housbondes ben from hem ago,
> That for the moore part they sorwen so,
> Or ellis fallen in swich maladye,
> That at the laste certeinly they dye . . .
>
> (ll. 2822–6)

[174] and sharp, perhaps ironic, observation on a more practical feminine approach to death:

> Why woldestow be deed . . .
> And haddest gold ynough, and Emelye?
>
> (ll. 2835–6)

The whole passage is left open to two kinds of interpretation: either Chaucer has decided, for the moment, to write "in character", giving expression to attitudes typical of the knightly speaker (a mingling of sentiment and worldly appraisal would not be out of possibility), or he is marking time while preparing for a more ambitious undertaking. In the light of other similar occasions in Chaucer's poetry,[15] the second explanation seems more likely. Exploratory, too, may be the brief statement of consolation given to 'olde fader Egeus', which tries out a simple answer to Arcite's dying question, 'What is this world?'

> 'Right as ther dyed nevere man', quod he,
> 'That he ne lyvede in erthe in som degree,
> Right so ther lyvede never man', he seyde,
> 'In al this world, that som tyme he ne deyde.
> This world nys but a thurghfare ful of wo,
> And we been pilgrymes passynge to and fro.'
>
> (ll. 2843–8)

This is the gist of one of Teseo's 'consolations' in his far longer speech from the *Teseida*:

> Così come alcun che mai non visse
> non morì mai, così si pò vedere
> ch'alcun non visse mai che non morisse.
>
> (XII, st. 6)

Just as a man who has never lived will never die, so we may see that no one who lives may escape death.

And for all the melancholy grace imparted to it by Chaucer's amplification into the pilgrimage theme, nothing could possibly disguise the fact that it is quite inadequate to come to terms with the more thoughtful, more difficult English poem. The abstracting of the statement from its original context must certainly signal the poet's intention to do more than simply translate Teseo's final reconciling words.

[175] Nothing could better mark the distance which by this time stretched between Chaucer's poem and Boccaccio's *Teseida* than the use of Boethius for the recasting of Teseo's speech. The provision of a new thirty-line preface and a later five-line insertion of material from the *Consolatio* is an act which surely registers the concern felt by Chaucer, at this stage of his work, to attempt a drawing-together of all the narrative and thematic threads of his new poetic fabric. And by beginning the speech on a high philosophic note, Chaucer encourages his readers, momentarily, to believe that, as he has engaged their interests in something more than Boccaccio's mannered tale of love and war, so he will satisfy their roused curiosity, their sense of being not simply observers but participants in a debate about the conduct of human life in a hostile universe. The first few lines seek to establish, in Boethian terms, the principle of cosmic order, the source and the nature of that force which infuses and binds all matter: the energy which drives the universe is divine love, and all is planned by divine wisdom:

> The Firste Moevere of the cause above,
> Whan he first made the faire cheyne of love,
> Greet was th' effect, and heigh was his entente.
>
> (ll. 2987–9)

But no restatement of the principle of divine order, love, and wisdom will be much help as a conclusion to this particular poem unless some attempt is made to relate it to those other 'divine principles' which seem to have been in full operation during the course of the narrative, and to those deities who have played so vivid a part in a drama principally of disorder. It is not long before it becomes clear that this will not be achieved. It gradually emerges that the speech will be in the nature of a substitution, a statement which will attempt to transcend difficulties, rather than to analyse and solve them. The brave words about 'heigh entente' and 'wise purveyaunce' are meant to redirect the reader's vision, away not only from the pain of the terrestrial drama, but also from the ignoble strife in heaven which has been, to a great extent, responsible for that pain.

Central in the process of redirection is the figure of Jupiter, who has appeared briefly in the poem—at his most prominent [176] as the hopeful one-line peacemaker in the turbulent scenes in heaven,

> . . . swich strif ther is bigonne . . .
> Bitwixe Venus, the goddesse of love,
> And Mars . . .
> That Juppiter was bisy it to stente.
>
> (ll. 2438–42)

Chaucer now begins to identify this figure with ultimate good, writing first of 'the firste moevere of the cause above', and then gradually revealing that the 'first mover' is Jupiter:

> What maketh this but Juppiter, the kyng,
> That is prince and cause of alle thyng,
> Convertynge al unto his propre welle
> From which it is dirryved, sooth to telle?
>
> (ll. 3035–8)

Indeed, Jupiter is the only member of that familiar pantheon who could possibly be brought forward to serve in such a role. But the attentive reader must surely remember that his anxiety to put an end to strife meant compliance with the dark counsels of his father Saturn, for Saturn's plans pleased everyone—

> he ful soone hath plesed every part . . .
>
> (l. 2446)

This acceptance by Jupiter of Saturn's harsh executive solutions is no less a feature of Chaucer's poem than their acceptance by Venus. And if the goddess of love is strangely served by the god of violent retribution, so too is the god of highest wisdom and justice who is not only 'prince and cause of alle thynge', but also the maker of 'the faire cheyne of love'.

It is, in fact, one of the most interesting paradoxes of the *Knight's Tale* that the Boethian sections of Theseus's speech, by which Chaucer sought so strenuously to blur the outlines of a bleak story, worked to throw an even clearer light upon its bleak nature. More questions are raised than answered by the equation of Jupiter, the anxious but passive member of the council of heaven, with the Boethian principle of cosmic power and love. Why speak of the exercise of divine love in the design of this drama, when the narrative has so openly exposed no more than the exercise of divine power and resourcefulness? [177] It is here that the relationship between Boccaccio's Italian poem and Chaucer's English poem is finally revealed as an uneasy treaty between a work of elaborate surface but of simple import, and a work of much reduced decorative substance but of markedly, even dangerously, increased thematic content. Boccaccio's poem has little to answer for at this point in its progress: the death of Arcita has a causal connection with his dedication to Mars, just as the marriage of Palemone will eventually have with his dedication to Venus. The 'malice of the gods' has been raised formally by the two Thebans as an issue but has been given limited development. The speech of Teseo needs to deal, therefore, with a situation of limited emotional significance. It has only to find solace for the pity of sudden death in vigorous and triumphant youth. Expediency can be at the very heart of its message, though it may cushion its acceptance of mutability by restating the enduring power of heroic reputation:

> e noi che ora viviam, quando piacere
> sarà di quel che'l mondo circunscrisse,
> perciò morremo: adunque sostenere
> il piacer dell' iddii lieti dobbiamo,
> poi ch' ad esso resister non possiamo.
>
> (*Teseida*, XII, st. 6)

And we who are now alive will therefore die when it shall please him who encompasses the world. Therefore we should now joyfully uphold the will of the gods, since we may not resist it.

> cioè d'alcun la morte il cui valore
> fu tanto e tal, che grazioso frutto
> di fama s'ha lasciato dietro al fiore;
> il che se ben pensassomo, al postutto
> lasciar dovremmo il misero dolore,
> e intender a vita valorosa
> che ci acquistasse fama gloriosa.

(XII, st. 12)

... the death of one whose courage was so great that the gracious fruit of fame is left after the flower (fades). Thus, if we live in faith, we should leave behind wretched misery, and devote ourselves to a life of valour which will acquire glorious fame for us ...

[178] Chaucer's poem, by contrast, has a great deal to answer for at this point: not only the pity but the justice of Arcite's death, not only the power but the motives of the gods. It is easy to see why he felt that Boccaccio's set-piece needed augmenting for a new occasion: it is not so easy to describe his methods of adjusting old and new material as both skilful and entirely scrupulous. The task of converting, through a retrospective philosophical haze, the ugly manoeuvres of the gods into dignified manifestations of a total beneficent purpose, was extremely ambitious; if Jupiter is credible in terms of the stark narrative, he is unlikely to be credible in terms of 'a thyng that parfit is and stable' (l. 3009). The pressure upon Chaucer to fresh composition is clearly felt, but the precise needs of the moment are hardly met. Having involved himself in matters far deeper than those suggested by his original, matters which required that the vision of evil, focused so particularly upon the terrible workings of Saturn, should be absorbed into a larger vision that all is ultimately good, Chaucer responds with a series of lesser statements, drawn from Boethius and Boccaccio, about the survival of the earthly generations 'by successiouns' (l. 3014), the necessity of resignation to death—

> Ther helpeth noght, al goth that ilke weye.
> Thanne may I seyn that al this thyng moot deye ...

(ll. 3033–4)

and the impractical waste of emotion in lament

> Why grucchen we? Why have we hevynesse?

(l. 3058)

The solace offered by the poem is curiously thin and formal, considering its offer of unlimited pain: even the transition, in Theseus's speech, from the grand Boethian chords of 'Greet was th' effect, and heigh was his entente' (l. 2989) to the sharper Boccaccian notes of

> Thanne is it wysdom, as it thynketh me,
> To maken vertu of necessitee,
> And take it weel that we may nat eschue . . .

(l. 3041–3)

and to the brusquely phrased finale, also Boccaccian—

> [179]   Kan he hem thank? Nay, God woot, never a deel,
> That both his soule and eek hemself offende,
> And yet they mowe hir lustes nat amende . . .

(ll. 3064–6)

reinforces the sense of a narrowing-down, not an expansion of the poem's issues. Suffering is answered, at best, by acceptance of the law of submission: no view of heaven, either Christian or pagan, is glimpsed by the suppliant. The invitation to exchange sorrow for joy in the marriage of Palamon and Emelye is a worldly argument for accepting a young hero's death, and was not nearly ambitious enough. The content and the tone of Teseo's speech, most of which Chaucer's Theseus proceeds to render fairly accurately, are no better a sequel to the events and issues of the English poem than Boethian philosophizing—nor, I would suggest, do we pass from one to the other with that sense of perfect artistic ease so often praised in studies of the *Knight's Tale.*

Chaucer provided Theseus with a speech which is not, in fact, a triumph of profound and integrated thought, and which protects itself against the charge of being called a patchwork affair by some impressive rhetorical phrasing:

> 'That same Prince and that Moevere', quod he,
> 'Hath stablissed in this wrecched world adoun
> Certeyne dayes and duracioun
> To al that is engendred in this place,
> Over the whiche day they may nat pace . . .'

(ll. 2994–8)

> 'And therefore, of his wyse purveiaunce,
> He hath so wel biset his ordinaunce,
> That speces of thynges and progressiouns
> Shullen enduren by successiouns'

(ll. 3011–14)

accompanied by the invitation to 'thanken Juppiter of al his grace' (l. 3069). But such is the memory of what has gone before that the announcement of this long-delayed union prompts relief rather than gratitude: the narrative, like the poem, exhausts itself.

In Boccaccio's *Teseida*, Chaucer seems to have discovered the material for a theme both sombre and dramatic—man's [180] confused encounter with the operation of destinal forces. Enriching that theme from his reading of Boethius and also, perhaps, from other late philosophers, he was still more strongly motivated by his feeling for the pathos of the human dilemma than by his conviction of that perfect ordering of the universe in which pathos should become irrelevant. If he was familiar with neo-platonic theory that the seemingly evil influences of planetary deities such as Saturn and Mars are only real in so far as they are brought into play by the imperfect, contradictory terrestrial world,[16] he did not allow that knowledge to dictate the emotional emphases of his poetry, nor to provide him with that great statement which might indeed have set the cruelties of the gods into a justifying context. As it is, those cruelties remain unjustified, unassimilated either into the narrative of the poem or into its stated philosophic system. For all the gravity of the language in which Theseus begins to attempt a reconciliation of suffering and happiness, Venus, Mars, and Saturn are never identifiable with the purposes of 'the Firste Moevere of the cause above' nor are their generally malignant influences properly subsumed into a benign law of life, administered by the creator of the 'faire cheyne of love', 'hym that al may gye'. Brought into harsh focus by the poet's vision of the pain for which they are responsible, they remain impressive, counselling nothing but obedience and endurance. Similarly no serenity, except perhaps that of 'all passion spent', is won through the unlikely metamorphosis, only acceptable on the most superficial verbal level, of Jupiter into "cause of all thyng", the burning fountain of creation.

The lasting satisfactions of the poem do not lie in Chaucer's search for some formal ordering, of both art and concept, which will serve to control the rich, often contradictory materials assembled from his reading of romance, astrology, medicine, and philosophy. Comprehensible as that search is in an age which was dedicated to belief in ultimate and all-embracing order, it did not draw upon Chaucer's imaginative energies to the full. The *Knight's Tale*, at its most remarkable, is an uneven work of 'sad lucidity', presenting a view of a world in which there is 'nor certitude, nor peace, nor help for pain', and expressing best not the great orthodoxies of medieval faith, but the stubborn truths of human experience. The importance of [181] this should not be underestimated. Only in certain limited contexts, and with limited emphases, did the medieval artist feel able to attend to those truths: when he did, he associated defiance, anger, despair, and doubt with a deficiency of moral strength and rarely with sensibility or intelligence. The medieval drama of protest is a religious drama, centred upon figures of unlawful rebellion and disbelief, from Lucifer to Cain, Noah's wife, Herod, and the unrepentant thief. The medieval Faustus is King Alexander, whose bid to defy his mortal destiny and scale the walls of Paradise was never more than an exemplum of vanquished pride. The *Knight's Tale* defends itself from criticism, to some extent, by preserving the form, if not the spirit, of a classical, non-Christian setting, and it comes, in the end, to rest upon conventional moral attitudes. But on the way to that ending, it allows its human beings a temporary freedom to act magnanimously and to speak movingly about their doubt of divine justice and benevolence. The fact that we can feel the power of what they say, and yet remain uncertain of Chaucer's over-all intention for his poem's meaning, still recommends the *Tale* as unusually well endowed with incentives to thought. Few other medieval poems offer us such a range of ironic reflection upon the confused nature of human affairs:

> Mind is a light which the Gods mock us with,
> To lead those false who trust it . . .

(Arnold, Empedocles and Etna)

Not only, then, for what it brings over into English of Italian pseudo-classical romance, but also for what it rejects and is stimulated to add, the *Knight's Tale* represents a major extension of the scope of medieval English poetry. Answering exactly to no particular literary genre of its time, either Italian or English, but indebted to many, it is an experimental poem of some distinction, in which we are able to see the making, not simply the confirming, of tradition.

Notes

1 For discussion of this possibility, and of the general nature of Chaucer's adaptation of the *Teseida* in the *Knight's Tale*, see Robinson's edition of Chaucer's *Works*, 2nd edn., pp. 669–70.

2 Chaucer's *Treatise on the Astrolabe*, II. 4, ll. 33–8 (*Works*, ed. Robinson, p. 551).

3 Chaucer's *Boece* (his translation of Boethius *De Consolatione Philosophiae*), Bk IV, pr. 7, ll. 12–14 (*Works*, ed. Robinson, p. 371).

4 As thus by J. A. W. Bennett, in his edition of *The Knight's Tale*, Harrap's English Classics (London, 1954), Notes, p. 118.

5 *Teseida*, Bk. IV, st. 13–14, 17, 82, 84–5.

6 See above, Chapter 5 [i.e., the previous chapter in Salter's book – ed.].

7 For a thorough discussion of this change, see Meg Twycross, *The Medieval Anadyomene: A Study in Chaucer's Mythography*, Medium Ævum monographs, n.s. I (Oxford, 1972).

8 e.g., J. A. W. Bennett, in his edition of *The Knight's Tale*, Notes, p. 131.

9 Statius, *Thebaid*, VII. 55–62; text and translation from the Loeb edition by J. H. Mozley, 2 vols. (London, 1928).

10 See Bennett's edn. of *Knight's Tale*, Notes, pp. 131–3; Walter Clyde Curry, *Chaucer and the Mediaeval Sciences* (Oxford, 1926; 2nd revised edn., New York, 1960), pp. 119–63 (esp. 121–4).

11 See Curry, *Chaucer and the Mediaeval Sciences*, pp. 123–4. For the 'children of Mars' and the incidents associated with them, see Raymond Klibansky, Erwin Panofsky, and Fritz Saxl, *Saturn and Melancholy: Studies in the history of natural philosophy, religion, and art* (London and Edinburgh, 1964), pp. 204–5.

12 See Klibansky, Panofsky, and Saxl, *Saturn and Melancholy*, pp. 205–7; also, F. Saxl, 'The Literary Sources of the "Finiguerra Planets"', *JWCI* 2 (1938), 72–4.

13 See Klibansky, Panofsky, and Saxl, *Saturn and Melancholy*, pp. 173–95.

14 An explanation suggested by Bennett, in his edition of *The Knight's Tale*, Notes, p. 144.

15 e.g., the preparation for the ending of *Troilus and Criseyde*, Bk. V, ll. 1765–1806.

16 See Dorothy Bethurum, 'Saturn in Chaucer's *Knight's Tale*', in *Chaucer und seine Zeit: Symposion für Walter F. Schirmer*, Buchreihe der Anglia Zeitschrift für Englische Philologie, vol. 14 (Tübingen: Niemeyer, 1968), pp. 149–61. See also, E. H. Gombrich, "Botticelli's Mythologies: A Study in the Neoplatonic Symbolism of his Circle", *JWCI* 8 (1945), 7–60; Jean Seznec, *La Survivance des dieux antiques*, Studies of the Warburg Institute, XI (London, 1940).

18 | The Wife of Bath and her four sisters: reflections on a woman's life in the age of Chaucer

MICHAEL M. SHEEHAN, CSB

Originally published in *Medievalia et Humanistica*, new series, 13 (1985):23–42. The original pagination is recorded within square brackets. The endnotes originally appeared on pp. 35–42. The first endnote originally appeared beneath the text on p. 23.

During the past decade many study sessions, numerous papers and collections of essays, and several monographs have been devoted to women's history in general or, more specifically, to the history of women in medieval Europe.[1] Much of this work is worthy of high praise. It is, however, not unfair to say that part of this literature suffers from a tendency to generalize: sometimes one wonders whether the notions advanced are applicable to any woman who actually lived.[2] To what extent can one write the history of "women" without further explication? In the description of attitudes, it is perhaps feasible to proceed in such general terms,[3] yet in several other areas of research, this approach is not entirely successful. There has been a tendency to forget that the study of the history of women in medieval Europe is by and large a new field of activity, one still at the stage of data collection and preliminary analysis. Much encouragement should be given to those who adopt a prosopographical approach, who seek to describe and reflect on the lives of individual women, and to those who concentrate their research on groups whose homogeneity permits the possibilities and realities of the lives of the women in question to be presented without danger of serious distortion.[4]

The second suggested approach, the analysis of homogeneous groups, will be employed in what follows, using the oldest tool of the social historian, the examination of law and its applications. In doing so, however, it is important not to fall into that error of vagueness criticized above. The intention is to identify and examine the lives of five women who will stand for groups within the three estates into which medieval authors long considered their society to be divided—those who pray, those who defend and govern, and those who work with their hands—and a fourth class, the merchants, whose importance was finally coming to be recognized. Chaucer can be of assistance in this enterprise: models are to be found in *The Canterbury Tales*, and to [24] the period of their composition—the last quarter of the fourteenth century—the following description applies.

First was the group whose law was the Common Law of England, the class that was landed and free. It extended through a wide spectrum of wealth and power, from the aristocracy, typified by Dorigen of the "Franklin's Tale", to a woman—the wife of the Yeoman, perhaps—whose husband possessed a little land and was free of the control of the manorial lord. But the Knight, whose Emily was the Dorigen of another age, was typical of that class. His wife—let us call her "Eleanor Knight"—can serve as model of the group.

Second were those women whose families provided the free burgesses, the citizens of the towns, a group that was growing in power in the period that is being examined.[5] Here, too, was a considerable spectrum of wealth and influence extending from the great merchant families down to those of the minor crafts; but all were citizens of the towns, and their lives were regulated by the customs of those towns. The Wife of Bath was one of them and, being involved in the cloth trade, enjoyed a position within the upper levels of urban society. Here it is not a question of those virtues that were especially her own and that would have propelled her to the head of any group, but of the advantages of the craft of which she was a member. She can serve as the model of the free townswoman.

Third were the women of the largest group in English society of the age, those whose rights and duties were stated in manorial custom. Two individuals can be isolated who would be typical of different classes among the peasantry. First was the wife of the Ploughman; let us call her "Joan."[6] If a little imagination is used, it is possible to say something of her. Since it was April, the heavy farm work of spring was finished, so the Ploughman could go on pilgrimage. There was still much to be done on the manor, and Joan was attending to it. She was married to a man who could afford to leave his land for a few days while he journeyed to Canterbury, who owned or had the use of a horse—not a very good one, but still a mount—and who was stoutly, if plainly, dressed. The Ploughman and his Joan can be seen as typical of the unfree peasants of some substance, tenants of a half or a whole virgate or even more, members of the group who constituted a third to a half of the village community.[7] Other members of this class had a more difficult lot. They extend from the quarter-virgator through the cottar, who held a few acres, to those nameless members of society who found a place in the village as servants or migrant workers. Within this group can be placed the Poor Widow of the "Nun's Priest's Tale," the woman who owned Chauntecleer. The opening lines of the tale make her spring into life:

> A povre wydwe, somdeel stape in age
> Was whilom dwellyng in a narwe cotage,
> Biside a grove, stondynge in a dale.

[25]
> By housbondrie of swich as God hire sente
> She foond hirself and eek hir doghtren two.
> Thre large sowes hadde she, and namo,
> Three keen, and eek a sheep that highte Malle.

A yeerd she hadde, enclosed al aboute
With stikkes, and a drye dych withoute,
In which she hadde a cok, hight Chauntecleer.[8]

Joan Ploughman lived a much easier life than did a cottar like the Poor Widow; she could be expected to live longer, and more of her children would survive.[9] Even so, in terms of their positions within their respective families, they were possessed of similar rights and bound by similar obligations: their lives were circumscribed within the custom of the manor. The Poor Widow, whom Chaucer has presented so well, can serve as the type of the peasant woman.

Fourth were the women of a similar, lowly estate, but who lived in the towns. The lives of the men and women of this group are the most difficult to describe. In London they were called "foreigns."[10] They might be English or even have been born in London itself, but they did not possess the freedom of the city, and the very word used to identify them spoke of their alienation. No class of documents describes their role in society; we meet them when their activity threatened the business enterprises of the burgesses, in pleas of debt, and when they were involved in crime. It is estimated that in London they outnumbered adult members of the citizen class by three to one.[11] This group provided the porters, the hawkers, the innkeepers, the servants, and the working men and women of many of the crafts, yet they remain the most elusive of all. The nameless women in the background of the "Cook's Tale" or of that world in which the Miller and the Pardoner were so much at home were members of this class. It will be difficult to say much of these women with certainty; perhaps the main accomplishment of this essay will have been to insist on their existence. One of them—"Rose Foreign" is a suitable name for her—can stand for her class.

The fifth group and the last to be identified, was never numerous in medieval England. They were the women who chose to change their state and become religious.[12] Women of any class could find a place within religious life; indeed, the four types who have been identified thus far might have been received as choir nuns or as lay sisters in the greater nunneries, or as sisters attached to hospitals and other charitable institutions. Choir nuns were usually drawn from the upper classes, and women of the noble and knightly families as well as those of well-to-do burgesses were the principal sources of vocations. The Prioress might well have been a relative of Eleanor Knight, although the reference to her affectations may have had a snobbish overtone, implying that the Prioress was born into a family rather lower on the scale within the free classes.

[26] The Prioress, Eleanor Knight, the Wife of Bath, the Poor Widow, and that unnamed woman of the towns whom we have called Rose Foreign will be the types to which the description that follows will refer. They have been isolated and identified because different sets of custom and law described, at least in part, the frame in which their lives developed. Before going further, however, it is important to recall that another kind of law was of general

application to all these women. For three centuries before the period under discussion, there had been a revival of speculation on man and woman and their respective roles, speculation that considered all levels of society. This was the work of theologians, philosophers, and lawyers. In time, some of their ideas came to be accepted as social norms or rules of moral guidance and, in greater or lesser degree, became enforceable regulations in the form of religious or canon law. Many of its rules were of universal application, so they touched the lives of the Poor Widow and Rose Foreign as well as the lives of their more wealthy sisters.[13] These sets of regulations were a force within medieval society pressing toward general and consistent usage, a usage that transcended differences of class.

One final distinction must be made. It makes little sense in an essay to refer to the rights and responsibilities of a woman without noticing where she is located along the path of life. Recall that in the "Prologue" to *The Canterbury Tales* there are radically different expectations of the Knight and the Squire:

> A Knyght ther was, and that a worthy man, . . .
>
> And everemoore he hadde a sovereyn prys:
> And though that he were worthy, he was wys,
> And of his port as meeke as is a mayde.[14]

In contrast to this wise, responsible, grave and rather dull man is the Squire:

> A lovyere and a lusty bacheler,
> With lokkes crulle as they were leyd in presse. . . .
>
> Embrouded was he, as it were a meede
> Al ful of fresshe floures, whyte and reede.
> Syngynge he was, or floytynge, al the day;
> He was as fressh as is the month of May.[15]

Yet, from the point of view of this presentation, the Knight and the Squire are the same person seen at different moments of a single life.

Having made all the necessary distinctions, we will examine the women of England—somewhat more than a million individuals[16] living in an area one-fifth the size of the state of Texas—in terms of the regulations that applied to them about the year 1380. They are distinguished as four typical women [27] within two traditional and one recently recognized lay groups: *bellatores*, *laboratores* and *mercatores*, and one typical of the status open to them all, that of *oratores*. Their rights and duties at each stage of life will be examined.

*   *   *

Birth

At birth all girl babies were allowed to live. The history of infanticide, especially female infanticide, is long, and there is evidence of it in various parts of Europe in the early Middle Ages.[17] Steady pressure to protect the life of the newborn was exerted by the leaders of society so that, well before the period that is the object of the present study, infanticide was forbidden and punishable in the courts. The research of Richard Helmholtz and Barbara Hanawalt during the past decade provides strong evidence that, in fourteenth-century England, the life of the newborn child was successfully protected by society.[18]

Childhood

Infant daughters of the free, landowning, and bourgeois classes could inherit and be recipients of landed property immediately after birth.[19] Rights, in fact, were vested even in the unborn child. Thus, in the case of uncertain inheritance, decisions as to the devolution of property were delayed until an expected child was born.[20] Money or chattels that came to little girls of these classes was considered to be the property of their fathers. Such, at least, was the law, although family attitudes on this matter are unclear and the practice revealed in testaments suggests that some, at least, intended that small children be the owners of legacies left to them.[21] If the father of little Eleanor Knight had died and she were his heiress, she and her estate would have been in the wardship of her feudal lord. If she were not the heiress, it is likely that her mother or other members of her family would assume the role, seeing to her nurture, administrating her property and, eventually, arranging her marriage. Guardianship of the Wife of Bath during her childhood would probably be in the hands of the person chosen by her father or, in some towns, was exercised by the borough administration.[22] In the rare instance when property came to a Poor Widow or a Rose Foreign during her childhood, it was probably in the control of her father or the head of the family who raised her.

We know little of the early care and socialization of infant daughters. In the landholding and bourgeois classes they were often put out to wet nurse; there is some evidence in Coroners' rolls that this was done among the peasants, as well.[23] At all levels of society it was expected that the little ones would have adequate care to protect them from danger. Episcopal statutes were especially exercised to prevent neglect.[24] The little girls of the upper classes were probably trained by their mothers and servants with emphasis on [28] obedience to their fathers. Some evidence suggests that from about ages four to seven the little peasant girls accompanied their mothers to work.[25]

Girlhood

At about seven, children were considered to come to moral responsibility. This did not touch their right to control property but meant, among other things, that they might be involved in the first step toward their adult vocation. Thus, little girls of the class of Eleanor Knight or the Wife of Bath, whose engagements were often made early (even before birth, on occasion), might take part in a betrothal ritual.[26] The Prioress, who would be drawn from those classes, may have entered a convent at this age, perhaps as a young student, perhaps as a postulant. And in this period of life between responsibility and majority, the lives of the four types of women would begin to diverge, and the fifth possibility become open to them. Eleanor Knight may have been attached to the suite of a great lady in a household other than her own where, in addition to training in deportment, she may have had some opportunity for the study of letters.[27] Young women of the Wife of Bath's group might enter apprenticeship in one of the crafts, such as the Silkworkers, in which women played a major role, or she may have become involved in her father's business in ways that were suitable for her.[28] The probability that she would take a place in the business world ensured that she would at least learn some mensuration; many city women were literate.[29]

In these years the future Prioress learned the round of convent life, including the recitation of the office in Latin, although probably by rote; her reading would be in the vernacular.[30] Young peasant girls like the Poor Widow's daughters found their places in the endless tasks of household and field; many became servants. It is clear from recent work by Judith Bennett that, on some manors at least, peasant girls maintained control of the money they had received so that, when it became time for their marriage, they themselves were able to pay the marriage fine (*merchet*) to the lord of the manor, rather than have it paid by their fathers or their future husbands.[31] Girls born into the foreign class of the towns, of whom Rose is the type, probably began to work as soon as they were able to be of use. Where their parents had established themselves as workers attached to but not possessing the rights of the craft guilds, they may have found a place by their side. A similar situation probably obtained where parents were innkeepers or offered food-services as hawkers. No doubt many were beggars and were already being drawn into prostitution.[32]

Majority

At age twelve, young women began to enter their majority. It is necessary to emphasize that this was but a beginning because, for them as for the young [29] women of our own age, majority came in stages: valid marriage became a possibility with the completion of the twelfth year, but the age at which disposition of property was permitted was considerably later.[33] At any rate, the time had come to think of a state in life. Marriage was the lot of most medieval women, but medieval society provided several honorable alternatives. One was religious life, considered to be a suitable vocation for women of Eleanor Knight's class or for that of the Wife of Bath. Their families would be expected to provide a dowry, although it would usually be considerably less than that for marriage. At this stage of life the young woman who had entered a convent in her childhood was permitted to take her final vows. The possibility of becoming a nun was also open to a woman at later stages of her life.[34] The fact that convents were often used as niches for women who had little or no desire for religious life was a constant threat to the monastic ideal and a cause of scandal as well: visitation records and the literature of the time leave no doubt in this regard.[35] The lay sisters (*conversae*) attached to the greater convents and those women who served in hospitals and other charitable institutions have not yet been studied. It is probable that some of them at least were recruited from the lower strata of society, that a Poor Widow or a Rose Foreign may have found a place among them.

Another possibility for the woman entering her majority was the single life in the world. The spinster in medieval England has proved to be a very elusive person but her name, at least, gives a clue to her place there. Spinsters probably existed in significant numbers among the sisters of the Wife of Bath and the Poor Widow, though they have left little trace. Testaments survive that are clear evidence of the activity of these women and, as well as other documents, have made it possible for scholars to begin the study of this group within English society.[36]

Marriage

The woman who became a wife and the married period of her life have thus far been the principal areas of research in the social history of her sex. Her betrothal and wedding, her rights during marriage, and the property distribution when her marriage ended have proved to be of special interest. At the social level of Eleanor Knight, the marriage of a woman at the minimum age of twelve was probably not uncommon, although a first union in the mid- or late teens would be more usual.[37] It will be remembered that the Wife of Bath insisted on her first marital adventure at twelve. She has sometimes been taken, at least in this matter, as a paradigm of the women of her class, but recent work suggests that first marriage usually occurred about five years later.[38] The possibility of a peasant woman finding a spouse was related to her succession to her parents' property at their death or retirement or the availability of land to the man she married. In either case the opportunity must [30] often have been slow in presenting itself. In the conditions that obtained after the Black Death, however, land was more available. Thus the age of first marriage seems to have fallen, especially for peasant women like the Poor Widow, whose families held but little land.[39]

As to Rose Foreign, little more than surmise is possible. The completion of her twelfth year would be a requirement for a valid union, of course. For the upper levels of her class at least, the possibilities were similar to those of the Wife of Bath. Her marriage was probably less related to possessions than was the case with the women of the other groups and, therefore, may have occurred when she was quite young; but in her case, as that of the others, the question must be examined with more circumspection than has often been the case in the past. The older stereotypes of very early marriage in each of the four groups under examination must be set aside until much research has been completed; there are indications that first marriage toward the end of the second decade of a woman's life will prove to be the more common pattern.

Of similar difficulty is the question of the different individuals and groups who were expected to be involved in the choice of a woman's spouse. It can be taken as axiomatic that the higher a woman's position within the class structure, the more her marriage was a choice involving a wide circle of advisers. Thus the betrothal and marriage of Eleanor Knight would be a more complex arrangement than that of the Poor Widow or Rose Foreign. Depending on the class of the bride, in most cases her parents and wider family, neighborhood and parish, feudal and manorial lords might be expected to intervene. The twelfth and thirteenth centuries had seen a careful examination of the ways in which marriage was constituted. It resulted in a decision that is an example, as mentioned above, of a regulation that touched women of every class: the final say in establishing the marriage bond lay with the bridal pair. At the level of canonical theory it was insisted that, unless the couple consented to their union, that union did not occur. This regulation was implemented and enforced, often with serious consequences that touched dynasties and fortunes as well as the lot of the individuals concerned. Furthermore, the ancient usage whereby marriage could be a private act, that is, made by an exchange of consent by the couple without announcement and without witness, was still accepted. In fact, that kind of marriage, with all its possibility of mutual or self-deception, was to remain in force in England until the Marriage Act of 1753.[40] The motive for the "free choice" of spouse was not necessarily romantic; many other intentions might be at play.[41] But the stereotype of the young woman forced to marry against her will does not stand. The way in which fourteenth-century English society resolved the claims of individual freedom and the wider interests of those with some claim on the persons or property of the couple is a problem that has exercised several scholars for more than a decade.[42] It still has many uncertain elements, but it must be understood that, if any of the four women under discussion [31] were to be married, she would have to consent to that union for it to occur.[43]

If the preparations for the marriages of Eleanor Knight and the Wife of Bath followed the path that society preferred, there would have been agreement between their parents or guardians and the future husbands and their families regarding the property that each would bring to the new menage and the settlement that would be made on the wife, were she widowed, and on the children born to the union. The women would be expected to bring a dowry (*maritagium*) to contribute to the household. In Eleanor's case this would likely involve some land and chattels as well. If she had no brother, her dowry might have been considerable indeed: potentially as much as her family inheritance. The Wife of Bath, too, may have brought tenements in the borough in which her family lived and other land as well, but chattels and money probably played a larger role in her case. Again, if there were no brother, to marry her might be to succeed to her father's estate and business. At the level of the peasantry a similar situation obtained, though the property involved would usually be much less. If a peasant woman had siblings, she probably brought some chattels—farm animals, linen, grain—to her marriage, and merchet would have been paid to the lord for her or by her. Once again, if she were an heiress, she would bring to her husband the parcel of land held by her parents. The Poor Widow's main contribution may have been her strong back and the ability to bear and nurture children.[44] As for Rose Foreign, once again records fail us. Presumably, if hers were a family that had found a place on the fringe of one of the trades, she would be expected to bring some dowry to her spouse; those of the poorest class would contribute what they could, presumably money and chattels that they had acquired themselves.

All four women came under the guardianship of their husbands when they married. The land that Eleanor Knight brought as *maritagium* and any land that came to her from family or other sources during her marriage passed into the control of her spouse.[45] He was not to alienate it although, as court records make abundantly clear, he frequently did so. In that case, if she survived him, Eleanor had an effective means of recovery at common law. If she died before a child were born, her land reverted to her family. If, as seems to have been Eleanor's case, a child survived its mother, her land was held by her husband during his lifetime, then passed to their offspring—in this case, the Squire. If the woman died giving birth to her child and the baby died too, as long as there was adequate proof that the infant was born alive—its cry was heard between four walls—then, by the courtesy of England, the husband held the property for his lifetime. On his death, it reverted to his wife's family. Any mobile property that Eleanor brought to the marriage, or that came to her later, by common law belonged to her husband. If she died before him, an attempt to dispose of these goods by testament was effective only inasmuch as he approved of it.[46]

[32] The brutal simplicity of the property rights of married couples before common law was somewhat refined in the boroughs and on many manors. Thus, quite aside from the moral and perhaps physical authority that the Wife of Bath exercised over her husband, her position by right with regard to him was stronger than was Eleanor Knight's in regard to her spouse. Although her husband would usually speak for her in court, she and women of her class were sometimes in business for themselves and were considered legally capable of controlling funds required for their business and of answering for that business in borough court.[47] Furthermore, she could acquire landed property jointly with her husband in some boroughs and, again depending on local custom, could bequeath chattels and even land.[48] Patterns of peasant life, revealed by the anthropologist, in which the wife plays a major role in family support, often working closely with her husband, obtained among fourteenth-century peasantry; there were similar consequences. In many manors, villein tenements of husband and wife coalesced into a common possession. Furthermore, like her more wealthy sister in the borough, the Poor Widow during the time of her marriage may well have been in business for herself. She would most likely have been a brewer and would have been responsible for purchases, payments, and the fines to which ale-wives were so often subject.[49] The testamentary right of the villein was

much debated in the fourteenth century. It can be demonstrated, however, that on some manors they did exercise that right and that some married women were included among the testators.[50] The testament of a Poor Widow would distribute small bequests and would likely be principally concerned with a gift in alms and her funeral.

When difficulties developed in a marriage, all four women had access to a remedy. It was the role of episcopal courts to protect the marriage rights of spouses and the bond that united them. Where the bond did not exist or proved to be intolerable, it was for the courts to provide an equitable separation. It is usually taken as axiomatic that the more wealthy were better suited to benefit from the remedies made available by the ecclesiastical courts. A first impression formed by a reading of papal registers and even those of the bishop's official is that Eleanor Knight and the Wife of Bath had a distinct advantage over the Poor Widow and Rose Foreign in these matters. It is clear that the marriage of Eleanor or of women of the higher aristocracy, was more likely to be considered in terms of its political consequences.[51] Yet it must be remembered that the jurisdiction in question functioned at the local level and that, by the time of interest to the present discussion, it was possessed of an efficient *ex officio* procedure. This meant that the hearing of cases touching marriage was not dependent on one of the parties being in a position to launch the case; hearings were often begun by the court itself when need was seen.[52] There is good evidence that assistance was available to men and women of the lowest levels of society.

[33] Throughout their married years women would, in the ordinary course, be in charge of the day-to-day direction of their households and often, in the absence of their husbands, would see to its wider needs as well.[53] In these same middle years of life the women who followed the vocation of the Prioress would have settled into the monastic routine. Some of them would have begun to take on responsibilities as an obedientiary, in charge of a monastic department such as housekeeping, the cellar, or the sacristy or, as the Prioress herself, have accepted the charge of a nunnery.[54] Although Chaucer spoke rather lightly of her, it should not be forgotten that he gave the Prioress the most numerous suite in the pilgrimage. As a superior of religious women she exercised one of the most responsible roles open to women during the Middle Ages. Not only the direction of a major economic enterprise, but also the spiritual care of her sisters and their dependents were in her hands.

Widowhood

With the deaths of their husbands, the women representing the four lay groups suddenly sprang into full legal personality as expressed in the class to which they belonged. For those who had been married in their teens this was birth into a new kind of civil existence; for those who had married after a period of full adulthood, it was a rebirth.[55] Eleanor Knight would normally receive one-third of the landed property that her husband held during their marriage; it was hers for life, and she could use it as she saw fit so long as she did not alienate it. In addition, all the property she had brought to the marriage, and any that had accrued to her by inheritance or gift since that time, came under her control. She would be required to surrender the principal house of her husband's estate to the heir within forty days. It was customary that she would also receive a third part—or half, if there were no children—of her husband's chattels. By the period that is of interest here, the customary division of chattels was weakening in southern England to the detriment of the widow's right but, if the evidence of testaments can be trusted, wives were well provided for from the chattels of the household.[56] The Wife of Bath and her class usually enjoyed at least as generous a share of landed property and, since in some boroughs husbands were allowed to bequeath land to their wives, they might receive much more.[57] The wife's share of chattels remained the custom in the boroughs well past the period that is being described. In many manors, the Poor Widow benefited from the system of community property as her more wealthy sisters did not. She continued to hold the property that she had shared with her late husband and did not have to pay an entry fine. Thus she excluded the heir until she died or chose to relinquish the estate.[58]

Thus the widow faced the future not only with the wisdom that experience had given her, but often with a considerable fortune as well. She was free to [34] remain single or to marry; in the latter case the choice of spouse was her own although, as was to be expected, she was often subject to much pressure in this regard. From many points of view, not least from that of wealth, the widow was an attractive candidate for marriage, and many of them entered into a second union soon after the deaths of their husbands.[59] On the other hand, it is clear that there were many widows at all levels of fourteenth-century society. Women like Eleanor Knight or a less matrimonially inclined Wife of Bath sometimes took vows and entered a convent. Others made a formal commitment to a life of continence and prayer while remaining in the world, even in charge of their own households. The study of this form of widowed life has only begun; it is impossible to state the numbers who chose this path, though it is unlikely that they were numerous.[60] Peasant women were usually allowed to maintain their property and remain un-married as long as they were able to acquit their obligations to their lord. Often the best solution to the problems of a Poor Widow was to remarry, although it is clear that many did not do so.[61]

As those who remained in the world grew older and their powers failed, they or their families sometimes arranged that they enter convents or hospi-tals as pensioners. In a similar circumstance the Poor Widow might choose to surrender her little property with the understanding that it would be trans-ferred to an heir, or even to a stranger, who would be responsible for her support and care during the years that remained. Manorial court rolls illus-trate this method of provision for old age and illustrate as well that these

198 Michael M. Sheehan

courts saw to the honoring of the agreement between the generations.[62] Religious like the Prioress could expect to be cared for by their communities until the end.[63]

Death and Burial

The description of the lives of these five typical women can be brought to a close with the final expression of affection and preoccupation with matters of the next world in their wills. According to the general law of the Church, religious were forbidden to own property and under ordinary circumstances were not to make wills.[64] In the somewhat relaxed state of monastic life in the later Middle Ages, however, these rules often proved difficult to maintain. Nuns accumulated chattels and sometimes sought to control their future use by will.[65] When one thinks of the Prioress, it is to wonder who next wore her brooch with the device "Amor vincit omnia"?[66] If Eleanor Knight died during her husband's lifetime she had no right to make a will, since she owned no chattels and landed property was not disposable by legacy. Moral guides urged that she make a will for charitable purposes and for the good of her soul, and Church courts would have given probate and would oversee its execution. They did not seek to exact that right from her husband.[67] If Eleanor were a widow, she had full control over all her chattels and could dispose of [35] them as she wished. As was mentioned above, the Wife of Bath had a somewhat better chance of having a right to make a will during her husband's lifetime. As a widow she could sometimes bequeath both chattels and real estate.[68] By the last years of the fourteenth century, on many manors, the Poor Widow would be allowed to dispose of her chattels by will.[69] Of the last will of Rose Foreign little can be said with certainty. The more general freedom of bequest that obtained in borough custom suggests that, if she did make a will, it probably received probate and was implemented.

Adults had the right to choose their place of burial, and many of them stated it in their wills.[70] Widows usually chose to be buried with their husbands, but some, like Margaret Paston, preferred to return to the family that gave them birth.[71] An Eleanor Knight might be buried in the church of an abbey with which her husband's family was associated. The Prioress would rest in the choir of her convent church. For most of the women of England, burial was in their parish: the Wife of Bath would likely seek a place within the church; the Poor Widow and Rose Foreign would find rest in the churchyard. Women of all groups, like their male counterparts, sought to arrange by their wills that surviving relatives and friends reach into the next life to assist them by their prayers. The date of death of the Prioress would be entered in the beadroll of her house so that each year her anniversary would be remembered in the liturgy and, possibly, by the distribution of a pittance in her memory to her sisters. If confraternity provided suffrages for the dead were established between her convent and other houses, she would be remembered more widely. In addition to the masses and other prayers offered for Eleanor Knight and the Wife of Bath soon after their deaths, it is possible that they would establish a chantry or be included in one founded by their husbands or other family. There they would be remembered for years to come, perhaps until chantries were suppressed in the sixteenth century.[72] The Wife of Bath would also benefit from the suffrages offered on her behalf by her guild. Unless she had risen to a position where she belonged to some craft or parish guild, Rose Foreign was probably quickly forgotten after her death; there would soon be little sign of her passing in the busy town churchyard. The Poor Widow, buried in the cemetery that surrounded her parish church, the cemetery through which her friends passed every week, might not be forgotten so soon. Although it is unlikely that she would be remembered in an anniversary mass beyond the first year or two, the physical proximity of her place of burial would help to preserve her memory for a generation. The poorest women, as the richest, would be remembered in a general way on the feast of All Souls.

Notes

This paper was presented as a Smith Lecture at the University of St. Thomas, Houston, in March 1982. An earlier form was read at the Caltech Invitational Conference, "Family and Property in Traditional Europe," 1981.

1 For retrospective bibliography see Carolly Erickson and Kathleen Casey, "Women in the Middle Ages: A Working Bibliography," *Mediaeval Studies* 37 (1975):340–59; and Joan Kelly-Gadol, *Bibliography in the History of European Women* (Bronxville, N.Y., 1976). For current work, see *International Medieval Bibliography* (Leeds, 1967–), since July–December, 1976, "General Index," s.v. "women." On possible tensions between the study of the history of the family and the history of women, see Barbara J. Harris, "Recent Work on the History of the Family: A Review Article," *Feminist Studies* 3 (1976):159.
2 See the reflections of Ria Lemaire on the limitations of the conference "La femme dans la société des Xe–XIIIe siècles," held at Poitiers, September, 1976: "En marge du colloque . . . ," *Cahiers de civilisation médiévale* 20 (1977):261–63. For this and several other references my thanks to Sharon Ady.
3 E.g., Bede Jarrett, *Social Theories of the Middle Ages 1200–1500* (1926; reprint New York, 1966); "Women," pp. 69–93; and, more recently, G. H. Tavard, *Woman in Christian Tradition* (Notre Dame, Indiana, 1973); Vern L. Bullough and Bonnie Bullough, *The Subordinate Sex, a History of Attitudes towards Women* (Urbana, 1973); several essays in *Religion and Sexism: Images of Woman in the Jewish and Christian Traditions*, ed. R. R. Ruether (New York, 1974); Carolly Erickson, *The Medieval Vision* (London, New York, 1975), "The View of Women," pp. 181–212; M.-T. d'Alverny, "Comment les théologiens et les philosophes voient la femme," *Cahiers de civilisation médiévale* 20 (1977):105–29; and M. C. Horowitz, "The Image of God in Man—Is Woman Included?," *Harvard Theological Review* 72 (1979):175–206.
4 Much progress has been made in obtaining data on the lives of individual women, including those of the lowest classes; see David Herlihy and Christiane Klapisch-Zuber, *Les Toscans et leurs familles* (Paris, 1978); for the English peasantry, see the work of J. A. Raftis in Toronto and R. H. Hilton in Birmingham and their students.

5 Although the population of London and a few other urban centers increased during the late fourteenth century, many English towns experienced serious decline: May McKisack, *The Fourteenth Century 1307–1399*, The Oxford History of England 5 (Oxford, 1959), pp. 380–81.
6 The Ploughman is seen here as the type of the substantial peasant, possessed of plough and team as well as land, rather than as the *famulus*, specializing in ploughing and attached to the demesne. Demesne farming was much reduced in the late fourteenth century, so there was little or no need for the ploughman in the older sense of *bovarius*: M. M. Postan, "The Famulus," *Economic History Review*, Supplement 2 (Cambridge, 1954), p. 12; and R. H. Hilton, *The English Peasantry in the Middle Ages* (Oxford, 1975), pp. 21–23.
7 In the changing conditions of the period, the economic position of this group was improving: see E. B. DeWindt, *Land and People in Holywell-cum-Needingworth* (Toronto, 1972), pp. 115–27, for the East Midlands; and Zvi Razi, *Life, Marriage and Death in a Medieval Parish* (Cambridge, New York, 1980), pp. 147–49 for Worcestershire; cf. M. M. Postan, "Medieval Agrarian Society in Its Prime; England," *Cambridge Economic History of Europe*, Vol. 1, 2nd ed. (Cambridge, 1960), pp. 630–32. On Chaucer's view of the Ploughman as the ideal laborer, see Jill Mann, *Chaucer and Medieval Estates Satire: The Literature of Social Classes and the General Prologue to the "Canterbury Tales"* (Cambridge, 1973), pp. 67–70.
8 Geoffrey Chaucer, *The Canterbury Tales*, ed. F. N. Robinson, *The Works of Geoffrey Chaucer*, 2nd ed. (Boston, 1957), p. 199, [vii] ll. 2821–23, 2828–31, 2847–49.
9 Razi, *Life, Marriage and Death*, pp. 140–49.
10 See *Middle English Dictionary*, ed. Hans Kurath and Sherman M. Kuhn, Vol. E–F (Ann Arbor, 1952), p. 735 a–b, s.v. "forein: 1". I am indebted to Professor R. H. Robbins for this reference and for valued assistance and advice touching many parts of this essay.
11 Elspeth M. Viale, "Craftsmen and the Economy of London in the Fourteenth Century," in *Studies in London History Presented to Philip Edmund Jones*, ed. A. E. J. Hollaender and W. Kellaway (London, 1969), pp. 136, 140–42, 163–64.
12 Eileen Power, *Medieval English Nunneries c. 1275 to 1535* (Cambridge, 1922), pp. 1–41; David Knowles, *The Religious Orders in England*, Vol. 2, *The End of the Middle Ages* (Cambridge, 1955), pp. 260–61.
13 René Metz, "Le statut de la femme en droit canonique médiéval," in *La femme*, Société Jean Bodin pour l'Histoire Comparative des Institutions 12, ii (1962):59–113; M. M. Sheehan, "The Influence of Canon Law on the Property Rights of Married Women in England," *Mediaeval Studies* 25 (1963):109–24.
14 Chaucer, *Canterbury Tales*, ed. Robinson, pp. 17–18, [i(a)] ll. 43, 67–69.
15 Ibid., p. 18, ll. 80–81, 89–92.
16 In a volume that, in spite of much criticism, has remained the benchmark of demographic study: *British Medieval Population* (Albuquerque, 1948), J. C. Russell estimated the population of England in 1377 at 2,232,373 (p. 146). In a review in *Revue Belge de philologie et d'histoire* 28 (1950):600–606, J. Stengers argued that numbers were considerably higher. Russell maintained that the population fell during the last quarter of the century (pp. 260–63), a position restated in *Late Ancient and Medieval Population*, Transactions of the American Philosophical Society, N. S. 48, pt. 3 (Philadelphia, 1958), pp. 118–19. For recent work on population trends 1350–1400, see Razi, *Life, Marriage and Death*, pp. 114–16. The numbers of men and women for this period were about equal: see Russell, p. 148, and S. L. Thrupp, "Plague Effects in Medieval Europe," *Comparative Studies in Society and History* 8 (1965–66):475.
17 Emily Coleman, "Medieval Marriage Characteristics: a Neglected Factor in the History of Medieval Serfdom," *The Journal of Interdisciplinary History* 2 (Autumn

1971):205–19, and "L'infanticide dans le haut moyen-âge?" *Annales: économies, sociétés, civilisations* 29 (1974):315–35. See Russell, *Late Ancient and Medieval Population*, passim.

18 R. R. Helmholz, "Infanticide in the Province of Canterbury during the Fifteenth Century," *History of Childhood Quarterly* 2 (1975):379–90; B. A. Hanawalt, "Child-rearing among the Lower Classes of Late Medieval England," *Journal of Interdisciplinary History* 8 (Summer 1977):1–22. The possibility that female infanticide is the explanation of the high sex ratios revealed in early fourteenth-century England and in London (1259–1330) is suggested by Russell, *British Medieval Population*, pp. 148–49, and by H. A. Miskimin, "The Legacies of London:1250–1330" in *The Medieval City*, ed. H. A. Miskimin, David Herlihy, and A. L. Udovitch (New Haven and London, 1977), pp. 220–21, though the latter points out that under-reporting is a plausible hypothesis. See Thrupp, "Plague Effects in Medieval Europe," pp. 474–83.

19 "Infant" is used to mean a very young child and not in the common-law sense of a minor. On the rights of the minor, see F. Joüon des Longrais, in "Le statut de la femme en Angleterre dans le droit commun médiéval," *La femme*, Société Jean Bodin pour l'Histoire Comparative des Institutions 12, ii (1962):148–63.

20 Testaments of the period provide for the child with which a wife is pregnant, or make bequests that are to be withdrawn if the pregnancy results in the birth of an heir.

21 Grandchildren are sometimes legatees; they would often be very young.

22 See *Borough Customs*, ed. Mary Bateson, Selden Society 21 (London, 1906), pp. 145–57.

23 Hanawalt, "Childrearing," p. 14.

24 See *Councils and Synods with Other Documents Relating to the English Church II* A.D. *1305–1313*, Vol. 2, ed. F. M. Powicke and C. R. Cheney (Oxford, 1964), p. 1411: "General Index," s.v. "Children: safety measures for."

25 Hanawalt, "Childrearing," p. 18.

26 "A woman hath seven ages for severall purposes appointed to her by law: as seven years for the lord to have aid pur file marier," according to Coke on the first age of woman, as cited by Frederick Pollock and F. W. Maitland, *The History of English Law*, 2nd ed. (1898; rpt. Cambridge, 1978), 2:439, n. 3.

27 "Although the evidence of literacy among women is less conclusive … it appears that the typical upper-class education for women included reading knowledge of the vernacular, whether French or English, or possibly both, but little or no knowledge of Latin or of writing": J. H. Moran, "Educational Development and Social Change in York Diocese from the Fourteenth Century to 1548," (Ph.D. dissertation, Brandeis University, 1975), p. 235, n. 18. See her *Education and Learning in the City of York 1300–1560*, Borthwick Papers 55 (York, 1979), passim; and F. R. H. Du Boulay, *An Age of Ambition* (London, 1970), pp. 118–19.

28 See Marian K. Dale, "The London Silk-women of the Fifteenth Century," *Economic History Review* 4 (1933):324–35; S. L. Thrupp, *The Merchant Class of Medieval London* (1948; rpt. Ann Arbor, 1962), pp. 169–70; Viale, "Craftsmen and the Economy of London in the Fourteenth Century" (see n. 11, above), pp. 150–51; and Maryanne Kowaleski, "Local Markets and Merchants in late Fourteenth-Century Exeter," (Ph.D. dissertation, University of Toronto, 1982), pp. 194–209, 220–25.

29 See Thrupp, *The Merchant Class*, pp. 170–71.

30 Power, *Medieval English Nunneries*, pp. 237–89, esp. pp. 245–50.

31 "Medieval Peasant Marriage: An Examination of Marriage License Fines in the *Liber Gersumarum*," in *Pathways to Medieval Peasants*, ed. J. A. Raftis (Toronto, 1981), pp. 193–246.

202 Michael M. Sheehan

Viale, "Craftsmen and the Economy of London in the Fourteenth Century," pp. 141–43. See J. A. Brundage, "Prostitution in the Medieval Canon Law," *Signs, Journal of Women in Culture and Society* 1, no. 4 (Summer 1976):825–45.

33 On the different ages of majority, see Pollock and Maitland, *The History of English Law*, vol. 2, pp. 436–39, and M. M. Sheehan, *The Will in Medieval England* (Toronto, 1963), pp. 239–41. On proof of age, see Russell, *British Medieval Population*, pp. 92–117, and Sue S. Walker, "Proof of Age of Feudal Heirs in Medieval England," *Mediaeval Studies* 35 (1973):306–23.

34 Power, *Medieval English Nunneries*, pp. 38–41.

35 *Ibid.*, pp. 25–38, 436–74, et passim; Sr. Mary of the Incarnation Byrne, *The Tradition of the Nun in Medieval England* (Washington, 1932), pp. 165–74; Mann, *Chaucer and Medieval Estates Satire*, pp. 128–37.

36 Annette Koren, "Provincial Women and Their Economic Status in Late Medieval England," a paper read at the Berkshire Conference of Women Historians, Vassar College, 1981. See the discussion of Cecilia Penifader, a spinster of Brigstock, Northants. (ca. 1316–ca. 1344), and her wide social network in Judith Bennett, "Gender, Family and Community: A Comparative Study of the English Peasantry, 1287–1349" (Ph.D. dissertation, Toronto University, 1981), pp. 108–13, 136, n. 63; and the earlier remarks of Eileen Power, "The Position of Women," in *The Legacy of the Middle Ages*, ed. G. C. Crump and E. F. Jacob (Oxford, 1926), pp. 411–15.

37 See Russell, *British Medieval Population*, p. 158.

38 See Thrupp, *The Merchant Class*, p. 196.

39 Razi found that, in the post-plague period, sons usually obtained land in the lifetime of their fathers and were able to marry earlier than had been the case before that time. They married at about twenty. The small sample that was available indicated marriage of women between twelve and nineteen. See Eleanor Searle, "Seigneurial Control of Women's Marriage: The Antecedents and Function of Merchet in England," *Past and Present* 82 (February 1979):3–43; and Chris Middleton, "Peasants, Patriarchy and the Feudal Mode of Production in England: A Marxist Appraisal. Part 2: Feudal Lords and the Subordination of Peasant Women," *Sociological Review* n.s. 29, no. 1 (1981):137–54.

40 See Christopher Lasch, "The Suppression of Clandestine Marriage in England: The Marriage Act of 1753," *Salmagundi* 26 (Spring 1974):90–109. The possibility of a secret but valid union must be kept in mind in the discussion of the marriage of all classes and in any analysis of the literature of the time; see K. P. Wentersdorf, "The Clandestine Marriages of the Fair Maid of Kent," *Journal of Medieval History* 5 (1979):203–31, and "Some Observations on the Concept of Clandestine Marriage in *Troilus and Criseyde*," *Chaucer Review* 15 (1980):101–26.

41 Cf. Jean Leclercq, *Monks on Marriage, a Twelfth-Century View* (New York, 1982), pp. 1–9, where the importance of the element of love in marriage is presented.

42 See Sue S. Walker, "Free Consent and Marriage of Feudal Wards in Medieval England," *Journal of Medieval History* 8 (1982):123–34. My thanks to Professor Michael Altschul for this reference and for other assistance in this essay.

43 See J. T. Noonan, Jr., "Power to Choose," *Viator* 4 (1973):419–34; and M. M. Sheehan, "Choice of Marriage Partner in the Middle Ages: Development and Mode of Application of a Theory of Marriage," *Studies in Medieval and Renaissance History* 1 (Vancouver, 1978):8–11.

44 B. A. Hanawalt, "Women's Contribution to the Home Economy in Late Medieval Europe," a paper read at the Berkshire Conference of Women Historians, Vassar College, 1981.

45 Joüon des Longrais, "Le statut de la femme," pp. 163–83; Pollock and Maitland, *The History of English Law*, 2:403–28.

46 William Holdsworth, *A History of English Law*, Vol. 3, 5th ed. (London, 1966), pp. 542–43. For a recent re-examination of the question, see Charles Donahue, Jr., "Lyndwood's Gloss propriarum uxorum: Marital Property and ius commune in Fifteenth-Century England," in *Europäisches Rechtsdenken in Geschichte und Gegenwart*, Festschrift für Helmut Coing zum 70. Geburtstag, ed. Norbert Horn (Munich, 1982), 1:19–37.

47 Thrupp, *The Merchant Class*, pp. 169–74, and Kowaleski, "Local Markets and Merchants in late Fourteenth-Century Exeter" (see n. 28, above), pp. 194–209, 220–25. See Bateson, *Borough Customs*, Selden Society 18:227–28.

48 Bateson, *Borough Customs*, Selden Society 21:106–11.

49 See J. A. Raftis, "Social Structures of Five East Midland Villages," *Economic History Review* 2 Ser. 18:1 (1965):91–92; DeWindt, *Land and People* p. 235 and n. 157; Hilton, *The English Peasantry*, pp. 103–6; and especially Bennett, "Gender, Family and Community" (see n. 36, above), pp. 141–91, 262–74, and 320–29.

50 Holdsworth, *A History of English Law*, 3:542, and n. 23; see n. 69, below.

51 "Ubi non est consensus utriusque non est coniugium ... nisi forte aliquando urgentissima interveniente necessitate pro bono pacis couniunctio talis toleretur." This text, c. 19 of the Council of Westminster (1175) was included in the *Extravagantes* of Gregory IX (4.2.2). See *Councils and Synods with Other Documents Relating to the English Church I* A.D. *871–1204*, ed. D. Whitelock, M. Brett, and C. N. L. Brooke (Oxford, 1981), 2:991, 967 n. 3; and the discussion in M. M. Sheehan, "Marriage Theory and Practice in the Conciliar Legislation and Diocesan Statutes of Medieval England," *Mediaeval Studies* 40 (1978):411. Dynastic and political aspects of marriage are well presented by H. A. Kelly in *The Matrimonial Trials of Henry VIII* (Stamford, California, 1975).

52 Slightly less than half of the marriage cases before the official of the bishop of Ely 1374–82 were *ex officio*. Several of them began because, at the reading of the banns of matrimony, objection was made to a proposed union. Learning of this, the court proceeded *ex officio* to investigate the case: M. M. Sheehan, "The Formation and Stability of Marriage in Fourteenth-Century England: Evidence of an Ely Register," *Mediaeval Studies* 33 (1971):256–62. On this matter generally, see R. H. Helmholz, *Marriage Litigation in Medieval England* (Cambridge, 1974), and *Select Cases from the Ecclesiastical Courts of the Province of Canterbury, c. 1200–1301*, ed. Norma Adams and Charles Donahue, Jr., Selden Society 95 (London, 1981), "Introduction," pp. 81–84.

53 See Eileen Power, *Medieval People*, 10th ed. (New York, 1963), Ch. 5, "The Menagier's Wife," pp. 96–119; *Medieval Women* (Cambridge, 1975), pp. 9–34; and Hanawalt, "Women's Contribution" (see n. 44, above). A remarkable sense of women's administrative activity may be gained from the correspondence of Agnes Paston (1440–79) and Margaret Paston (1441–1484): *Paston Letters and Papers of the Fifteenth Century*, ed. Norman Davis, 2 vols. (Oxford, 1971–6), nos. 13–34, 434–36, and 124–230, 707–36.

54 Power, *Medieval English Nunneries*, pp. 42–95, 131–60.

55 Joüon des Longrais, "Statut de la femme," pp. 183–235; Pollock and Maitland, *The History of English Law*, 1:482–85.

56 See William Holdsworth, *A History of English Law*, pp. 554–56; M. M. Sheehan, "The Family in Late Medieval England, Extended or Nuclear? Evidence from Testaments," a paper read at the Fifth British Legal History Conference, University of Bristol, 1981.

57 Bateson, *Borough Customs*, 21:cviii–cxv.

58 On the customary rights of the peasant widow and the acquittal of the obligations of her holding, see George Homans, *English Villagers of the Thirteenth Century*

(1941; rpt. New York, 1975), pp. 184–88; J. A. Raftis, *Tenure and Mobility* (Toronto, 1964), pp. 36–42; Edward Britton, *The Community of the Vill* (Toronto, 1977), pp. 20–22; and Hilton, *The English Peasantry*, pp. 98–100.

59 On the removal of the required interval of at least a year and a day between death of a husband and the remarriage of his widow, see Sheehan, "The Influence of Canon Law," p. 112.

60 A preliminary study of these women was presented by Sharon Ady in "Vows of Chastity and the Medieval English Widow" at the Sixteenth International Conference of Medieval Studies, University of Western Michigan, Kalamazoo, 1981. See J. R. Shinners, Jr., "Religion in Fourteenth-Century England: Clerical Standards and Popular Practice in the Diocese of Norwich" (Ph.D. dissertation, Toronto University, 1982), pp. 334–35.

61 See B. A. Hanawalt, "Widowhood in Medieval English Villages," a paper read at the Sixteenth International Conference of Medieval Studies, University of Western Michigan, Kalamazoo, 1981. Razi notes that peasant widows seem to have found it more difficult to marry in Worcestershire after the plague (*Life, Marriage and Death*, p. 138).

62 See Homans, *English Villagers*, pp. 144–46; Raftis, *Tenure and Mobility*, pp. 42–46; S. R. Burstein, "Care of the Aged in England from Medieval Times to the End of the 16th Century," *Bulletin of the History of Medicine* 22 (1948):738–43; and Elaine Clark, "The Quest for Economic Security in Medieval England," a paper read at the Medieval Conference: "Aging and the Aged in Medieval Europe" Part 1, Toronto, February 1983.

63 Power, *Medieval English Nunneries*, p. 57.

64 The religious superior posed a special problem in this regard; see Sheehan, *The Will in Medieval England*, pp. 250–53.

65 Power, *Medieval English Nunneries*, pp. 315–40; see Knowles, "The Wage-System and the Common Life," *The Religious Orders of England*, Vol. 2, pp. 240–47. For Bishop William of Wykeham's injunctions against the making of wills by nuns (1387), see Power, op. cit., p. 337 and n. 6.

66 Chaucer, *The Canterbury Tales*, ed. Robinson, p. 18, [*GP* i(a)] ll. 158–62.

67 Sheehan, "The Influence of Canon Law," pp. 119–71; *The Will in Medieval England*, pp. 234–41. See n. 46, above.

68 See n. 48, above.

69 In the diocese of Rochester (1347–48), the testaments of 127 men, 33 married women, 20 widows, and 5 women (who were probably spinsters) were probated in groups. Many of these were the testaments of the very poor; see *Registrum Hamonis Hethe*, ed. C. Johnson, Canterbury and York Society 49 (Oxford, 1948), 2:923–26, 1000, et passim.

70 See Antoine Bernard, *La sépulture en droit canonique du Décret de Gratien au Concile de Trente* (Paris, 1933), pp. 85–104.

71 "First, I betake my sowle to God ... and my body to be beried in the ele of the cherch of Mauteby byfore the ymage of Our Lady there, jn which ele reste the bodies of divers of myn aunceteres, whos sowles God assoile" (4 February 1482): *Paston Letters and Papers*, no. 230, 1:383.

72 See K. L. Wood-Legh, *Perpetual Chantries in Britain* (Cambridge, 1965), pp. 8–29, et passim; and Rosalind Hill, " 'A Chaunterie for Soules': Chantries in the Reign of Richard II," in *The Reign of Richard II: Essays in Honour of May McKisack*, ed. F. R. H. Du Boulay and Caroline M. Barron (London, 1971), pp. 243–55.

19 | Chaucer's representations of marriage and sexual relations

DAVID AERS

Originally published as the beginning of chapter 4 in David Aers, *Chaucer* (Brighton: Harvester Press, 1986, pp. 62–75). Reprinted by permission of Simon and Schuster International Group. The original pagination is recorded within square brackets. The endnotes originally appeared on pp. 107–8 and are here partially renumbered. In the rest of chapter 4, Aers discusses the *Knight's Tale*, the *Franklin's Tale*, the *Book of the Duchess*, and *Troilus and Criseyde*.

Over thirty years ago an American scholar studying medieval romances wrote:

> It is a commonplace that throughout the Middle Ages marriage was an arrangement of convenience, an enforced legal contract designed to secure certain political, military, or economic advantages. With such ends in view, it was inevitable that the desire of the woman should be the least significant element in the bargain.[1]

Although the evidence supporting Margaret Gist's statement is overwhelming, the 'commonplace' she outlines with the link she rightly makes between the material foundations of marriage and the dismissal of female desire in a patriarchal society, is still not often foregrounded by teachers of medieval literature. Her summary of the basis of Christian marriage points us towards the contexts in which human beings experienced marriage and its sexuality. These were the contexts within which, and potentially against which, [63] imaginative explorations of marriage took place.

The mentality fostered by respectable medieval marriages can be illustrated from the diary of a fourteenth-century merchant, Georgio Dati:

> I had an illegitimate male child by Margherita, a Tartar slave whom I had bought ... [1391] We [business associates] renewed our partnership on 1 January 1393, when I undertook to invest 1,000 [gold] florins. I did not actually have the money but was about to get married—which I then did—and to receive the dowry which procured me a larger share and more consideration in our company ... I married my second wife, Betta, on 22 June.... On the 26th of that same June, I received a

payment of 800 gold florins from the bank of Giacomino and Co. This was the dowry ... On 5 July 1402 ... Betta gave birth to our eighth child. After that my wife Betta passed to Paradise.... The [business] partnership is to start on 1 January 1403 and to last three years ... I have undertaken to put up 2,000 florins. This is how I propose to raise them; 1,370 florins are still due to me from my old partnership.... The rest I expect to obtain if I marry again this year, when I hope to find a woman with a dowry as large as God may be pleased to grant me.

'God' duly obliged the merchant, and he records that in May 1403 he was betrothed and 'The dowry was 1,000 florins: 700 in cash and 300 in a farm'. He had eleven children by this wife. She died in childbirth, 'after lengthy suffering', and he writes: 'I then took another wife.... The dowry was 600 florins ...'.[2] This man is in no way deviant. His diary exemplifies what Gist correctly described as 'commonplace'; a respectable man's outlook and the practice of Christian marriage in a society like the Wife of Bath's where 'al is for to selle' (*Wife of Bath's Prologue*, 1. 414). The human effects of this economic foundation to medieval Christian marriage can hardly be ignored.

Another major force shaping the contexts in which [64] Chaucer lived and out of which he wrote is orthodox Christian teaching on marriage and marital sex, the norms the Church *tried* to impose from the pulpit, through the apparatus of the confessional, through a massive array of didactic writings, through formal theological and legal texts. Chaucer's fictions work over the conventional teachings I shall summarise, put them into solution, explore them and their likely effects on human identity and relationship. Grasping the ideological contexts of his poetry here will help us engage with the resonances of the texts we study and help us grasp the achievements and horizons of his imagination.

The chief purposes of Christian marriage were the procreation of children to be reared in the orthodox Catholic Church, and the channelling of sexual drives: without such marriage, by definition, 'fornication' would flourish. The Church proved incapable of seeing that the deepest love could be fully and profoundly expressed in sexual union. Indeed, it constantly excluded the expression of mutual love and delight as a legitimate purpose of specifically sexual union between married people. The prevalent clerical attitude was authoritatively expressed by St Augustine: 'I feel that nothing more turns the masculine mind from the heights than female blandishments and the contact of bodies without which a wife may not be had' (*Soliloquies*, I. 10). No wonder the Church prohibited priests from marriage. Nor is it surprising that this outlook should become articulated in an ideology which taught that focus on the enjoyment of sexual union within marriage was a sin, probably a mortal sin. It is characteristic of this tradition that Pope Gregory the Great forbade people to enter a church or receive communion after marital sex because he feared that all sex involved some pleasure of the flesh which entailed sin. J. T. Noonan's comment is relevant: 'A barrier was set against the consideration of marital values other than procreation; consideration of a value such as love was blocked.'[3] Similarly, [65] H. A. Kelly found that in doctrines about the purposes of Christian marriage taught by theologians and canonists (church lawyers), 'mutual love between the spouses is notably absent'.[4] In fact, as Noonan's research shows, throughout the Middle Ages 'there is no integration of the ideal of personal love with the purpose of [marital] intercourse.'[5] This Christian tradition had powerful propagandists and its mark on our culture was to be long-lasting. William Blake was still struggling with its survival in the nineteenth century, as he writes in his magnificent *Jerusalem*:

> Have you known the Judgement that is arisen among the
> Zoas of Albion? where a Man dare hardly to embrace
> His own Wife, for the Terrors of Chastity that they call
> By the name of Morality.

On the contrary,

> every Minute Particular is Holy:
> Embraces are Comminglings: from the Head even to the Feet.
>
> (*Jerusalem*, Plates 32 and 69)

But instead of Blake, let us listen to some orthodox Christian voices, remembering that these passages are explicitly about sexual love between couples married within the Christian sacrament of marriage.

We catch the core of the tradition in the infinitely repeated formula asserting that 'the too ardent lover of his own wife is an adulterer'. Instructing confessors on how to be guided in their inquiries into the lives of married people, J. P. Foresti advised:

> If one was too immodest in touches, embraces, kisses and other dishonourable things [*inhonesta*], it sometimes might be mortally sinful because these things are not consonant with sacred [66] matrimony.... If he knew [sexually] his wife not for offspring or for paying the debt [i.e. the so-called marital debt to alleviate the spouse's lust, to prevent adultery], but only for his own insatiable and uncontrollable pleasure ... he has exposed himself to the danger of serious sin.[6]

It was only a licit intercourse, 'paying of the debt' (the adoption of such Pauline language itself tells a revealing story), if the spouse did so *without* intention of taking any pleasure in the sexual act. This is standard teaching which Chaucer knew in detail.

He translated its stock commonplaces in the penitential manual he gives to the Parson as his 'myrie tale in prose' in those unfinished writings he called 'the tales of Caunterbury' (*Retractions*). As noted in the last chapter, there are grounds for reading the *Parson's Tale* and its *Prologue* as involving a critical treatment of both Parson and the orthodox Christian line on marital sex.[7] Whatever readers may finally decide about the place of this work, it at least demonstrates Chaucer's intimate knowledge of fully-elaborated Christian ideology in the sphere of marital sex. His writing discloses that his fascination was with the human implications of standard Christian teaching, and its explorations were profoundly imaginative and highly critical.

Let us stay with the *Parson's Tale* for a moment. Having used the word 'ordure' to denote excrement (l. 428), the Parson proclaims that married couples who make love in and for mutual 'delit' commit the mortal sin of adultery, proving the devil himself has control over them and that they have 'yven hemself to alle ordure' (ll. 903–5). With relish he proclaims the Christian view of the eternal punishment 'adulterers' will suffer 'in helle in a stank brennynge of fyr and of brymston' (l. 840). The only kind of marital sex the Parson approves is a joyless penitential suffering: 'she hath merite of chastitee that yeldeth to her housbonde the dette of [67] hir body, ye, though it be agayn hir likynge and the lust of hire herte' (l. 940). The human consequences of such ideas of virtue can be painfully followed in Margery Kempe's account of her own marital experiences, an account that should be read and carefully considered by all interested in medieval writing and culture as well as by those studying specifically female experiences in our history.[8] (Comparison between her work and Chaucer's could also focus on Chaucer's horizons and the limits of his insight.) Chaucer himself depicted some aspects of the appalling human reality such Christian ideology fostered in his representation of May and the Wife of Bath enduring their Christian husbands' unwanted sexual intercourse, practising what the Parson describes as the 'merite . . . that yeldeth to hire housbonde the dette of hir body . . . agayn hir likynge'. The Parson's text drives home conventional Christian ideology: 'if they [a married couple] assemble oonly for amorous love . . . to accomplice thilke brennynge delit . . . it is deedly synne' (l. 942). The teaching and its language manifest the complete degradation of the erotic, the total separation of love from sexuality, of sexuality from one's full and true humanity. It is just here that the Christian ideology of sex joins hands with the most degenerate pornography to fragment the human person, to split off and debase sexual love. The Parson's ideal is a sexless marriage: 'Man sholden loven hys wyf . . . as thogh it were his suster' (l. 860). (He is not, presumably, recommending incest!)

There is one more point worth making about the Christian doctrine displayed in the *Parson's Tale*. That is, its unexamined but characteristic union with the economic foundations and interests of marriage, ones under exclusively male control. For example, in treating adultery the text describes this as including sin against *property* rights: 'This synne is eek a thefte; for thefte generally is for to reve a wight his thyng' (l. 876). The woman is represented as a mere [68] object, a piece of property owned by the Christian male, 'his thyng'. Furthermore, through adulteries, 'comen false heires ofte tyme, that wrongfully occupien folkes heritages. And therefore [sic!] wol Crist putte hem out of the regne of hevene, that is heritage to goode folk' (l. 883). Whereas Christ in the New Testament taught and followed a path of poverty, of disengagement from property, family and wealth, orthodox Christianity managed to turn him into the great defender of established property rights, punishing humans with eternal torments for breaking the patterns of family inheritance of property.

This combination of economic structure and interests joined with Christian sexual ideology to shape medieval marriages. It is the material that formed the dominant contexts and horizons with which Chaucer's fictions work, actively, in powerful imaginative exploration. Whether the specifically literary heritage of romance and courtly poems of love offered important and genuinely alternative models of sexual relations is a question I shall take up later in this chapter.

*   *   *

In discussing Chaucer's representations of society we considered the significance of the *Shipman's Tale* and I now wish to recall that poem.[9] Chaucer left signs that he attributed it at some stage to a female speaker, presumably the Wife of Bath (ll. 10–19). It displays very crisply the fate of marital and extramarital sexual relations in the world it figures. If the practice and ethos of the market pervades a society, if human relations become predominantly mediated through a cash nexus, the forms human sexuality takes and the language in which they are spoken, will be profoundly affected. The *Shipman's Tale* displays this in a thoroughly jovial mode. The merchant's wife views sexual activity as an economic [69] exchange: in exchange for her husband's support she will 'paye' him in bed, simultaneously fulfilling the Church's command that spouses should 'pay the debt' (ll. 413–24). She perceives her own body as a commodity. Her genitals become an accountbook, and the poem concludes with a pun which fuses genitals, the sexual act, the poem itself and financial accounting:

> For I wol paye yow wel and redily
> Fro day to day, and if so be I faille,
> I am youre wyfe; score it upon my taille,
> And I shal paye as soon as ever I may.
> . . . . . .
> Thus endeth now my tale, and God us sende
> Taillynge ynough unto our lyves ende.
>
> (ll. 414–17, 433–4)

Nor is extramarital sex any different. The wife agrees with the monk, 'That for thise hundred frankes he sholde al nyght / Have hire in his armes bolt upright' (ll. 314–15). Crude, but symbolising the kind of crude reduction of human relations where the cash nexus is central.

Chaucer elaborates his vision of this situation in the poem he did give to the Wife of Bath. Her famous *Prologue* exhibits the fate of woman as a commodity to be bought and used in marriage, one whose economic and religious task was to 'pay the debt' in a society where 'al is for to selle' (l. 414). In exchange for the sexual use of her body, her first three husbands give her economic security (ll. 204, 212). This has been a normal enough state of affairs in our civilisation but Chaucer's satire brings out its nastiness:

> For wynnyng wolde I al his lust endure,
> And make me a feyned appetit;

> And yet in bacon hadde I nevere delit,
[70]   That made me that evere I wolde hem chide.
>
> (ll. 416–19)

The frustration and degradation of sexual life in such a culture is sharply evoked. It is one, as we noted above, supported by the Church's command to 'pay the debt': the Wife has good cause to cry out, 'Allas! allas! that evere love was synne!' (l. 614). Yet, as in the passage just quoted, Chaucer shows how she, like the wife in the *Shipman's Tale*, accepts the practices and ethos of the market. She rebels against male domination, confirming the fears embodied in the anti-feminist tradition she knows so well and judges so accurately as the outpourings of psychically crippled and unreflexive males (ll. 692–710). But she does so within the framework of market relations, and seeks power through the accumulation of property, grounded in the sale of her labour-power and her body. As Alfred David observes, she 'regards "love" like any other commodity to be bought and sold in the world's market place'.[10] The attitudes of this female rebel thus give us further insight into a culture which teaches her that marriage is a relationship grounded in the exchange of commodities and the domination of one human by another. Even when she achieves the freedom to marry 'for love and no richesse' (l. 526) she claims to 'love' her young husband because he was stand-offish, thus making himself a more valuable commodity to the purchasing Wife:

> Greet prees at market maketh deere ware;
> And to greet cheep is holde at litel prys.
>
> (ll. 522–3; see too ll. 513–16)

The language discloses a form of life, the culture which generates it. That her fifth marriage fails to transcend the economic conflicts and struggles for domination fostered in her society, is hardly surprising (ll. 627–827).

> ∗   ∗   ∗

[71] In the *Merchant's Tale* Chaucer offers one of the most disturbing visions of traditional Christian marriage as an institutionalisation of human and sexual degradation. Its critical perspective, subtlety, imagistic resonance and overall organisation cannot meaningfully be attributed to the perverse shallowness of the misogynistic merchant who is its formal pilgrim-teller. As throughout the *Canterbury Tales*, there is simply no hard-and-fast rule about the relations between author, fictional tellers and tales, nor is there always a consistent narrative voice in even one tale. It is important that the reader neither seeks nor imposes the kind of 'coherence' here that Chaucer's texts seem quite uninterested in.

The poem opens with a lengthy and ironic reflection on normal male assumptions about the ends of marriage—that is, the 'paradys terrestre' the male hopes to experience in marriage, and the risks he runs of not having his expectations matched (ll. 1245–468). This passage is replete with long-lasting masculine stereotypes of women, fixing their role as the male's obedient economic, domestic and, of course, sexual instrument. She is also, inevitably, the lost, nurturing and all-accepting mother. The old knight who wants a wife is affluent enough to afford a wide range of choice. Chaucer presents this activity in a brilliantly evocative image:

> Heigh fantasye and curious bisynesse
> Fro day to day gan in the soule impresse
> Of Januarie about his mariage.
> Many fair shap and many a fair visage
> Ther passeth thurgh his herte nyght by nyght
> As whoso tooke a mirour, polisshed bryght,
> And sette it in a commune market-place,
> [72] Thanne sholde he se ful many a figure pace
> By his mirour ...

(ll. 1577–85)

Here again are the possible psychic consequences of inhabiting a society where, in the Wife of Bath's words, 'al is for to selle'. In this imaging, women are, typically enough, denied all subjectivity—they only exist as objects in the acquisitive male field of vision, commodities to be purchased and consumed.

This version, as already noted, has its material foundations in contemporary social organisation and Chaucer proceeds to illustrate normal practices in the arrangement of *respectable* marriages. The knight's kin and friends make the legal and economic contracts whereby the woman he desires 'Shal wedded be unto this Januarie' (ll. 1692–8). The female's desire, as Margaret Gist observed about the reality of standard marriages, is irrelevant, written out. She is made totally passive. Any genuine marriage will, of course, be an orthodox Christian one, a holy sacrament, and Januarie's is certainly that—a church wedding blessed by the priest (ll. 1700–8). Chaucer emphasises the role of the Church, for after the wedding feast he shows the passive bride being 'broght abedde as stille as stoon' and the priest blessing the bed of the marriage the Church has sanctified (ll. 1818–9). Thus the text reveals the total involvement of the Church (something that was a long struggle for it to achieve) in the perpetuation of a marital institution based on economic power and male enthralment of females. As Chaucer evokes the meaning of loveless marriage and the compulsory sex that went with it, we may remember J. T. Noonan's analysis of the Church's 'failure to incorporate love into the purpose of marital intercourse'.[11] The poet's satire embraces the ideology and practices of the Catholic Church in a way that many pious commentators and teachers still evade. He [73] makes the priest's blessing of the bed lead straight into the sharply detailed and hideous representation of aggressive sexuality, the death of tenderness and the absence of any mutuality—an outstanding passage too long to quote here (ll. 1820–50). Marital sex is exhibited as an arena where the male may use the female body in a self-gratifying exercise of 'manly' power and domination. Chaucer's finely particularised satire evokes and decisively judges male attitudes which are still manifest, be it in living reality, in pornography, or in 'respectable' literature such as Lawrence's *The Plumed Serpent* or parts of *Lady Chatterley's Lover*.[12] Male sexuality is presented, in an image often chosen by men, as a 'knyf', a weapon used 'on the job' to carve up the 'yong flessh', 'the tendre veel' in terms of which the woman has already been imagined (ll. 1840, 1832–3, 1418–20; cf. *Parson's Tale*, ll. 855–60). Chaucer concludes this memorable passage by inviting his readers to reflect on a perspective habitually occluded both in traditional literature and its conventional teaching in our institutions of education: 'God woot what that May thoughte in hir herte' (l. 1851). Or, as he ironically asks us to consider after another sacramental encounter in the marital bed, 'whither hire thoughte it paradys or helle' (l. 1964). We understand how the male's 'paradys terrestre' (l. 1332) may create and be the female's 'helle'. The text which sponsors such reflection never encourages any conventional moral judgements against May as it depicts her desperate attempt to alleviate her subjection to this legalised rape by turning to Damyan. As he did in the *Wife of Bath's Prologue*, Chaucer stimulates reflection on the domination of life and literature by unexamined male assumptions and images:

> By God! if wommen hadde writen stories,
> As clerkes han withinne hire oratories,
> They wolde han writen of men moore wikkednesse
> [74]   Than al the mark of Adam may redresse.
>   . . .
> The clerk, when he is oold, and may noght do
> Of Venus werkes worth his olde sho,
> Thanne sit he doun, and writ in his dotage
> That wommen kan nat kepe hir mariage!
> (*Wife of Bath's Prologue*, ll. 693–6, 707–10)

This male poet cannot of course be substitute for the silenced voices and buried experience of half the human species: but his texts can awaken the kind of awareness which is an essential aspect of the long struggle to challenge and dissolve the male hegemony which continues to deform the lives of women *and* men.

The poem's concluding play with mythological deities also encourages such reflexivity by satirising its absence. Watching May's attempts to loosen Januarie's enslavement of her, Pluto complains about the wickedness, the 'untrouthe and brotilnesse' of women, deploying assorted clichés from the anti-feminist tradition (ll. 2237–61). In the self-righteous notes of conventional male wisdom he tells her:

> Th'experience so preveth every day
> The tresons whiche that wommen doon to man.
>
> (ll. 2238–9)

Chaucer's contexts explode this stance in a burst of ironic laughter, for he has just told us how the authoritative speaker had himself 'ravysshed' Proserpyna, fetched her 'in his grisely carte' and forced her to be his wife in hell (ll. 2225–33)—an obvious image of Januarie's marriage to May. All too representative of male moralisation, he then has the gall to complain about women's 'tresons' to men! Chaucer continues to mock the masculine stance as it expresses solidarity with the 'honourable knyght', the 'worthy knyght' Januarie, absolutely certain that it is *simply* because he is [75] old and blind that May seeks another man (ll. 2252–61). She seeks another man, of course, but because she is miserably locked in a marriage she did not make. Furthermore, the poet exposes the male god's use of the Bible as one centred on the self-righteous maintenance of crude sexism (ll. 2242–51): he does so by allowing the wife a thoroughly cogent refutation of Pluto's 'auctorites' and the use he tries to make of them (ll. 2276–304). Indeed, Chaucer gives the woman the same exegesis and arguments that Prudence offers in her decisive defence of women against traditional anti-feminist cant in the *Tale of Melibee* (ll. 1056, 1069–78). The fact that some scholars try to teach us that the poem is anti-feminist is risible, although such responses would hardly have surprised the poet who writes into his work the Host's mindlessly sexist response to the *Clerk's Tale*.

Notes

1 M. A. Gist, *Love and War in the Medieval Romances* (University of Philadelphia Press, 1947), p. 17. See the invaluable introductory study by E. Power, *Medieval Women* (Cambridge U.P., 1975).
2 In J. O'Faolain and L. Martines (eds), *Not in God's Image* (Harper & Row, 1973), pp. 184–5.
3 J. T. Noonan, *Contraception. A History of its Treatment by Catholic Theologians and Canonists* (Harvard U.P., 1966), p. 151.
4 H. A. Kelly, *Love and Marriage in the Age of Chaucer* (Cornell U.P., 1975), p. 247.
5 Noonan, *Contraception*, pp. 196, 248–54.
6 *Confessionale*, section 'Concerning the lechery of married couples', translated in T. N. Tentler, *Sin and Confession on the Eve of the Reformation* (Princeton, 1977), p. 176.
7 [Aers refers here to the previous chapter in his book – ed.]
8 See *The Book of Margery Kempe*, ed. S. B. Meech (Early English Text Society, o. s. 212, 1940). And S. Delany, 'Sexual economics, Chaucer's Wife of Bath and the Book of Margery Kempe', *Minnesota Review*, 5 (1975), 104–15.
9 [Aers refers here to an earlier chapter in his book – ed.]
10 Alfred David, *The Strumpet Muse. Art and Morals in Chaucer's Poetry* (Indiana U.P., 1976), chapter 9.
11 Noonan, *Contraception*, pp. 256–7.
12 See Kate Millett, *Sexual Politics* (Abacus, 1972): on Lawrence, chapter 5.

20 | Deconstructing
The Canterbury Tales: pro

PEGGY A. KNAPP

Originally published in *Studies in the Age of Chaucer*, Proceedings
no. 2 (1987):73–81. Reprinted by permission of the New Chaucer
Society. The original pagination is recorded within square brackets.
The endnotes originally appeared as footnotes.

Why would any sane person advocate turning to so outrageous a scheme as
deconstruction for help in interpreting a medieval text, especially so plain and
beloved a text as *The Canterbury Tales*? After all, Jacques Derrida alleges that
"there is not a single signifier that escapes ... the play of signifying references that constitutes language."[1] In contrast, "every good and true Christian," including Chaucer, would doubtless agree with Saint Augustine that,
"wherever he may find truth, it is his Lord's" and that "by means of corporal
and temporal things [including signs] we may comprehend the eternal and
spiritual."[2] For Augustine, the word is ultimately guaranteed by the Word
made flesh, Christ, who is Wisdom. For Derrida, the word is not guaranteed
at all; it is part of a system in which its significance is marked only by its
difference from other signs, and therefore continually in play.

I am not going to try to erase or trivialize the distance between these
two conceptions of discourse, but to suggest the role that postmodernist
theory might be made to play in an interrogation of Chaucerian text and
"meaning."

To deconstruct is, in one sense, to unbuild, to disassemble, to see the
incongruous parts of a constructed thing, and to resist reassembling the parts
to assert an integrated and unitary "meaning," based on authorial intention,
stable reference to the "real" world, or thematic consistency. The characteristic difference between this and other systems of analysis is this prohibition
against *centering*, providing an axis on which the disassembled features of a
text can be reintegrated. I will attempt to discuss, first, some of the uses of
deconstructive strategy for students of *The Canterbury Tales* and [74] then,
briefly, the necessity of our offering a critique of it from the particular
vantage point we occupy. I do not see deconstruction as the end point or
final solution for the development of the philosophy of discourse, but as one
of our own era's contributions to the very old and continuing debate about
signs and meanings in which medieval thinkers were deeply involved.

Centering in Authorial Intention

Deconstructionists do not doubt that texts have historical authors who may intend a particular meaning or range of meanings as they write; they are authors themselves. The issue is whether that intention can control meaning for readers and hearers, whether the range of possibilities for words, figures, and genres can be delimited by an individual act of will. Derrida argues that language is too vast a system to be controlled by an individual will, even when we may feel that we can describe that will:

> ... the writer writes *in* a language and *in* a logic whose proper system, laws, and life his discourse by definition cannot dominate absolutely. He uses them only by letting himself, after a fashion and up to a point, be governed by the system. And the reading must always aim at a certain relationship, unperceived by the writer, between what he commands and what he does not command of the patterns of the language that he uses.
>
> (*Grammatology*, p. 158)

This formulation modifies the force of authorial intention, but does not exclude it from consideration.

Limitations on the control of meaning by authorial intention is no news to medievalists. In the *Confessions*, Augustine describes an offhand classroom remark of his which startled him by leading to the conversion of his student Alypius. The child's "Tolle, lege" ("Take, read"), so central to Augustine's own conversion, is another example of authorial intention's lack of control over the effects of discourse.[3] Although Augustine sees Presence, the will of God, in these meanings, he acknowledges a system of significance the human author "does not command." Even Scripture may contain meaning not available to its human author. In *On Christian Doctrine* anachronistic reading is allowed because "the Spirit of God, who [75] worked through that author, undoubtedly foresaw that this meaning would occur to the reader or listener" (3.27.38).

Consider, in terms of authorial intention, Nicholas's persuasion of John the Carpenter in *The Miller's Tale* (lines 3574–76):

> "Whan that grete shour is goon away,
>   Thanne shaltou swymme as myrie, I undertake,
>   As dooth the white doke after hire drake."[4]

The immediate author, Nicholas, is conning John into sleeping apart from Alison and out of the way of his planned adultery. His persuasion, however, is based on another text, the biblical description of the Flood. Nicholas is aided by the power of that text in evoking the apocalyptic cleansing of the world and its idyllic aftermath, and by its pervasiveness and authority in his culture. The whole scam relies on John's belief in God's intent and Nicholas's ability to interpret it through astrology. But for Nicholas, it depends on there being no such revealed intention and no moral force which would punish him for his blasphemy.

Nicholas's author, Robyn the Miller, allows Nicholas to succeed at his stratagem. Presumably his intent, as Robert Miller has argued, is to discredit the clergy as well as the nobility by showing its learning as a cynical exploitation of the word with which it is entrusted. Ignorant, and perhaps jealous, of the "real motives" of the "higher" kinds of life, Robyn reduces the profession of learning itself as he reduces Nicholas.[5]

Chaucer's authorial intentions, of course, must be seen as extending over all the others—it is he who created Robyn the scoffer, Nicholas the con man, and the credulous John. The Miller is there with his scandalous un-Boethian story to fill out the picture of the estates and conditions of fourteenth-century England. In a common view, he is coarse and ribald, but beloved. In another, he is unmasked as depraved, but still a part of the grand plan of the whole to make a universal moral signifying system clear through a series of emblematic links with biblical types: Robyn's bagpipes would lead the companye to helle. In both these views, Chaucer's intentions organize and orchestrate the other levels of significance, and like the others, they are deduced from the interpretation of the text and its contexts.

[76] Suppose we try to imagine instead all these imputed intentions in a kind of free play along with the immediate rhetorical force of the lines themselves. The white duck passage is too close to its biblical antecedent, too idyllic, too winning, to be entirely subordinated to Nicholas's selfish intention to con John. It glancingly evokes a cleansed, shimmering world familiar to religious piety, even while the countermovement is clearly in the reader's mind: Isn't this a clever joke? Floating in loose suspension are the power of the Scripture itself, the hilarious hoax of Nicholas, and John's foolish, but not altogether unthinkable, credulity. This sense of "play" loosens the grasp of all the authorial intentions involved. It might be taken to show Nicholas's linguistic force touching him, briefly, too deeply, an effect of the language he uses that he cannot fully command. It might go some way toward rehabilitating Robyn's intent, as if he gives unwilling acknowledgment of the power of mythic vision, even in circumstances as reduced as these. It also subtly casts Chaucer's overall intention in doubt: perhaps he allows a drunken Miller (as well as an avaricious Pardoner) to present the *companye* with sudden insight, including him in a wide arc of uncentered valuation.

Centering Fictions in Reference to the "Real" World

Deconstruction takes issue with any interpretive scheme which privileges verisimilitude. It holds that language does not transparently convey nonlinguistic "reality," but rather constructs the reality we see by organizing the material world to be grasped by comprehension. This is Paul de Man evoking the semiology of Charles Sanders Peirce:

The sign is to be interpreted if we are to understand the idea it is to convey, and this is so because the sign is not the thing but a meaning derived from the thing by a process ... not ... dependent on a univocal origin. The interpretation of the sign is not, for Peirce, a meaning but another sign: it is a reading, not a decodage, and this reading has, in its turn, to be interpreted into another sign and so on *ad infinitum*.[6]

The world is not directly, literally, or properly readable into texts.

Again, the medievalist is not surprised. Augustine dealing with reference comes to a similar formulation:

[77] However, when true accounts of the past are given, it is not the things themselves, which have passed away, that are drawn from memory, but words conceived from their images. These images they implanted in the mind like footsteps as they passed through the senses.

(*Confessions* 11.23)

We know from *On Christian Doctrine* that the images may be literal or allegorical, but like Peirce, Augustine insists that they are linguistic. Reference, then, becomes indirect and problematical, dependent on signs invoking sign systems rather than simply on reference to things in the world.

In his description of Absolon, the Miller mentions his elaborately styled shoes with "Poules wyndow corven" on them (line 3318). This detail is explained as an allusion to a particular fourteenth-century fashion and presumably marks Absolon as an aspiring man-about-town. You have to be thinking about possessions, appearances, and impressions, the argument goes, to wear shoes like his. A set of assertions about Absolon's social and moral situation can easily be built up around a detail like his shoes, and in this case corroborated by many other details in the *Tale*.

That approach would be directly referential and sufficiently satisfying to interpretation, but seeing language as a coded set of differentiations also has its explanatory power, even in a simple case like this one. The Parson does a lot of walking—to the "ferreste" in his "wyd" parish—and he goes "upon his feet," but no shoes are mentioned. The necessary conclusion is not that he goes discalced (although that is lightly suggested) but that a contrast between his unconcern with shoes and Absolon's attention to them is constructed. Note that here readers are doing the building, constructing a grid of likenesses and differences; we can also notice that the Parson *walks* the length of his parish to perform his pastoral duties, while the Monk *rides* well-groomed horses "huntyng for the hare." A rich, and theoretically limitless, set of oppositions can be traced among the pilgrims and characters in the *Tales* and also between any of the created characters and an array of culturally familiar types (as Robertson's work has shown). The Parson's description as (at least metaphorically) unshod, especially in the same line as mention of the staff, suggests an evangelical poverty and service denied in the portraits of the monk and friar: biblical discipleship.

But a third code cannot be ruled out. Wyclif's itinerant "poor priests" were, as Chaucer wrote, walking barefoot, with staffs and vernacular Bibles, to preach "Goddes word" in English villages. They, like the Parson, never went "to Seinte Poules / To seken ... a chaunterie for soules" (lines [78] 509–10). In both *The General Prologue*'s description of the Parson and the Miller's description of Absolon, Saint Poules has connoted unseemly self-interest, worldliness, and pride (it is also where the Sergeant of the Law meets his clients). Saint Paul's would serve as an apt symbol of the institutional church, wealthy, likely to draw parish priests away from their duties, and the source of persecution for those who preach "Goddis word," in a Wycliffite coding. Saint Poules and fancy shoes, then, versus the countryside and bare feet.

These are all referential systems, each claiming some "real" world object, but once we have noticed that several are in play at once, we have turned "real" into a problem rather than a guide to interpretation. The direct observation of fashion leads to particularization (Dryden's "God's plenty"), which might or might not be reconcilable with a broad kind of moral typing, and the potential allusion to the contemporary phenomenon of the "poor priests" cannot be made to mesh well with the other two. Moreover, we can never be sure that we have exhausted all of the relevant intertextual possibilities. It does not take deconstructive logic to produce any of these three readings, but it takes deconstructive energy and resolve to keep all of them in play.

Thematic Centering

Derrida takes up the philosophical weaknesses of "thematizing" in his essay "Plato's Pharmacy." The more subtly and ruthlessly words and figures are scrutinized, the less stable meanings and patterns of meaning appear. Plato's seeming assertion of writing as a remedy leads to its identification as poison, and vice versa.[7] Readers seem invited by texts to apprehend thematic consistency, but with more probing they may discover that the same text suggests a given "theme" no more readily than its opposite. The most important insight here is the *constructed* nature of themes; they are found *through* the efforts of readers not *in* the fabric of texts.

Once more I turn to the method of Augustine. Augustine thematized the whole body of Scripture when he designed the test of *caritas* to ensure reliable reading. Since sign systems may be read either literally or figuratively, and since Scripture contains both modes, the reader must distinguish one from the other by some principle. This principle is claimed to [79] be the theme and core of the entire message God encoded for his people: love for God and the use of the world in the service of that love. Note that Augustine himself had to interpret the Bible, with its various linguistic and figural difficulties to intuit that central theme, then locate the theme *in* the text as its center, and then control the interpretation of individual passages by their congruence with it. He brilliantly demonstrated how recalcitrant meaning may be contained within thematic bounds and, in the process, noted the institutional loyalty which prompted his choices (*On Christian Doctrine* 2.8.12 and 2.15.22).

Exactly this is what we normally do when we produce a thematically unified interpretation—build a thematic center from a selection of textual details (not all, since that would involve repeating the whole texts more than once), link the details into a proposition, and then explain the leftovers in terms of that proposition. Derrida's critique is of this practice.

Griselda's old coat will serve as a useful example. Chaucerians who take *The Clerk's Tale* as an allegory of the Christian's proper obedience to God will find this detail a pathos-inspiring instance of Griselda's difficult but right-minded patience. Coming back to her father's house in her smock after her dismissal by Walter, she resumes her former life of poverty and work without complaint. Janicula, however, has not mastered his daughter's story as an allegory. He has saved her old coat because he thinks she is living out the familiar seduced-and-abandoned pattern in which a jaded aristocrat plays briefly with the affections and virginity of a peasant girl, and he says so (*ClT* 906–10):

> For evere he deemed sith that it bigan
> That whan the lord fulfild hadde his courage,
> Hym wolde thynke it were disparage
> To his estate so lowe for t'alight,
> And voyden hire as soon as ever he myghte.

The Clerk, near the end of his telling, articulated one theme for his story, Janicula quite another. Both versions can claim considerable textual warrant.

It might be argued that Janicula made his reading before the conclusion in which Griselda was reinstated socially. It is certainly true that he does not have all the "facts": the existence of the living children, Walter's plan to eventually take his wife back, and the like. But Janicula is a stubborn reader and might find the full conclusion more damaging to Walter than the [80] penultimate interpretation he gives in this passage. Full knowledge might judge Walter less respectful of Griselda, more certain of his overwhelming power over her, less responsible to his duties to his people than even he had imagined.

The "olde coote" does not fit. The fabric is rude, and the woman is older. Perhaps her fuller figure is the result of Griselda's childbearing. She can never have back her only dowry, her maidenhood, as she says herself. The reader who interprets this gloomy tale of exploitation as a confident allegory has to be aggressive indeed in turning aside from its plain rhetorical effects. It would seem that we have here one of those "gaps" or "fissures" so familiar in the deconstructionist program of undoing thematic unities, a textual detail which, like Janicula, stubbornly resists being implicated in such unities. Although the passage does not invalidate an allegorical reading of *The Clerk's*

Tale, it embarrasses such a reading. A coat which fit the outcast Griselda would have served the Clerk's stated theme better by presenting an undisrupted return to her old life, rather than calling attention to the physical change the woman's body has undergone. Moreover, the importance of the ill-fitting coat is enhanced by its not having been forced on the Clerk by its inclusion in the Petrarchan source. A deconstructive reading will see this tension (and others with the same structure) not as resolved but as *operating* in the *Tale* and throughout *The Canterbury Tales*.

Deconstruction for Chaucerians

Although I have argued for the scrupulousness of deconstructive readings for medieval texts, I also want to suggest the need for medievalists to offer a critique of deconstruction. For while the nature of language may be to keep intention, reference, and thematic meaning in undecidable play, we are continually reminded that people do in fact produce definite, centered readings and, I would claim, allow those readings to influence their ideology and their lives.

It is, therefore, necessary not only to appreciate the radical openness of language and textuality but to see how historical conditions work to close them, to enable certain readings to seem natural or obvious for a particular interpretive community. This task necessitates the return to a study of the particularities of history, but it is history with a difference to which we return. The interpretative task is no longer served by settled generalizations about "the medieval world view" to stabilize authorial intentions or thema[81]tic likelihood or by the compiling of historical instances as a direct referential model for Chaucer's fictions. Instead that task is nothing less than the reimagining of the past, recognizing that most of our knowledge of it comes from texts, each of which bears a complex and problematic relation to events and practices themselves. But that is another story.

The language in which deconstructionists have phrased themselves is irreverent and prickly, deliberately, it seems, uncongenial to most other schemes for interpretation. But if they are right that language decenters as well as organizes perception, just this strangeness could have the effect of forcing Chaucer studies to reexamine its critical practices, to reconsider, deconstruct, and send out some new plumb lines before building its interpretations of text and history.

Notes

1 Jacques Derrida, *On Grammatology*, trans. Gayatri Chakravorty Spivak (Baltimore, Md.: Johns Hopkins University Press, 1974), p. 7.
2 Saint Augustine, *On Christian Doctrine*, trans. D. W. Robertson (Indianapolis: Bobbs-Merrill, 1958), 2.18.28 and 1.4.4.
3 Saint Augustine, *The Confessions*, trans. John K. Ryan (Garden City, N.Y.: Image Books, 1960), 6.12 and 12.29.

4 For quotations of Chaucer I have used John Hurt Fisher, ed., *The Complete Poetry and Prose of Geoffrey Chaucer* (New York: Holt, Rinehart and Winston, 1977).

5 Robert P. Miller, "The *Miller's Tale* as Complaint," *ChauR* 5 (1970):147–60.

6 Paul de Man, *Allegories of Reading* (New Haven, Conn.: Yale University Press, 1979), pp. 8–9.

7 Jacques Derrida, *Dissemination*, trans. Barbara Johnson (Chicago: University of Chicago Press, 1981), p. 71.

21 | Deconstructing *The Canterbury Tales*: con

TRAUGOTT LAWLER

Originally published in *Studies in the Age of Chaucer*, Proceedings no. 2 (1987):83–91. Reprinted by permission of the New Chaucer Society. The original pagination is recorded within square brackets. The endnotes originally appeared as footnotes.

Let me start by acknowledging that I am a beginner at understanding deconstruction and that I have made this beginning as a kind of reparation for aggressive ignorance. Ever since I first heard the word and gained a vague notion of what it meant, I have been instinctively opposed to it. "Blessed be alwey a lewed man, / That noght but oonly his bileve kan," my motto was—and my "bileve" consisted in historical philology, close reading, and common sense. But I have come to feel that it is immoral to reject out of hand a method and a set of principles that not only are there and will not go away but are held and used by people I admire. I realized that one cannot claim to reject deconstruction on "humanist" grounds when a good number of one's quite human colleagues and students take it seriously. I committed myself to writing this paper as a way of forcing myself to understand the method and experiment with it.

My understanding is still far from complete. It depends chiefly on a thorough reading of Robert Scholes's *Textual Power*, supplemented by a partial reading of Vincent Leitch's *Deconstructive Criticism* and Jacques Derrida's *Of Grammatology*.[1] I have a long way to go to understand it fully. I have purposely avoided reading arguments against deconstruction, since I wanted both to study it without prejudice and to make a personal, not a canned, response. In this essay I shall try to present a moderate or qualified argument against applying deconstructive methods wholesale to *The Canterbury Tales*. I want to grant a certain usefulness, and show that usefulness, but then to show what its limits are. I may have gotten a bit [84] more caught up in the usefulness than in the limits, maybe because of my desire to make amends, more likely simply because of the excitement of doing something different. Nevertheless, it is the insistence on limits that is my theme.

Next let me try to put into words my understanding of deconstruction, especially as it applies to literary interpretation. This is not meant to instruct anybody, but simply to make my own understanding clear. I think of deconstruction as a way of analyzing any system or member of a system. As applied to a text or discourse, which is a system of words and ideas, it is the process of revealing how far it "constructs" its object, how it is not referential, not a mimetic representation of reality, but a "construct" made in part by the "subject" or author, in part by the language and cultural categories he inherits. Its major principle is that language is not referential, or at best is imperfectly so; a corollary of that principle is that "difference" or differentiation is a function of the mind, or of language, not of reality. Reality is seamless, or at least more seamless than our thoughts about it are, and therefore any differentiation is likely to be a violence on, or "appropriation of," reality. Binary oppositions, the most characteristic mode of Western thought, are, in Scholes's words, "the most basic and most violent acts of differentiation."[2] An obvious example is gender: though the difference between men and women is real enough, our language and our cultural habits require us to differentiate between them in thousands of situations where no real need to do so exists. Thus a major way to deconstruct a text is to reveal its constitutive polar oppositions, the fundamental dichotomies that it is constructed around and from which its apparent meanings flow. This is to lay bare the special violence it imposes on reality. It is important to note that the author does not intend such violence, indeed does not recognize the poles in his own thinking, or embedded in the language. One "deconstructs" these oppositions by showing how each term shares certain attributes with its opposite. And one deconstructs the author's intentionality by showing the blind spots or ambivalences in his understanding of his own terms and concepts. To my mind the most salient, and potentially the most problematic, feature of deconstructive criticism is this drive to undermine our trust in the author's controlling power.

Thus a second major deconstructive technique is to look for signs of counterintentionality. Here one breaks down the illusion of authorial control by showing that the author's text or construction is a compromise [85] between, or even suppression of, conflicting intentions; commonly this is done by detecting the signs of that conflict or suppression in moments of division or aporia, that is, "impasse." Especially one looks for contradictions. To find them is to reveal that the text "deconstructs itself."

Since what "constitutes" or "constructs" the text is a combination of cultural assumptions or anxieties embedded in language and personal assumptions or anxieties embedded in the author's subconscious mind, one replaces the unknowable object by focusing either on the medium or on the subject, that is, either on cultural or on authorial constructions. Another way to say this is that, if language is not referential, then the point of interest in any discourse is not the object, not the statement about some event or phenomenon or process, not the "subject matter"—but rather the subject, that is, the speaker, the constructor of the discourse, and what it reveals about him. Thus Marshall Leicester has argued for a "voice-oriented reading" of *The Canterbury Tales*, a reading that sees each tale as "about its speaker," even their referential aspects mere functions of the "I" or reflexive "evidence of the speaker's character."[3] And Allen Shoaf has shown how Troilus and Pandarus and the narrator all construct versions of Criseyde that have far more to do with their own intentions and presuppositions than with Criseyde (whom we therefore cannot know).[4] Deconstruction could presumably also show us more about Chaucer as subject, show in a "deep" way how what look like his insights into "human nature" are culturally relative, "partial" products of his inevitable confinement to the preoccupations of his time and place, and finally reveal his characteristic anxieties, particularly if we were sure we could get beyond the subjects of personae he creates to him as creating subject.

The example I shall give tends somewhat in the last direction, but I shall stop well short of what seems to me the arrogance or at least futility of psychoanalyzing Chaucer. I am content rather to use the technique to explore the implications of a few contradictions and a few sets of generative binary oppositions. *The Canterbury Tales* is in some obvious ways a deconstructor's dream: not only an unfinished and so indeterminate text, with lots of evident discontinuity and self-contradiction, but a nonreferential or self-referential or mediated text, both because many tales ask us to focus as much on the teller as on the subject matter and because such [86] outward references as it has point regularly not to reality but to more texts. I want to concentrate on some indeterminacies but then, I hope, move past them to concentrate on determinacy.

When I first worked out my essay, it had an analysis of the various indeterminacies embedded in the *General Prologue* line, "he moot as wel seye o word as another," then of some contradictory polarities in *The Prioress's Tale*, and finally of an extremely troublesome simile in *The Squire's Tale*. But it was too long, and since the *Squire's Tale* part was really my major exhibit, I have decided to move directly to that.

The simile I have in mind, one wrenched from its original context in Boethius, occurs in part 2 of *The Squire's Tale*, near the end of the jilted falcon's long complaint to Canacee about the tercelet who "falsed" her (lines 606–27):[5]

> "Whan it cam hym to purpos for to reste,
> I trowe he hadde thilke text in mynde,
> That 'alle thyng, repeirynge to his kynde,
> Gladeth hymself'; thus seyn men, as I gesse.
> Men loven of propre kynde newefangelnesse,
> As briddes doon that men in cages fede.
> For though thou nyght and day take of hem hede,
> And strawe hir cage faire and softe as silk,
> And yeve hem sugre, hony, breed and milk,
> Yet right anon as that his dore is uppe,
> He with his feet wol spurne adoun his cuppe,
> And to the wode he wole, and wormes ete;
> So newefangel been they of hire mete,

And loven novelries of propre kynde;
No gentillesse of blood ne may hem bynde.
  So ferde this tercelet, allas the day!
Though he were gentil born, and fressh and gay,
And goodlich for to seen, and humble and free,
He saugh upon a tyme a kyte flee,
And sodeynly he loved this kyte so
That al his love is clene fro me ago;
And hath his trouthe falsed in this wise."

[87] The simile would have us believe that a male falcon who drops a female falcon for a kite is like a caged bird who abandons soft straw and a diet of sweets to fly back to the woods and eat worms: both, we are told, are seeking newfangledness.

There are many confusions here. First, on nature: the falcon is naturally noble, of gentle birth, and yet somehow "repairs to its kind" by seeking a new, baser partner; its nature is divided between falconness and maleness, and one nature contradicts the other. Furthermore, even if we grant that it is unnatural, a denial of his genes, for a falcon to love a kite, surely for a caged bird to seek freedom is neither unnatural nor newfangled but a reassertion of its birthright. The whole concept of nature seems to be a contradictory construction. A second confusion involves the relation of nature to gentillesse: the gentle life is represented as at once natural (for the falcon, something in his blood) and artificial (for the woodbird, a matter of captivity, training, nurture)—and yet this captivity is called, in the most strained moment in the passage, "gentillesse of blood." Third, on the moral status of gentillesse: as imaged in the falcons, particularly the female, it is clearly good, a source of "truth"; but as imaged in the soft floor of the cage and the soft diet, it is meretricious and effete, as against the substance or "truth" of woods and worms. Fourth, on gender: males are aligned with fickle behavior, females with fidelity; but this is so patent an attempt to rescue the simile by using the specious idea of male newfangledness to cover over the other confusions that whether or not it is true to experience is virtually irrelevant here. Finally, we are surely meant to despise the falcon, but the simile then asks us to despise the woodbird for preferring worms to sugar out of a passion for variety, when actually we applaud the bird and despise instead the brainless colonialism of the cager. I pass over the additional absurdity of a bird turning another bird into a man and then illustrating men's behavior by comparing them to birds.

What shall we make of these confusions? I think the deconstructive way would be to say, first, that they depend on a series of polar oppositions everywhere evident in Chaucer: male/female, nature/art, social status/moral worth, surface/substance, plain/fancy, stability/change; and, second, that the confusions deconstruct the binary oppositions, that is, show them to be society's or the author's constructions, appropriations of reality, by revealing both that any attempt to align them consistently breaks down and that even within a single polarity each side shares properties with the other. Maybe you could even say further that the contradictions reveal [88] Chaucer's anxieties: about gender, say, that his patently false attempts to assert that women are true, men fickle merely reveal an instinctive tendency to believe the opposite; or about gentillesse, that, despite various attempts in his poems to insist that virtue, not birth, matters, he really was a snob; or about the plain and the fancy, that, for all his praise of plain speaking and plain living, plainness in fact was mere worms to the artist in him. I am willing to do just that, but to do it in a spirit of praise, to acknowledge that we all struggle with inner contradictions that are not just in the words, and to honor Chaucer for making poetry out of the struggle. For it is precisely these "constructions" that make the poems possible in the first place; they are constructive in the good sense of creative and enabling as well as in the putatively bad sense of appropriations of reality.

I should now like to argue that not only this troublesome passage but the whole *Squire's Tale* is generated by a series of creative binary oppositions. If we put aside its apparent incompleteness and take the tale as it stands, we see that its own structure is binary: two parts, one "realistic," public, and urban, the other "romantic," private, and rural. The issues of part 1— Cambyuskan's birthday party and the reception of the strange knight with his gifts—are "male," political, and adult, focusing on royal celebration, the accommodation of a major guest from outside, the problem of the crowd's misperceptions, etc.; the issues of part 2—Canacee's meeting with the jilted falcon—are "female," personal, and adolescent. This division corresponds to a division among the four gifts the strange knight brings: horse and sword are "male," ring and mirror "female." There is a contrast of style, too: the style of part 1 is varied and digressive, and one often feels the intrusions of self-conscious rhetoric; the style of part 2 is integrated, consistent, and sustained. Part 1 concentrates on art: on the formal world of courtly procedures, on the technology of the flying horse, on the rhetorical art of the narrator: part 2 takes place in the green world (though a park), puts Canacee in touch with one of its denizens (though a courtly one), and eventually raises the questions of nature I have spoken of. Altogether, one could say that we have in miniature in *The Squire's Tale* the major oppositions we are accustomed to identifying in Chaucer's oeuvre. Part 1 is like *The Canterbury Tales*: public, varied, digressive, scholastic, Jean de Meun its patron; part 2 is like *Troilus* or the dream poems, a distanced, conventional world in which courtship is the consuming issue; its patron is Guillaume de Lorris.

What is to be made of this binary structure of the whole tale? Well, first I would like to report that I never thought of the poem in this way until the problem I felt with the birdcage passage forced me to try to deconstruct it, [89] and so to analyze it in binary terms. Whereas I had always thought of it in temporal, narrative terms, as the first two events in a complex but linear story that Chaucer never developed, I have now come to see it in terms of a "spatial" contrast: two blocks of poetry set against each other and capable of generating an almost endless series of meanings from the contrast. One is tempted initially, perhaps, to deconstruct the polarities by claiming that one set of poles, the male, public set, is unconsciously "privileged," the other "marginalized." This is perhaps how we tend to first read the poem. We take its real action to be probably political and certainly human, and so regard the Canacee plot, and certainly the falcon plot, as marginal—a product of a fatal dalliance with pretty conventions, whether by the Squire or by Chaucer. But I think it takes only a little reflection to see that part 2 is full of interest and that both sides of all the polarities carry weight. What Chaucer has created is a diptych, similar to various such diptychs in *The General Prologue* or between tales, in which the juxtaposition of sharply opposed elements generates meaning. I certainly do not claim that Chaucer could not have gone on with the narrative; but thinking of the tale as binary helps me see how he might have seen it as able to stand on its own.

Those who write on deconstruction are fond of speaking of gaps, of disconnection, of difference and dissimilarity rather than "presence"—above all they speak of the disconnection between words and the entities they purport to represent. Their methods have helped me see why Chaucer's simile is a kind of dis-simile, revealing unlikeness more than likeness. Returning to it, one can discern another level at which it emphasizes a gap: the little story it tells of the caged woodbird is a story of an attempt at synthesis, an attempt to bridge the binary oppositions wild/tame and even beast/man. Of course the simile says that the attempt fails: the woodbird abandons "presence" to reassert its "difference." Interestingly, the four gifts also seem directed at the problem of difference. All are meant to synthesize or bridge intractable natural divisions: the horse bridges divisions of time and space; the sword, though it makes wounds with its edge, makes them whole again with its flat; the ring bridges the gap between us and the animal and vegetable worlds, with a view to healing wounds, "al be [they] never so depe and wyde"; the mirror bridges the gap between one mind and another, a gap that speech often creates. And the action of part 2, so far as it goes, is synthetic, too: the one thing that happens is that Canacee rescues the suffering falcon.

I think it is right to say that the discontinuities and contradictions so rife in the simile are repaired in the episode at large, in the rescue, because there a connection is made, a gap is bridged. The force feeding of civilized [90] values to the caged bird in the simile is replaced by Canacee's sympathetic listening. One is made to feel that the magical ability the ring gives her to understand the falcon's "leden" is minor in comparison to the moral sympathy she offers, though both are needed: Canacee herself synthesizes the polarity of mind / heart, and it is her wholeness that effaces the difference between her and the falcon. And when she brings the falcon home, wraps her "softely" in plasters, and "by hire beddes heed ... made a mewe, / And covered it with veluettes blewe" (lines 636, 643–44), it might be said that the disharmonies of the simile have been quite specifically repaired. If the poem momentarily "deconstructed itself" there, it has reconstructed itself here. Of course one can still deconstruct this happy union of woman and bird by simply asserting that we are more aware of the difference between them than the similarity, or perhaps by arguing that only in a hopelessly nonreferential form such as romance can our dreams of overcoming difference be accomplished. But to do so would surely put the critic in the company of the false fowls painted on the mew, or perhaps of the magpies painted next to them whose function is to "crye and chyde." Canacee offers us a model of right reading: to understand the "leden" and to be moved by sympathy.

Thus what my attempt to deconstruct the bird simile leads me finally to do is to assert that the poem treats—in Chaucer's terms, of course, not Derrida's—the very issue that deconstruction treats: difference, gaps, discontinuities, and, both by its own failure to continue and by effecting a sharp contrast between its two finished parts, acknowledges difference. Furthermore, the failed bird simile—not to mention the failed love affair in which the tercelet's language does not refer to the state of his heart—seems further to acknowledge the width of gaps. On the other hand, the knight's four gifts are designed to bridge gaps, and in the second part we see Canacee using the ring to bridge the very gap between nature and civilization that the simile presents as unbridgeable. In short, where Chaucer parts company with Derrida is in his willingness to give us narratives of presence and closure: in place of the deconstructionist's skepticism, he offers us faith.

It is faith that is the gist of my objection to a wholesale use of deconstruction in interpreting Chaucer's poetry. Faith, and patience as well. Deconstruction is the poetics of skepticism and distrust: distrust in language and distrust in our poets' ability to use language creatively to instruct and please us. And it is finally arrogant. I do not mean that individual critics are arrogant, but that the method seems essentially arrogant. It places the critic in too superior, too condescending a role. In everyday life we insist that [91] criticism be "constructive." Literary criticism ignores the standards of everyday life at its peril. What Chaucer urges on us, again and again, is patience, or "patient suffrance": Canacee's mode, not the tercelet's. There is an important sense, of course, in which deconstruction is not arrogant: it refuses to "master" the text, to force closure on it. It refuses to cage the bird; it asserts instead that the bird will always elude the cager's attempt to dominate it. But once again Canacee provides a corrective: she does cage the bird, but in a way that represents a meeting of minds and wills, not domination. As the falcon speaks to Canacee, trusting that she will understand and be moved to take what it says to heart, so I think Chaucer speaks to us, confidently, vividly, seeking and expecting a trusting, patient, vivid response. We may need the edge of the sword of deconstruction to "wound" the text, but we also need the flat, healing stroke of patient, trusting good will. Patient analysis guided by faith and good will: that is also the horse, bridging the gap of centuries; the ring, enabling us to understand the "leden"; and the mirror, effecting a meeting of minds.

Notes

1 Robert Scholes, *Textual Power: Literary Theory and the Teaching of English* (New Haven, Conn., and London: Yale University Press, 1985); Vincent Leitch, *Decon-*

structive Criticism: An Advanced Introduction (New York: Columbia University Press, 1983); Jacques Derrida, *Of Grammatology*, trans. Gayatri Spivak (Baltimore, Md., and London: Johns Hopkins University Press, 1974).

2 Scholes, *Textual Power*, p. 112.

3 H. Marshall Leicester, Jr., "The Art of Impersonation: A General Prologue to the *Canterbury Tales*," PMLA 95 (1980):213–14 [see above – ed.].

4 R. Allen Shoaf, *Dante, Chaucer, and the Currency of the Word* (Norman, Okla.: Pilgrim Books, 1984), pp. 107–57.

5 Quotations from Chaucer are taken from F. N. Robinson, ed., *The Works of Geoffrey Chaucer*, 2d ed. (Boston: Houghton Mifflin, 1957).